THE NATION
OF ISLAM

P9-DID-914

THE NATION OF ISLAM

Understanding the "Black Muslims"

STEVEN TSOUKALAS

Foreword by Carl F. Ellis Jr.

P&R
PUBLISHING
P.O. BOX 817 • PHILLIPSBURG • NEW JERSEY 08865-0817

Page design by Tobias Design
Typesetting by Michelle Feaster

Printed in the United States of America

Library of Congress Cataloging-in-Publication Data

Tsoukalas, Steven, 1956-
    The Nation of Islam: understanding the "Black Muslims"/Steve Tsoukalas; foreword by Carl F. Ellis.
        p. cm.
    Includes bibliographical references and index.
    ISBN 0-87552-474-5 (pbk.)
    1. Black Muslims—Controversial literature. 2. Black Muslims—Relations.
3. Christianity and other religions—Black Muslims. I. Title.

BP222.T77 2001
297.8'7—dc21

                                        2001021023

To Joe Titone,
whose unfailing passion for ministry
to the church in the city
inspired me to write this book

Contents

Foreword

by Carl F. Ellis Jr.

"SO WHAT!"

I was anticipating new experiences and new ideas on this crisp October Sunday afternoon. My father's words were still ringing in my ears: "Even if we don't agree with him, we should at least hear what he has to say." The all-male line necessary to enter the Chicago Amphitheater puzzled me. But, as I stepped through doors, the reason for the gender segregation became clear. We were being searched! Not exactly the new experience I was looking for.

A sea of women in white, flowing robes arrested my attention as we entered the balcony of the main arena. This exotic sight gave me the impression of a Middle Eastern setting.

The opening of the program was preceded by a line of uniformed men in lockstep forming a tight human corridor down the middle aisle. As the platform celebrities passed through this corridor, I knew this would be no ordinary meeting.

It was Saviour's Day, 1962—my first encounter with the Nation of Islam. I learned later that those uniformed men were none other than the Fruit of Islam, a well-disciplined paramilitary security force. The four-hour meeting had an ambiance of strong masculinity that captivated me. New feelings of pride, protest, and defiance welled up in me, *and I liked it!*

About an hour into the proceedings, a young, tall, tan-skinned,

red-haired man took the podium. He spoke with a fire and compe-
tence I had never seen demonstrated before. His name was Malcolm. He electrified the crowd with his pithy wit and thorough
grasp of the issues we faced as a people. Malcolm also reminded the
crowd that as Muslims they were preaching self-love, not hatred of
others, as the white press had been asserting. Throughout his dis-
course, he expressed his undying devotion to Elijah Muhammad.

With Mr. Muhammad's turn at the podium, I was mystified by
Malcolm's devotion to him. Muhammad's speech was unclear and
difficult to understand. About halfway through his address, my
mother nudged me and pointed out a man wearing a swastika arm-
band. Speculation about the significance of the Nazi presence tem-
porarily displaced my efforts at deciphering the ramblings of Elijah
Muhammad.

Having heard Malcolm, I would have followed him anywhere.
But Elijah Muhammad: that was another matter. His religious doctrines seemed superfluous.

Just prior to the closing of the meeting, the master of cere-
monies announced that George Lincoln Rockwell, leader of the
American Nazi Party, wanted to address the assembly. A crescendo
of boos erupted from the crowd, and I joined in. Just then Malcolm
X came forward and admonished us, saying, "Wait a minute, broth-
ers and sisters. I must be in the wrong meeting. Aren't we Muslims?
We're intelligent, aren't we? We can think for ourselves, can't we?"
With each of Malcolm's questions the verbal affirmations increased.
Then, in the exact words of my father, Malcolm said, "Even if we
don't agree with him, we should at least hear what he has to say."
With those words, we all sprang to our feet in applause. Malcolm's
power of persuasion was amazing!

Mr. Rockwell's address was standard Nazi rhetoric containing
several promises of favor toward the Nation of Islam once they gain
power. He ended his speech by declaring, "Elijah Muhammad is the
Adolf Hitler of the black man." This remark triggered an immediate and angry cacophony of boos and epithets that was quelled only
when Rockwell was escorted from the amphitheater.

Once order was restored, Malcolm warned us that the "white
devils" would publish twisted reports identifying the Nation of Islam
with the American Nazi Party.

That evening, the Chicago newspapers did exactly as Malcolm predicted. Their screaming headlines and incriminating photographs clearly communicated that the "Black Muslims" and American Nazis were virtually one and the same. I was outraged!

That very day, in defiance, I became a fifteen-year-old avid student of Malcolm X and a strong sympathizer of the Nation of Islam. Many people tried to dissuade me by pointing out that the Nation of Islam preached "black supremacy." I would quickly retort, "So what! We already live under white supremacy. If given a choice, I'd rather have black supremacy."

CLOSET FOLLOWERS

In those days, we referred to ourselves as American Negroes. Ethnic identity was not on our radar screens. After all, the majority of us were committed to the time-honored strategy of assimilation into the dominant culture. We were committed to winning friends and influencing people among the white American population. We did not dare to speak our minds in front of "white folks," especially when it came to issues of race. Our expressions of anger about racism were restricted to the times when they were not present.

The civil rights movement was at its height, and we looked to the strategy of nonviolent demonstrations as the key to our progress. Malcolm X, however, inaugurated a paradigm shift for many of us, especially among young men. We began to question the strategy of moral persuasion exemplified by Dr. Martin Luther King Jr. We began to challenge the notion of turning the other cheek. We also began to suspect the black church and its theology of suffering as a means of pacification. Malcolm led us to discover new cultural issues—issues the church was not addressing. Thus, for us Christianity was beginning to resemble what the Nation of Islam had dubbed it to be, namely, "the white man's religion."

We loved Malcolm because he was the only black man who had the nerve to speak his mind to the general public. Yet we hated him for this machismo because we had not yet fully abandoned our commitment to assimilation. This love/hate response Malcolm invoked made him fascinating yet irresistible. Most of my peers, even the churchgoing ones, were closet followers of Brother Malcolm. Though we shared sympathies with the Nation of Islam, we never seriously considered joining it. Malcolm was the hero, not Elijah Muhammad.

SMOKE AND MIRRORS

The appeal of Malcolm X then is similar to the appeal of Louis Farrakhan today. Witness the tremendous turnout at the Million Man March (October 16, 1995). It is estimated that more than 60 percent of those who gathered in Washington, D.C., were Christians. It cannot be demonstrated that these Christian men were followers of Farrakhan. On the contrary, many of them were outspoken about their Christian witness. However, the response to Farrakhan's call to march does reveal his considerable influence. There is no Christian leader of any stripe who could have convened a million Christian and non-Christian men to take a stand for righteousness.

While it can be argued that Louis Farrakhan employs theological smoke and mirrors in his lengthy diatribes, it cannot be denied that he touches on cultural core issues of great concern to many African Americans, especially young men.

The Bible deals with all these important issues better than any other book does. This is why Mr. Farrakhan quotes from it so much. Yet we in the Christian community tend to focus on private fire insurance almost to the exclusion of biblical teaching and kingdom principles addressing issues young African Americans are wrestling with. This is not to say that a passport from hell to heaven is not important. The point is that the gospel says so much more that demands our attention and implementation (Mic. 6:8).

INDISPENSABLE

Although membership in the Nation of Islam for me was out of the question, I was on the well-traveled road from Christianity to Islam—orthodox Islam. My satisfaction with the church was on the decrease, and my curiosity about the mosque was on the increase. Malcolm X was my trailblazer. When he broke with Elijah Muhammad and started the Organization of Afro-American Unity (OAAU), I would have followed him. When he embraced orthodox Islam, I probably would have eventually done the same.

But in June 1964, I met Jesus Christ. The young men who introduced me to Jesus did so by addressing my issues and answering my questions with the Word of God. Since then, God has given me the privilege of introducing hundreds of others to Christ in the same way. And yes, most of them were in the mosque or on the road to the mosque.

Today, hundreds of thousands of others like me are traveling this same mosque-bound road, looking for answers only the Word of God can supply. We can make a breakthrough for Christ among these disaffected men and women by understanding the psychology behind their drift toward Islam. Engaging them in conversation and hearing their stories are key to this understanding. Before such conversations can happen, however, walls of distrust and suspicion must come down. I have seen these walls crumble as they discovered I understood their beliefs.

Steve Tsoukalas has given us an excellent resource in *The Nation of Islam*. This well-researched book will prove to be indispensable as we fulfill the Great Commission among our African-American brothers and sisters caught in today's nexus of theological confusion.

In this day of political correctness, many Christians make the mistaken assumption that only African Americans can minister to African Americans. This assumption approaches the status of irrefutable fact when it comes to those in the Nation of Islam. While cultural savvy has its advantages, it does not follow that the lack of such savvy cancels the power of the Word of God (Isa. 55:11).

Bill Garvey is a colleague of mine who happens to be white. Yet he has been amazingly effective in his ministry to entrenched members of the Nation of Islam. As they discover that Bill really understands them, their doctrinaire view that "the white man is the devil" begins to disintegrate. They become open to the gospel as they learn how it addresses their concerns. Brother Garvey loves them and prays for them. He takes the time to understand their core issues and wisely applies the Word of God to them.

After reading *The Nation of Islam,* I was left with one regret—that it was not published earlier. The positive effects of this valuable book would have been enormous.

Whether you reside in the 'hood or the 'burbs, whether you are African American, white, Hispanic, or "other," whether God has called you to home missions or foreign missions, you cannot afford to let Steve Tsoukalas's magnificent work sit on the shelf.

Truly, *The Nation of Islam* is a *must read.*

Preface

In 1964 I was eight years old when I saw a beautifully honed, muscular black man win the heavyweight boxing championship of the world. I watched him "float like a butterfly and sting like a bee" to knock out Sonny Liston. When it was over, Cassius Clay hopped on the ropes with eyes glaring, mouth wide open, and threw jabs toward the crowd in an "I told you so" manner.

Moments later he was interviewed by a reporter who was obviously entertained by his claim, "I'm the prettiest thing that ever lived!" "I am the greatest," he shouted. I recall several times watching replays of the fight and viewing again that ringside interview. The media's attention was and still is focused on Clay's boast of prettiness and greatness. To this day comedians repeat these words when they impersonate the champ. He was truly an amazing personality.

What went over my head, and what is usually not emphasized by the media and the world of comedy, were his remarks, "Almighty God was with me. . . . I talk to God every day!" I remember Clay saying these things, but after all, many an athlete has stated "I thank God" after a victory. I considered these words commonplace, something that was nice and expected after a victory.

After researching the Lost-Found Nation of Islam (NOI), I realized that in Clay's mind, "Almighty God" was the stranger who came to Detroit in 1930—Wallace D. Fard. Clay had come into contact with the NOI in 1959, about five years before his match with Liston. And for at least three years before the fight he was attending NOI meetings. Since according to NOI doctrine Fard is Allah in the flesh, Clay believed W. D. Fard was God. Days after he won the

heavyweight title, Clay became Muhammad Ali, signifying his identification with Allah (Fard) and the NOI.

My exposure to the NOI came after I became a Christian. During some time off from delivering a series of lectures at a church in
New York City, a friend and I decided to take a walk in Manhattan.
My eyes focused on a young black man selling books on the sidewalk.
Curious as to what was on his table, I walked toward him. After looking over the books, I began to ask questions. As the young man sat
in his chair, he turned away from me at a 45-degree angle and answered me with short, hurried words. Though he was willing to sell
me books, it was obvious I made him uncomfortable. Being new to
this city, I thought that perhaps this was the street-corner dynamic of
downtown. I thought no more of the encounter.

Four years later a friend asked me to teach Christians about the
NOI. I had never studied it, but I accepted the offer. In the months
of preparation I subscribed to *The Final Call*, the movement's newspaper, and ordered several books from its Chicago headquarters.
Then, just as the experience with Muhammad Ali had become clear,
it also became clear why that young man on the Manhattan street
corner treated me the way he did. In his eyes I was a devil, as all
whites are. I was a liar and a deceiver, and I was inferior to him by
nature. Welcome to the world of the NOI.

This book is a sociological, historical, and theological study of
the NOI. The movement's doctrine cannot be truly understood
without studying the sociological and cultural soil from which the
NOI grew. Thus, in this study I will probe the mindset of nine-
teenth- and early twentieth-century black nationalism and the religious components that made black nationalism before I examine
NOI theology. With this I hope to give the reader not only knowledge of the NOI but also an understanding of the NOI.

Most people call the movement the "Black Muslims," but some
in the NOI, including Malcom X, have frowned on this label. I have
chosen, therefore, to use the movement's official designation.
Sometimes, however, people think that "the Nation of Islam" refers
to traditional Islam. For that reason the phrase "Black Muslims" appears (with quotation marks) in the title of this book, to help po-
tential readers identify the content. I will not use that designation
in the book itself, except in quotations from other writers.

I wish to thank P&R Publishing for its decision to put this work in print. I am also gratefully indebted to Carl Ellis and Jerry Buckner, two fine scholars and theologians, for their careful reviews of the manuscript and their kind words about it. Between them are scores of years of experience with the NOI, a fact that has made this book much better than it would have been without their input.

ONE

Sociological and Religious Soil

In her study of the Nation of Islam, Martha F. Lee writes, "The Black population of the United States has long struggled to find its identity in the context of the society and republic in which it must exist. . . . The political question 'who are we?' must be answered by reflection upon and interpretation of the past."[1] Lee adds that blacks' struggle for interpretation of the meaning of their existence has been satisfied within the context of religion and that "while many Blacks found orthodox religious faith to be sufficient, many others stretched its boundaries. . . . By far the most successful is the Nation of Islam."[2]

The Nation of Islam (NOI) is a product of the times. The movement, which began in 1930, did not appear within a vacuum. Several cultural, anthropological, and theological influences from the nineteenth and early twentieth centuries spawned it. Consequently, the movement cannot be understood without mention of slavery and the attitude it birthed among certain black people or without a study of a few key black leaders who promoted black nationalism[3] and who preceded the rise of the NOI.

HEROISM, HATE, AND BLACK NATIONALISM—THE NINETEENTH CENTURY

American slavery and racism, vicious and degrading as it was,[4] fostered two basic attitudes among blacks in the nineteenth century—heroism or an outright detestation of whites. Wilson Jeremiah Moses writes of the "myth of Uncle Tom," alluding to Harriet

1

Beecher Stowe's *Uncle Tom's Cabin* (1852). This myth (*myth* here is not meant to convey an imaginary phenomenon) among nineteenth-century blacks was one of Christian heroism, in which they saw themselves as a race whose example of suffering, endurance of shame, and forgiveness of their oppressors would lead ultimately to vindication and reward. According to Moses,

> Mrs. Stowe, of course, meant for Uncle Tom to symbolize the black race's innate propensity for Christian heroism. It was because the African race possessed the traits of patience, long suffering, and forgiveness that they would ultimately become a messianic redeemer race.[5]

Moses therefore speaks of black "messianism" and in part defines it corporately as "the redemptive mission of the black race."[6] He also defines the term individually: "the expectation or identification of a personal savior—a messiah, a prophet, or a mahdi."[7] This latter concept as well was evident in black culture of the nineteenth century. Witness David Walker's and Henry Highland Garnet's *Walker's Appeal and Garnet's Address to the Slaves of the United States* of 1848,[8] in which Walker calls black people out of their ignorance, out of their playing the white man's game, and into an awareness of their mighty African heritage.[9] Walker spoke against the racial slanders of Thomas Jefferson[10] and against "*Christian* Americans" who poured their "wretchedness and miseries" upon blacks.[11] Consequently, Walker "prophesied that God would soon be sending black Americans a great leader."[12] As we shall see, both these concepts of messianism, the corporate and the individual, would come to play an important part in the early black nationalist movements preceding the NOI and in the ideology, anthropology, and theology of the NOI.

Walker and Garnet, to be sure, had black leaders who disagreed with them. Moses notes that the messianism of Walker and Garnet "was filled with the rhetoric of violence."[13] Growing in this period was a sense among many blacks that their slave masters were using Christianity's teaching of turning the other cheek as an excuse to oppress them and beat them in the name of Christianity.[14] "Stand still," Walker wrote, "and see the salvation of God and the miracle he will work for our deliverance from the wretchedness of the Christians!!!!!!"[15] Add to this Walker's word to Americans:

> Americans, unless you speedily alter your course, you and your *Country are gone!!!!!!* . . . I call God—I call angels—I call men, to witness that your DESTRUCTION *is at hand,* and will be speedily consummated unless you REPENT.[16]

Slowly, then, the view symbolized in *Uncle Tom's Cabin* was to become by the early twentieth century a "symbol of misguided altruism,"[17] and Mrs. Stowe's Uncle Tom was "entirely distorted" into "a selfless, stoical, fatalistic martyr."[18] It was replaced in the minds of many black people with a fresh awareness that blacks were of noble origin, in some cases nobler, even to the point of ontological superiority. This was their newfound identity. They were God's chosen race. Therefore they could boldly rise up with pride and speak against their white oppressors both politically and religiously. Perhaps this was due more and more to blacks agreeing with David Walker and Henry Highland Garnet and with those who preached their message.[19]

This nineteenth-century cultural, political and religious soil produced the early twentieth-century black nationalist activists who in turn influenced the NOI. Two of those activists were Marcus Garvey and Noble Drew Ali.

BLACK NATIONALISM–THE TWENTIETH CENTURY

Marcus Garvey's Universal Negro Improvement Association (UNIA) and the Moorish Science Temple of Noble Drew Ali were in essence the political and religious forerunners of the NOI. Some scholars believe that Garvey's movement emphasized more the political and social, while Ali's group was largely religious.[20] Ali's movement was almost totally religious, but Garvey did not discount religion.[21] He was keen enough to know that history has proven that religion moves the masses.[22] Though Garvey's use of religion did not reach that of Noble Drew Ali, it cannot be stated that he neglected religion.[23]

Marcus Garvey

Marcus Garvey came from Jamaica. By the time of his death and even beyond, he had influenced millions and had fashioned "the largest mass movement in the history of the African American."[24]

Garvey touched the lives and philosophies of W. D. Fard and Elijah Muhammad, both early NOI leaders, and after his death Garvey influenced Malcolm X. This is indicative of the power Garvey possessed. Though he once was described with retaliatory vigor as "fat . . . with protruding jaws . . . and [a] rather bulldog-like face. . . . Boastful, egotistical, tyrannical [and] intolerant,"[25] Garvey did much to raise millions of lower-class African Americans to a standard in which they viewed themselves as an important people with a destiny reserved only for them.

Garvey's Calling. C. Eric Lincoln mentions that during the summer of 1914, after returning to Jamaica from a visit to London, Garvey was moved to recognize his mission after reading Booker T. Washington's autobiography *Up from Slavery.*[26] Even though many black leaders hated Washington for his "strategy of compromise and accommodation,"[27] Garvey reacted in another way:

> I read *Up from Slavery* . . . and then my doom . . . of being a race leader dawned upon me. . . . I asked: "Where is the black man's Government? Where is his King and his kingdom? Where is his President, his country, and his ambassador, his army, his navy, his men of big affairs?" I could not find them, and then I declared, "I will help to make them."[28]

During his time in London in 1912, Garvey came under the influence of the African nationalist Duse Muhammad Ali. From him Garvey learned "Africa for Africans."[29] Separatism, therefore, would come to be an important ingredient in Garvey's solution to his people's problems.

The UNIA. In 1914 Garvey organized the UNIA in Jamaica. In 1916 he brought his movement to the United States (Harlem), "screaming out of the British West Indies onto the American stage."[30] It was to become "the largest black social movement in

American history," with "nearly two thousand branches around the world and up to six million dues-paying members in the United States."[31]

The UNIA was founded to bring lower-class, oppressed blacks to a sense of racial pride and self-containment, both commercially and educationally. On the flip side, Garvey would utilize his newly founded organization to scathe the "so-called Negro[32] leaders" of the United States. The "so-called Negro leaders," said Garvey, "had no program, but were mere opportunists who were living off their so-called leadership while the poor people were groping in the dark."[33] For Garvey, the black intelligentsia was as much the enemy as were the whites. They had bought into the whites' scheme of things, and the whites, in Garvey's mind, were content to allow a few blacks high status if it would keep the rest of the black population inoculated to the real white agenda—domination.

Garvey's Ideology. Garvey's black nationalism was tenacious. Though the UNIA agenda in part called for racial unity among blacks, race pride and love, the establishment of secondary and higher learning schools, and independent commerce and industry,[34] backing this agenda was an attitude of color prejudice. For example, Garvey claimed that mulattoes in leadership roles were a mixed race, were deceptive,[35] and "were to think of themselves as monstrosities to be bred out of existence."[36]

Garvey further prided himself in the superiority of the black race. "Every student of history, of impartial mind," said Garvey, "knows that the Negro ruled the world, when white men were savages and barbarians living in caves."[37] This theme would become popular with Elijah Muhammad's NOI, as would Garvey's assertion that whites know this but hide this truth from blacks.

One of these civilizations was Egypt, but Garvey's view of "the greatness of colored civilizations" did not originate with him. Mary Lefkowitz says, "The notion of such a specifically black Egyptian heritage appears to have been well established by the turn of the century. It was taken up by the historian W. E. B. Du Bois (1868–1963)."[38] And Edward W. Blyden (1832–1912), another black nationalist leader, must have influenced Du Bois: "Blyden likewise insisted that all Africans were the true heirs of the great civilization of ancient Egypt."[39] Though Lefkowitz challenges "the notion," and it is not the role of this book to enter into the debate, we should nonetheless note the influence such writers had upon Garvey.

Garvey, says Lefkowitz, also joined the Masons.[40] Prince Hall Masonry (Freemasonry for blacks) played an important part in molding Garvey's organization of the UNIA:

> To a large extent, the UNIA was organized along Masonic lines: it had a significant benevolent function; it had a constitution based on the Masons'; it also had a "potentate," analogous to the "imperial potentate" of the black Masonic Ancient Egyptian Arabic Order of the Nobles of the Mystic Shrine. Both organizations favored large-scale public displays, and the UNIA potentate's helmet closely resembled the ceremonial hat worn by Masons in special parades.[41]

Because he was a Mason, Garvey was probably familiar with black Masons' adoption of the Egyptian heritage of blacks.[42] Lefkowitz adds that an anonymous writer of an article in *The Colored American Magazine* (1903) spoke out against white Masons' refusal to accept blacks in their lodges. He labels Europeans "naked barbarians" and calls attention to the fact that on Egyptian soil was a civilization "far exceeding that of Greece or Rome today. . . . Here the landmarks of Masonry were born."[43] Other authors have noted this black Masonic concept of history.[44]

Garvey's vision was to move African Americans back to their homeland of Africa in a fifty-year time span.[45] He would propagate this view largely through his *Negro World* newspaper, which had a circulation of two million by June 1919.[46] This oddly placed Garvey in agreement with such white supremacist segregationist groups as the Ku Klux Klan. According to Dinesh D'Souza, Garvey in 1922 "arranged a secret meeting with the Grand Cyclops of the Invisible Empire of the Ku Klux Klan" to seek financial aid to transport blacks to Africa.[47]

Garvey's public speaking was no laughing matter. In 1920 the UNIA held its first international convention in New York. Twenty-five thousand black people from twenty-five countries attended. Garvey thrilled the crowd with these words:

> We are the descendants of a suffering people; we are the descendants of a people determined to suffer no longer. . . .
> We shall now organize the 400,000,000 Negroes of the world into a vast organization to plant the banner of freedom on the great continent of Africa. . . . If Europe is for the Europeans, then Africa shall be for the black peoples of the world. We say it; we mean it.[48]

Garvey's target for the emigration of African Americans was Liberia. At the end of the speech, Garvey proclaimed, "Up, you mighty race! You can accomplish what you will!"[49]

In all this Garvey was reacting against The Oppressor—the white race. And he would not stop with Liberia. His dream of establishing a homeland for blacks would extend in his mind and plans to the whole of Africa. To this effect he is reported as saying, "We shall not ask England or France or Italy or Belgium, 'Why are you here?' We shall only command them, 'Get out of here.' "[50]

Self-Sufficiency. Marcus Garvey's impact upon black culture in the United States was so great that a million dollars was gathered in order to fund the UNIA's Black Star Steamship Line for the express purpose of bringing the blacks of America back to their homeland.[51] Yet even with this backing, the project of emigration was never realized. But that did not stop the Garveyites, who still were able to realize part of Garvey's dream of independence in commerce and trade, a phenomenon that influenced, and to this day characterizes, the NOI.

> They gloried in the cooperative possession of grocery stores, laundries, restaurants, and hotels. They took an unconcealed pride in staffing the Universal Black Cross Nurses, the Universal African Motor Corps, the Black Eagle Flying Corps, and other UNIA auxiliaries with black men and women.[52]

Such accomplishments gave millions of blacks new social identity, social molding, and a bond that most likely never existed anywhere else in the history of blacks in the United States. Garvey was their social messiah. He undoubtedly possessed a great mind coupled with an extraordinary measure of charisma. The following statement by Arthur J. Magida regarding the accomplishments of the Garvey movement is a tribute to his genius of persuading millions to follow him and his ideals:

> As would the Nation of Islam, the Garvey movement turned skin into the arbiter of virtue and greatness; economic self-sufficiency into the vehicle for liberation from white domination; and land into the means for ultimate emancipation.[53]

Clifton E. Marsh virtually duplicates these comments with a list of four Garvey accomplishments that influenced Elijah Muhammad's NOI:

1. Black Factories Corporation—black business
2. Back to Africa culturally while developing a nation within a nation in the United States
3. Race pride and African consciousness
4. Black nationalist credo—red for the blood of the race, black for the color of the race, and green for an independent homeland[54]

Garvey and Religion. It is logical to assume that a leader like Marcus Garvey would not forget an important dynamic in his moving of countless blacks to personal, political, and economic freedom. Religion was important enough for Garvey to weave it into his ideology, for it was vital to the majority of the black populace. After all, the emigration of blacks to Africa involved an exodus that could not excuse the thought of a destiny, a chosen spiritual destiny, for blacks. This, Garvey thought, must involve God. "One God! One aim! One destiny!" therefore became "the favorite rallying cry of the movement."[55] God was on their side, and Garvey was a modern-day Moses.

Though Garvey did not possess a theology that identified his movement, his goal was to ally himself with theologians of different faiths[56] who shared his view that anything white is of no good to blacks. For him this was safe ground. The white God therefore was of no advantage to blacks. With religion as well as other parts of their lives, blacks should have their own identity, their own identifiable God, a God with whom they could relate. Garvey's genius was to teach that blacks could do this in the context of their personal religion, whatever that might be (except the "Christianity" of the whites).[57]

Garvey first secured the services of a former Episcopalian rector, George Alexander McGuire, and named him Chaplain General of the UNIA.[58] Under McGuire the UNIA had its personally sponsored African Orthodox Church (this is different from saying that Garvey founded the church). Blacks needed a God with whom they could identify, and the theologian McGuire was just the man to set the wheel in motion: "Forget the white gods. . . . Erase the white gods from your hearts."[59] Not too long after this, a black Mother Mary and a black Jesus "became a standard picture in the homes of the faithful."[60] And, to the protests of both the black press and non-UNIA black clergy,[61] McGuire called for the faithful to "tear down and burn any pictures of the white Madonna and the white Christ found in their homes."[62] The doctrine that God the Father and Jesus were black later became a tenet of the NOI.[63]

It is important to note that George Alexander McGuire and others were reacting to (if not wholly, at least in part) the mistaken notion, represented in many portraits as well as in many minds, that Jesus was or at the least looked like a white European. Jesus was not white European. He was Semitic and therefore a Jew.

Garvey and the Law. Since its inception the UNIA, Garvey in particular, was under the eyes of the law enforcement officials, not to mention various colonial governments.[64] Like the Garveyites, the soon-to-come NOI would come under constant surveillance by the law.

Garvey was known in government official eyes as a seditious person. In 1922, the government finally had its opportunity to place Garvey in jail. The young leader was indicted for mail fraud. He was charged with using fraudulent means to promote stock for the Black Star Steamship Line, which belonged to the UNIA. Tension rose even higher with the murder (to this day unsolved) of a key ex-Garveyite and supposed prosecution witness, James W. H. Eason. As a result, more effort was made to prosecute Garvey, and letters to law enforcement officials by black leaders who opposed him helped to speed the process.[65] Garvey spoke out against these "good old darkies,"[66] and years later he identified with the persecution of Jesus Christ: "They framed him. They said he was preaching sedition."[67] Garvey spoke these words during an Easter Sunday speech in Jamaica in 1929, for by that time he had been deported from the United States a few years after being convicted of mail fraud in 1923.

Leaving a Mark. Marcus Garvey died in London in 1940, but he had left a permanent mark upon the consciences of blacks in America. Of all the black leaders, Garvey would be the most influential upon leaders of the NOI. His independent commerce and industry, his desire for a separate state, his particular brand of racism that saw whites as the inferior race, and his support of a black God were all to become trademarks of the NOI. Millions of blacks adored him. Even the young Malcolm Little, who later became Malcolm X, wept when he learned that Marcus Garvey was dead.

Noble Drew Ali

Born in 1886, Timothy Drew of North Carolina became known as "The Prophet" and changed his name to Noble Drew Ali. Noble Drew Ali did as much to feed the religious ideas of the NOI as Garvey did the anthropological, political, and economic. Elijah Muhammad praised Ali on many occasions, for Muhammad's teachings are drawn from the doctrinal well of Ali (sometimes with variations).

Beginnings. In 1913[68] Noble Drew Ali established the Moorish Science Temple Divine and National Movement of North America after moving to Newark, New Jersey. In 1926 Ali changed the name of his movement to the Moorish Science Temple of America. Temples were established in several urban centers in the United States. Considering numbers alone, the Moorish Science Temple was not as influential as the Garveyite movement. Probably only thirty thousand people became members.[69]

Ali's religion was Islam.[70] Tradition has it that on a visit to North Africa, Timothy Drew "received a mission from the King of Morocco to teach Islam to the Negroes in the United States."[71] Additionally, in order to prove that he was a prophet of Allah, Drew had to meet the challenge of finding his way out of the pyramids of Egypt. He was placed inside them, and he found his way out. He was *the* prophet.[72] Soon Morocco became the place of origin for the blacks, who were, according to Ali, "Asiatics." All whites were European, while all olive- and dark-skinned people (all non-Caucasian) were Asiatics. Blacks were in reality "Moors" and descendants of the ancient Moabites; thus came the designation Moorish Science Temple.

Separatism. Whites were the enemy and the devil: "Noble Drew Ali felt the Caucasians were the embodiment of evil, . . . which is Satan."[73] Ali, like Garvey, promoted the idea of racial superiority of blacks (Asiatics) and the eschatological hope of the "destruction of the Europeans [whites]."[74] As we shall see, Ali instituted a number of practices and policies that reinforced this idea for his followers.

A number of Garveyites simultaneously belonged to Ali's cult,[75] which viewed the blacks as God's chosen race.[76] Ali, however, did not seek the emigration of blacks to Africa[77] or anywhere else. But he did possess a separatist mindset when it came to religion: "Christianity is for the European (paleface); Moslemism is for the Asiatic (olive-skinned)."[78] Membership, therefore, was open only to Asiatics.

Once again we need to be reminded that this was a reaction that rose out of the oppression of black people. Institution of a Moorish origin for blacks, separation in the context of religion, and the ultimate destruction of the oppressors were all answers to the fundamental problem facing blacks. Noble Drew Ali would give thousands identity, social and religious adhesion, and hope for the future.

All this could not be founded upon mere political and social foundations, as Garvey knew. Religion must play a role. At the very least, Garvey used religion as an important afterthought. In Ali's thinking, religion was foremost.

Other Moorish Beliefs and Practices. The Islam of Noble Drew Ali is in many ways not classical Islam. It mixes the Islamic expressions of Ismailiyya, Ahmadiyya, and Sufism with Freemasonry,[79] the gnosticism of Eliphas Levi, and black nationalism.[80] Additionally, he believed he was the third reincarnation of Islam's prophet Muhammad and that Muhammad was a reincarnation of Jesus.[81]

11

The Moors desired not only religious separation; they wanted separation in all areas of life, including marriage. Interracial marriages were forbidden, for they led to union with the gods of the whites (Europeans). Mixed marriages would defile Moors and anger Allah. Moors were also strongly exhorted to abstain from infidelity, alcohol, and general unproductiveness, as these would only serve as a bad witness, not to mention first and foremost Allah's displeasure at such vices. Moorish men and women wore distinctive clothing, marking themselves as followers of Allah and Islam. Men and women also remained separated during worship services and prayed three times a day while facing Mecca.[82] To solidify Moorish members' new identity and true nationality, Noble Drew Ali instituted the practice of giving new names to adherents. All new members, for a fee, added "Bey" or "El" to their names. They were issued identification cards that included the member's new name, the symbol of the star and crescent, and the following statement:

> This is your nationality and identification card for the Moorish Science Temple of America, and birthright for the Moorish Americans. We honor all the divine prophets, Jesus, Mohammad, Buddha, and Confucious. May the blessings of God[,] of our father[,] Allah, be upon you that carry this card. I do hereby declare that you are a Muslim under the Divine Law of the Holy Koran of Mecca[83]— Love, Truth, Peace, Freedom, and Justice. "I am a citizen of the USA."[84]

Unlike Garvey, the Moors desired to remain a part of the United States. This did not stop Ali's followers, though, from walking the streets and harassing the white enemy by flashing their identification cards at them. They paraded their newfound identity and boasted of their freedom from European domination.[85] After the police became involved due to complaints from whites, the Prophet issued orders to cease this practice.[86] "Our work," said Ali, "is to uplift the nation."[87]

The main text of the Moorish Science Temple is *The Holy Koran of the Moorish Science Temple of America*. This is not to be confused with orthodox Islam's Qur'an. The *Holy Koran* (1927) is a work of more than sixty pages containing the teachings of Noble Drew Ali. Its philosophy is much akin to gnostic, esoteric thought. Scholars also have noted Ali's plagiarism of Eliphas Levi's *Aquarian Gospel of Jesus the Christ* (published in 1907) and a Tibetan document titled *Infinite Wisdom*.[88] According to Mattias Gardell, "the introductory chapter of the *Holy Koran* is taken verbatim from an introductory text of the *Aquarian Gospel of Jesus the Christ*. . . . The only deviation is that the word 'God' has been replaced by 'Allah.' "[89] Gardell notes that according to Abbie Whyte, "a large part of the *Aquarian Gospel of Jesus the Christ* was plagiarized by Noble Drew Ali."[90]

Influence upon the NOI. The following list summarizes Ali's direct influence on the NOI, not counting some of the gnostic speculations of Ali.[91]

1. The ancient Moabites are the divine Asiatic nation and all blacks are Asiatics, "the original inhabitants of the earth and the progenitors of all nonwhite nations."[92] (This bears some semblance to the NOI's Yakub myth, in which an evil scientist named Yakub grafted, through a series of birthing experiments, the white race from the original black race approximately sixty-six hundred years ago. In this way the NOI sees the black man as Asiatic and as the "progenitor" of the whites. For this reason Ali, and later the NOI, hated the designations "Negro" and "colored.")
2. The Caucasians are "colored";[93] they are the unnatural ones.
3. Whites, therefore, cannot be members since Christianity is for whites and Islam is for Asiatics.
4. Jesus was black.
5. "Noble Drew Ali is Jesus Christ and the prophet Muhammad [of Islam] reincarnated."[94] (The Messenger Elijah Muhammad of the NOI taught that Wallace Fard [his teacher] was "Allah in person," God to the NOI.)
6. Ali's mission was apocalyptic, warning of the wrath and destruction of Allah upon the earth.[95] (Elijah Muhammad's God-man Wallace Fard was incarnated for this reason—he was to usher in a new era for mankind by beginning God's

work of cleansing the earth and elevating blacks to their promised blissful afterlife.)

7. For Ali and his followers the white man is the devil. (One cannot read material from the NOI for long and not find this teaching.)
8. Mixed marriages are forbidden.
9. Women are separated from men during meetings.
10. Whites will be destroyed.
11. Asiatics are the superior race.
12. The Star and the Crescent is a symbol of the movement.
13. Members are given identification cards.
14. Members change their names.
15. Ali's movement aspired to be self-sufficient in industry and commerce.
16. Members must abide by a strict moral code and dietary sanctions (infidelity, slothfulness, alcohol, meat, and eggs are taboo).

Greed and the Death of Noble Drew Ali. In relation to point 15 above, Gardell observes,

> Following the example of Marcus Garvey, the Moors established "the Moorish Industrial Group" and founded small businesses in various fields. Besides operating restaurants and barber shops, the sale of religious paraphernalia proved to be a lucrative venture.[96]

This proved to be the beginning of the end for Ali. Profits came from the independent business ventures of the cult, and greed and the lust for power arose within the ranks. With the growth of the Moorish Science Temple came delegation of authority. Ali, of course, remained The Prophet, but several men came under him in authority.[97] One in particular would come to bring the prophet's downfall. Claude Green, a Moorish Science Temple "sheik," challenged Ali's authority and eventually led a splinter group that literally removed Ali from his Moorish Science Temple headquarters in Chicago. A few days later Green was found murdered.[98] Even though Ali was nowhere near Chicago at the time of the murder, police arrested him and later released him. Ali died a few weeks later, on July 20, 1929. Ali was ill to begin with and never recovered, though other theories as to the cause of his death are given.[99]

Who Would Succeed Ali? As is characteristic of many religious groups, the death of the founder invites spiritual claims to succession. The Moorish Science Temple was no exception. By 1929 Ali was dead and Garvey was deported. There was a void in black nationalism. Two men would compete for leadership.

John Givens El, Ali's chauffeur, allegedly fainted after the prophet's death. His eyes were examined, and in his eyes appeared the Star and the Crescent, symbols of the Moorish Science Temple. This was confirmation that John Givens El was the new Prophet.[100] Present-day Moors are followers of John Givens El and believe that Ali "reincarnated into his chauffeur."[101]

The other man vying to fill the void was W. D. Fard, "the mysterious stranger from the East." It was Fard who fashioned the NOI and personally taught Elijah Muhammad.

SUMMARY

In this chapter we have explored the sociological and religious soil of black nationalism in the nineteenth and early twentieth centuries—a must if we are to understand the rise of W. D. Fard's and Elijah Muhammad's NOI. Several factors birthed by America's black nationalist movements shaped their beliefs, the most important being the reaction by blacks to slavery and all its accompanying racist phenomena. A spirit of unity dominated the black community within the cultural milieu of black nationalism, a spirit forged with inherent black pride and identity. As this grew, so did various black leaders with their expressions of black nationalism, black theology, and black anthropology.

Marcus Garvey and Noble Drew Ali stand in the forefront of many blacks' minds as the fathers of black nationalism. But even they had their predecessors. Men like David Walker, Henry Highland Garnet, Alexander Crummell, Edward W. Blyden, Martin Delaney, Booker T. Washington, and W. E. B. Du Bois,[102] among others I may have neglected to mention, must not be forgotten.

All these, in some measure, contributed to the social and religious black nationalist movement and religion known as the NOI.

W. D. Fard: The Stranger from the East

The forms of black nationalism taught by Garvey and Ali combined to influence millions of blacks. But with Marcus Garvey's deportation and Noble Drew Ali's death, the soil was rich for someone to come along and plant a new movement that would continue and promote their foundational views. "The stranger from the East" would start a movement that continues to this day—the Nation of Islam (NOI).

To many people who have not studied the NOI but have merely glanced at it through the media's eyes, the NOI is synonymous with Elijah Muhammad, Malcolm X, or Louis Farrakhan. These three, however, are really products of this powerful figure—the stranger from the East.

Like those of his predecessors, the stranger's movement catered to the sociological and religious needs of blacks. Like his predecessors, he would end up influencing millions of people.

THE MYSTERIOUS APPEARANCE

The stranger from the East is Wallace D. Fard, also known as Mr. Farrad Mohammad, Mr. F. Mohammad Ali, Professor Ford, Wallace Fard Muhammad, and Mr. Wali Farrad. The NOI knows him as Master Fard Muhammad or W. D. Fard. When he made his "appearance" among blacks in Detroit in the summer of 1930, no one knew who he was or where he came from. He would soon, however, be noticed by many people.

Who was he? Why did he come? There were two options. To some he was a charlatan who capitalized on the absence of Garvey and Noble Drew Ali. To others he was the messenger sent by God to continue the work of these two men. Whatever the case, the NOI held the latter view (and later claimed a higher view of Fard) and openly challenged any and all who disagreed.

Fard's Method

On July 4, 1930, Independence Day,[1] Fard arrived in Detroit. He was convinced that he had an important message to spread and a vision to fulfill, a mission to undertake, and he would use whatever means possible to realize his goal.

Prior to coming to Detroit, Fard most likely had come under the influence of both Noble Drew Ali and Marcus Garvey.[2] This view is strengthened, albeit not conclusively, by the fact that Fard claimed to be the reincarnation of Noble Drew Ali. Fard, of course, could have heard of Ali in passing as he talked with people, but it seems unlikely, given this claim. To claim this, Fard would have to be in political and theological agreement with Ali, which in turn implies familiarity with Ali's teachings.

Fard came as a traveling salesman of raincoats and silks. Apparently this was common practice among Arab and Syrian peddlers at that time.[3] Some people, therefore, thought that he might be an Arab. Fard said he was from Mecca, the holy city, and that he came among the blacks of Detroit as a messenger of Allah to set his people on the road to freedom and newfound identity. Sister Denke Majied, the former Mrs. Lawrence Adams, tells of Fard's method of getting into the homes[4] of blacks in order to gain a hearing:

> He came first to our houses selling raincoats, and then afterwards silks. In this way he could get into the people's houses, for every woman was eager to see the nice things the peddlars [sic] had for sale. He told us that the silks he carried were the same kind that our people used in their home country and that he had come from there. So we all asked him to tell us about our own country. If we asked him to eat with us, he would eat whatever we had on the table, but after the meal he began to talk: "Now don't eat this food. It is

poison for you. The people in your own country do not eat it. Since they eat the right kind of food they have the best of health all the time. If you would live just like the people in your home country, you would never be sick any more." So we all wanted him to tell us more about ourselves and about our home country and about how we could be free from rheumatism, aches and pains.[5]

Sister Majied's reaction is typical, as were the reactions of the others she described. In the Great Depression, hope of escape from the toils and sufferings of everyday life was what people needed. Or perhaps at the very least some kind of diversion—a simple escape if only for the moment—from these toils and sufferings was welcomed. Whatever the case, Fard provided that hope or diversion with his tableside talks. And his charisma must have been extraordinary, for what started out as after-dinner speeches soon became public lectures.

From Peddler to Christ Figure

Slowly Fard began to make more authoritative claims about himself. Meetings became so packed with people that more spacious accommodations were needed. At first the attendees were sectioned into several groups. They were then told when they could hear Fard speak. Of course, it was Fard who told them when and where.[6] In time this became an organizational nuisance, so followers contributed funds to rent a hall and called it The Temple of Islam.[7]

As his audience grew, so did the quantity of Fard's words. Accompanying his claim that he came from the East—the holy city of Mecca—was this claim: "More about myself I will not tell you yet, for the time has not yet come. I am your brother. You have not yet seen me in my royal robes."[8]

A sense of mystery followed Fard from the beginning and continues today, and the claim of royal robes, if nothing else, left room for speculative fantasy on the part of Fard's followers as to the origin of this stranger from the East. Some believed he was from the Arab tribe of Koreish and that he came from wealthy stock. For these people this was no coincidence, for Muhammad, the prophet of Islam in the seventh century, was said to be of that same tribe.[9]

19

Fard, therefore, was divinely destined for his role as The Messenger. In his followers' eyes he was the one for whom the world had been waiting. Indeed, Fard himself said that he had come to "awaken the dead nation in the West."[10]

But the claims did not stop there. One devotee of Fard, Yussuf Mohammed, boasted, "When the police asked him who he was, he said: 'I am the Supreme Ruler of the Universe.' "[11] Several decades later, Imam Wallace D. Muhammad (Elijah Muhammad's son, who had defected from his father's teachings) stated that Fard told his flock that he was a "Christ figure to displace the old Christ that Christianity gave black people."[12] To back up these powerful assertions, Fard performed "feats of magic," such as taking a collection of hair from his audience, placing the hair in a pile, and lifting up the pile with a single strand of his own hair. Fard, after performing this feat, then stated, "Lift me up and I will draw all men unto me."[13]

From 1930 to 1933 W. D. Fard drew eight thousand people into the newly organized NOI.

WHO IS WALLACE FARD?

Surprisingly, according to the NOI, Fard is half black and half white. Following are the words of Elijah Muhammad:

> He said his father went often in the mountains there in their country where some Caucasians were living. . . . He said he got one of these women and took her for his wife so he could get a son to live more like this civilization of the whites so as to be able to get among them and they will not be able to distinguish him.[14]

But Fard has a criminal record, contrary to the statement from Elijah Muhammad, and law enforcement officials have him classified as white, born in Portland, Oregon, in 1891 to Hawaiian immigrants. Arthur J. Magida reports,

> Whenever Fard was arrested, and wherever he was booked, he identified himself as a *white* man. His standard story was

that he had been born in 1891 in New Zealand to a Polyne-
sian mother and an Englishman who arrived in New
Zealand on a schooner. Occasionally, he claimed he was
born in Portland, Oregon, and that his parents, Zared and
Beatrice Ford, had both been born in Hawaii.[15]

Other stories of Fard's background made their rounds among
the public. Some thought Fard was "a black Jamaican whose father
was a Syrian Moslem."[16] Others thought Fard was "a Palestinian
Arab who had participated in various racial agitations in India,
South Africa, and London before moving on to Detroit."[17] Or perhaps "he was educated at a London university in preparation for a
diplomatic career" to serve the Arab nation and free the blacks of
America from the oppression of the "Cave Man"[18] (whites). Many
years later, *The New Crusader*, a Chicago newspaper, said that Fard
was "a Turkish-born Nazi agent [who] worked for Hitler in World
War II."[19] All these theories are highly unlikely. Three other theories, however, seem plausible.

Three Theories

Nothing has been conclusively proved as to the origin of W. D.
Fard, but Mattias Gardell lists three theories that "have proved to be
the most enduring."[20] First is that Fard was a member of Noble
Drew Ali's Moorish Science Temple; second, that he was a rabbi of
a black Hebrew congregation in the 1920s; and third, that he was a
fraud.

Fard a Moor. As for Fard being a member of Noble Drew Ali's
cult, this could account for his claim that he was the reincarnation
of Ali. Further, it is suggested that upon the death of Ali two factions
arose—one faithful to Ali, and the other, led by Fard, being faithful
to Fard.[21] The faction staying faithful to Ali remained as the Moors,
while those following Fard became the NOI. Evidence that suggests
this theory is unfounded is the absence of Fard's reincarnation
claims in the beliefs of the NOI, absence of Moroccan identity for
adherents of the NOI, and Fard's alleged expulsion of converts for
sharing Moorish teachings with members of the NOI.[22] In light of
the numerous similarities between Moorish beliefs and those of the

NOI, this is difficult to believe, unless Fard was so prideful that he did not allow his followers to label or associate his teachings with those of Noble Drew Ali.

Fard Is Ford. Howard Brotz sets forth the second theory that Fard was a rabbi of a black Hebrew congregation. Brotz claims that Fard's name was false and that his real name was Rabbi Arnold Josiah Ford.[23] Ford was from Barbados, became a close friend of Marcus Garvey, and represented one of a number of faiths associated with the Garveyites.[24] Ford and Garvey later had a falling out when Ford tried to persuade Garvey to claim Judaism as the religion for blacks. Garvey's eclectic ideology made this impossible, and the resulting tension eventually led to Ford's expulsion from the UNIA in 1923.[25] Ford later organized the Kabbalah-based Beth B'nai Abraham. There he taught the path of *gnosis,* knowledge of the self leading to liberation. His movement faltered for six long years and disbanded in 1929. According to Brotz, Ford then disappeared from New York in 1930, and this happens to be the time of his mysterious appearance as W. D. Fard in Detroit.[26] Fard came from the East, but not from Mecca!

Gardell suggests that this theory is far-fetched:

> The Fard-is-Ford thesis . . . is hardly convincing. Could Ford, a renowned personality in black nationalist circles, have managed to change his identity and establish a nationalist religious movement without being recognized?[27]

Robert A. Hill and Barbara Bair state that Ford moved himself and a small band of his followers to Africa, obtained a parcel of land from Emperor Haile Selassie of Ethiopia, and headed up a group of repatriates. This movement failed, most of the followers returned to the United States, and Ford died in Addis Ababa in 1935.[28]

Fard a Fraud. W. D. Fard came to Detroit, and it was not long before he came under the scrutiny of the police and later the Federal Bureau of Investigation (FBI). There were two reasons for this. First, his message, like that of Garvey and Ali, was that blacks were superior to whites. Whites were the devil, the oppressor of the black race. Fard fostered an attitude among his followers that they should rise up and not take it anymore. Word travels quickly, even in a city, and the police were quick to take notice of possible social unrest. Second is the widely publicized human sacrifice said to have been performed specifically because of Fard's teaching.

Human Sacrifice in Detroit. On the morning of November 20, 1932, Robert Harris (renamed Robert Karriem[29]) built a sacrificial altar in his home at 1249 Dubois Street and sank a knife into the heart of his neighbor,[30] John J. Smith. Harris told Smith that if he offered himself as a sacrifice, Smith would become "the Saviour of the world."[31] Harris also told Smith that Harris had been "commanded to kill some one by the Gods of Islam," and that Smith had to fully agree to be sacrificed. As Harris's wife, "Queen" Bertha, held a clock to signal the appointed time, Harris asked Smith, "Smith, do you want to die?" Smith said yes but then changed his mind and started to resist. Harris, "to quiet him," abruptly struck Smith on the head with a seventy-five-pound rear-wheel axle, crushing his skull. Harris then lifted him onto the altar and plunged the eight-inch knife "to the hilt" into Smith's heart.[32]

Why did Harris and Smith believe this? According to E. D. Beynon,

> [Fard] taught explicitly that it was the duty of every Moslem to offer as sacrifice four Caucasian devils in order that he might return to his home in Mecca. The prophet also taught that Allah demands obedience unto death from his followers. No Moslem dare refuse the sacrifice of himself or of his loved ones if Allah requires it.[33]

The police arrested Harris, who admitted to the ritual killing of Smith. In addition to believing that Smith would become a savior, Harris told the police, Smith's act of sacrificial killing was predestined fifteen hundred years ago.[34]

Though it is debated whether or not Harris and Smith were members of the NOI or whether or not Fard gave orders for the killing,[35] "belief in blood sacrifices was definitely a part of early Muslim [NOI] doctrine, notwithstanding Fard's denial."[36] In fact, "it is a matter of record that the Muslims did teach sacrificial killing at that time."[37] There exist, say researchers, 154 lessons of W. D. Fard. Portions of them have been quoted in secondary sources. If these sources are accurate there is little doubt that at the very least a person could be persuaded to kill in the name of Fard's teaching. A portion of Fard's lessons follows:

> [Q:] Why does [Fard] Mohammad and any Moslem murder the devil? What is the duty of each Moslem in regard to four devils? What reward does a Moslem receive by presenting the four devils at one time?
>
> [A:] Because he is one hundred percent wicked and will not keep and obey the laws of Islam. His ways and actions are like a snake of the grafted[38] type. So Mohammad learned that he could not reform the devils, so they had to be murdered. All Moslem[s] will murder the devil because they know he is a snake and also if he be allowed to live, he would sting someone else. Each Moslem is required to bring four devils, and by bringing and presenting four at one time his reward is a button to wear on the lapel of his coat, also a free transportation to the Holy City of Mecca.[39]

Comparing this lesson with the ritualistic murder of Smith by Harris reveals that Harris was not following Fard's teaching verbatim.[40] This again and in part has led some people to say that Harris's involvement with the NOI is doubtful.

Nonetheless, when reports of the murder reached the public, the reaction was strong, and further reports about Fard's "Voodoo Cult" revealed a "death list" of names that included Gladys Smith and Margret Adele. Both women were social workers who were in part responsible for declaring Harris ineligible to receive welfare aid.[41] Other public officials, including Mayor Frank Murphy and Judge Edward J. Jeffries, were targeted.[42] Though this is no excuse to place names on a death list, being in the Great Depression and having one's name removed as a welfare recipient could influence an already unstable person to commit murder.

More than a week later the Detroit police arrested Fard and NOI teacher Ugan Ali, only to release them after five hundred members of the NOI protested the arrest and after both Fard and Ali promised to disband the NOI.[43] As for Harris, "[he] was declared insane by a sanity commission and committed to the Ionia Institution on December 14, 1932."[44] This shows that the police did not have much evidence to implicate Fard in the sacrificial murder of Smith by Harris. But this is not to say that a teaching such as that found in Fard's *Lesson #1* could not have been used as an excuse to commit murder. Perhaps Harris was to some degree familiar with Fard's work.

Decades later another homicide occurred. If the account is true, there is no doubt that Fard's lesson on the murder of white devils was taken literally and verbatim:

> One-man wars were waged. One afternoon in the early 1970s, when Ali K. Muslim, then Charles 41x (there were 40 Charleses registered in the Newark mosque before he joined[45]), was guarding the temple, a man carrying a sack asked to meet a temple official. The man, thoroughly confused about Elijah Muhammad's teachings,[46] believed that if he killed four white "devils" he would win a star-and-crescent lapel pin and a trip to the Holy Land. He had come to redeem his prizes. In the sack, Ali K. Muslim says, were four severed heads.[47]

Enter the FBI. Fard later came to be a subject for study by the FBI. In 1958 the NOI was under the leadership of Elijah Muhammad after the "disappearance" of Fard in 1934. FBI file #105-63642-22, February 3, 1958, stated, "Any information developed concerning the actual origins and life of W. D. Fard is extremely important to the investigation of the NOI and should be pursued vigorously and imaginatively."[48]

Inquiry into Fard's past began, and it was later found that Fard's fingerprints matched those of convict Wallie D. Ford, born in Portland, Oregon, on February 25, 1891, the son of Hawaiian immigrants.[49] The fingerprints were on file in the Los Angeles Police Department and in San Quentin Prison.[50] Ford had been arrested on drug charges and served three years in the prison, from June 12, 1926 to May 27, 1929.[51] After his release from San Quentin, Wallie

D. Ford told his former fiancée, Hazel Brown, that he was going to move to the Midwest to sell silks.[52] The NOI claimed the FBI had doctored the evidence of the fingerprint matching.[53]

It is theoretically possible that the fingerprints were doctored. The question is, though, has it been proven? Until then, it is not unreasonable to maintain that Fard is Wallie D. Ford, based on the available evidence. Further, in Claude A. Clegg III's *An Original Man,* there appear three pictures—a San Quentin mug shot of W. D. Ford, a Los Angeles Police Department photograph of Ford, and an NOI photograph of W. D. Fard (Wallace Fard Muhammad). The reader is encouraged to form an independent opinion, but my opinion is that the three photographs are of the same man. Clegg, it seems, shares my opinion, for he relates the above evidence of the arrest of Ford but uses Fard's name.[54]

THE DISAPPEARANCE OF WALLACE FARD

The Smith murder left a sour taste in the mouths of the police, even though nothing could be pinned upon Fard by way of evidence. The image of "The Voodoo Cult" lingered. Fard was arrested two more times after the Smith murder. The arrests were on charges of disturbing the peace with "cult activities."[55] Finally, on May 26, 1933, Fard was "ordered out of Detroit."[56] Later an article appeared in *The Detroit Free Press* titled "Voodoo's Reign Here Is Broken."[57]

It does seem that the evidence needed to place Fard behind bars was lacking. Moreover, why was he banished rather than placed in prison after these arrests? The most plausible reason for his banishment from Detroit is social unrest caused by his popularity. According to Clegg, the Detroit police department's dealings with the NOI had served to bring many blacks "to view the whole situation as a racist assault on their community."[58] Situations like this can only strengthen an oppressed group and make its leader all the more the hero. Clegg then asserts, "As an alternative short of making a martyr of the leader, the Detroit police department decided to banish him from the city."[59]

This is not to excuse Fard from any wrongdoing. It is possible that he was a racketeer. Clegg reports that a police transcript reveals what Fard told authorities during questioning. Starting the NOI was "a racket," and his purpose was to get "all the money out of it he could."[60] Clegg then adds that Fard's motive in this confession may have been to get the police off his back by telling them what they wanted to hear, or that the police concocted the confession, or it was "the ugly truth."[61]

Fard, having already groomed Elijah Muhammad for leadership, left for Chicago, and most likely led the Detroit branch of the NOI through Supreme Minister Muhammad. Chicago was a logical move, for in 1932 Elijah Muhammad established NOI Chicago Temple No. 2. But not long after his arrival in Chicago, Fard was arrested on September 26, 1933. The charge was disorderly conduct.[62]

A Rousing Farewell

As is the case with his origin, so it is with his disappearance—no one knows for sure what happened to W. D. Fard.

Before his mysterious disappearance, Fard gave a rousing farewell speech to the faithful. Some compared him with Marcus Garvey, who in the 1920s had been deported. Some, no doubt, compared his experiences with those of Jesus Christ, while still others (or at least one—Elijah Muhammad) saw him as *the* messiah. With the following there is little doubt that Fard claimed for himself the title of Messiah for the NOI. Poised near his automobile, Fard shouted to the admiring crowd, "I am with you; I will be back to you in the near future to lead you out of this hell."[63]

During a time together with Elijah Muhammad, Fard used the same messianic and apocalyptic language to console him. Perhaps Fard knew it would not be long before he had to relinquish leadership for good. Perhaps to secure that Muhammad would still include Fard as the central point of the movement, Fard said to Muhammad, "I love them [black people]. I will destroy the Nations of the Earth to save them and then die myself."[64]

Because of the law, Fard's time in Chicago was short. After yet another arrest, Fard summoned the Supreme Minister to give him final preparations for leadership. In a series of events, Fard pronounced him "Messenger of Allah,"[65] gave him a copy of the Qur'an and a list of 104 other books, wrote him letters concerning organizational matters, and assured him with the words, "You don't need Me anymore."[66] Elijah Muhammad's last contact from Fard was a letter from Mexico.[67]

What Happened to Fard?

There are several speculations as to the fate of this charismatic black leader—some more plausible than others.

Critics of the NOI call attention to the "coincidence" of Elijah Muhammad's rise to power at the same time Fard disappeared. Rumors circulated that Muhammad offered Fard as a sacrifice to Allah, but C. Eric Lincoln rebuts this, saying, "Muhammad's rise was neither sudden nor unchallenged. . . . Muhammad simply cast his lot on the side that eventually prevailed."[68] Some say Fard was spotted "aboard a ship bound for Europe," but this, says Lincoln, "is unsubstantiated."[69] Unsubstantiated as well are reports that Fard met his death at the hands of the law or angry ex-members of the NOI or angry whites who hated Fard because of his attacks on the "white devils."[70] Yet another theory is that Fard went from Chicago to Los Angeles "driving a new car and garbed in flowing white robes."[71] After some time in Los Angeles, Fard sold his car and headed for New Zealand aboard a ship.[72]

One other startling claim remains, but we must move up forty years to examine it. On February 25, 1975, Elijah Muhammad, the beloved leader of Fard's NOI, died of congestive heart failure. One day later (ironically enough, on Saviour's Day, an annual celebration commemorating the birth of Master Fard Muhammad), NOI National Secretary Abass Rassoull stated to twenty thousand members of the NOI that Minister Wallace D. Muhammad would assume leadership of the movement.[73] Wallace was the seventh child of Elijah Muhammad.

A little more than a year later, Wallace D. Muhammad, or Warith D. Muhammad, rocked the NOI world with new information about W. D. Fard. As we shall see in chapter 4, Elijah Muhammad believed Fard was "Allah in person," "God in person." Wallace, however, never could accept his father's deification of W. D. Fard (due to Wallace's study of traditional Islam), and as a result he had a stormy relationship with the Elijah Muhammad-led NOI.[74] But with things supposedly patched up between him and his father, now deceased, Wallace announced that W. D. Fard was simply an ordinary Muslim and that "Master Farad [Fard] Muhammad is not dead . . . he is physically alive and I talk to him whenever I get ready. . . . I go to the telephone and dial his number."[75] Fard is supposed to have changed his name to Abdullah, a mysterious Muslim seen by many, and died in the early 1990s.[76] According to Wallace, Abdullah did not admit directly to him that he was Fard because he would incur his rage, perhaps for leading people astray from real Islam. This, like many of the other theories about Fard, is not substantiated with solid evidence. Fard remains a mystery.

SUMMARY

Whatever may be said of W. D. Fard, one thing is certain—he started a massive black nationalist movement from the humble beginnings of a silk peddler. Indeed, he went from silk peddler to Christ figure in the span of a few years. He was a powerful, intelligent, and charismatic man.

In this chapter I have explored Fard's mysterious origin, his methods, and his mysterious disappearance. But there is something else to Fard other than his power, intelligence, and charisma. To the post-Fard NOI he is Master Fard Muhammad, Allah in person, God in the flesh.

What did Fard teach that would attract these thousands of people? And why would his successor, the Honorable Elijah Muhammad, come to believe that Fard was and is God in the flesh? That is the focus of our next chapter.

THREE

The Teachings of W. D. Fard

With the rise of black nationalist movements in the nineteenth and early twentieth centuries came a new sense of identity, social adhesion, and hope for a better life to come for millions of oppressed blacks. The successful black nationalist leaders knew that the spiritual dimensions addressing the needs of the people must not be neglected, so they incorporated in their ideologies this dimension of human existence.

Marcus Garvey and Noble Drew Ali are among the most notable of these black leaders. They in turn had a profound impact upon W. D. Fard's Nation of Islam (NOI). But there were other influences upon Fard's theology. The Freemasons, the Jehovah's Witnesses, and Baptist fundamentalism, through the preacher Frank Norris, would also contribute to Fard's theological scheme.

In this chapter I shall briefly summarize Garveyite theology and the theology of the Noble Drew Ali's Moorish Science Temple of America, and I shall detail Fard's theology. I shall also mention, in places, its similarities with Freemasonry and the Jehovah's Witnesses. Obviously Fard's teachings are not exactly like those just mentioned in all doctrinal areas. This would be impossible even for Fard, given their contradictions when compared one to the other. But there are similarities.

THE SHAPING OF A THEOLOGY

Fard possessed the ability to edit and apply the teachings of Marcus Garvey, Noble Drew Ali, Freemasonry, and the Jehovah's

Witnesses to his theological framework. He sifted out what he did not consider worth keeping, made use of blacks' social and economic struggles, and brought to his people teaching that in their opinion came directly from the divine. E. D. Beynon once wrote,

> The prophet's message was characterized by his ability to utilize to the fullest measure the environment of his followers. Their physical and economic difficulties alike were used to illustrate the new teaching. Similarly, the biblical prophecies of Marcus Garvey and Noble Drew Ali were cited as foretelling the coming of the new prophet. As additional proofs of his message, the prophet referred his followers to the writings of Judge Joseph Rutherford, of Jehovah's Witnesses, [and] to a miscellaneous collection of books on Freemasonry and its symbolism.[1]

As is characteristic of most heterodox religious movements, especially at their inception, truth cannot be obtained by followers without the aid of the group's leader. Fard's movement was no exception. Though Fard directed his NOI to Rutherford's teachings and books on Masonic symbolism, he also "explained to the people that the recommended books and [radio] addresses [of Rutherford] were symbolic and could be understood only through the interpretation which he himself would give at the temple services."[2] Fard was God's Messenger from the East, the holy city of Mecca; and he would be, indeed he alone could be, the only one through whom Allah would speak.

Marcus Garvey

Marcus Garvey's[3] Universal Negro Improvement Association (UNIA) was founded in Jamaica in 1914 and brought to America in 1916 largely for political and social reasons. But Garvey, like all other astute leaders of mass movements, did not neglect religion. His view of the black race together with the theology of UNIA-sponsored clergy did much to shape Fard's anthropology and theology. And Garvey himself was not averse to making theological statements. To an extent the UNIA was a religious movement.

Garvey insisted that in ancient times blacks ruled the world. Long ago white men were mere barbarians living in caves while blacks were heading the human race in every category. The ontological superiority of the black race was a staple in the Garveyite message—everything black was good, everything white was of the devil. Garvey also favored separation. He dreamed of transporting all blacks back to their homeland, Africa.

Garvey capitalized on an African-centered theology. With George Alexander McGuire, Chaplain General of the UNIA and a leader of the UNIA-sponsored African Orthodox Church, at the helm, Garvey opted for a black God and a black Jesus. Blacks were called to erase the white gods from their hearts.

"One God! One aim! One destiny!" was the rallying cry of the movement. Garvey told black people that God was on their side, that God was against the whites, and that God indeed had destined the four hundred million blacks of the world to plant the banner of freedom on the continent of Africa. But not only were they to enter Africa, they were to tell the colonizing countries to "get out!"

The Garveyites were to some degree self-sufficient economically and educationally. They owned and operated their own steamship line, motor corps, restaurants, hotels, and laundries and had as part of their agenda the establishment of secondary schools and institutions of higher learning. In short, they were almost a nation within a nation.

Noble Drew Ali

Ali[4] did as much to influence W. D. Fard theologically as Garvey did politically. Ali's meshing of the social moorings of black nationalism with Islam was unique and found its expression in Ali's Moorish Science Temple of America.

When he established his temple in 1913 in Newark, New Jersey, Ali taught that all blacks and olive-skinned people were Asiatics. They came from the original race, the ancient Moabites. These Moabites were the progenitors of all nonwhite peoples. Since the darker-skinned people were the original people, it was the whites who were "colored." The homeland for Ali's Asiatics was not Liberia, as Garvey espoused, but Morocco (thus the designation Moorish Science Temple). Unlike Garvey, however, Ali did not look to transport his people to Africa. They could remain in the United States. Further, whites were devils, while Asiatics were ontologically superior to whites. Consequently, God's true people, the Asiatics, would one day triumph over the white devil Europeans, who would be destroyed for their wickedness.

With Christianity being the religion of the whites and Islam being for Asiatics, membership in the Moorish Science Temple was open only to olive-skinned and dark-skinned people. Ali would allow no devils in his temple. As was the case with Fard's NOI, Ali's group was far removed from the theology of traditional Islam.

A strict moral code characterized the movement. Infidelity, alcohol, meat, eggs, and slothfulness were taboo. Further, Asiatics were forbidden to marry a white (European). Not only was this bad for the offspring, who would be tainted with the nature of the devil race, but this would also lead to religious syncretism—Islam could in no way be yoked with Christianity. To drive this point home, the Moors would further distinguish themselves from the whites by adopting new names, complete with Moorish Science Temple identification cards. New names were given by adding "Bey" or "El" to the old name.

Ali favored religious separation, and this commanded his view of social separation and his criticism of integrationists. Though he did not demand emigration of dark-skinned people back to Africa, he articulated in no uncertain terms a separate existence for them within the United States.

The Moors have as their chief textbook *The Holy Koran*. Not to be confused with traditional Islam's Qur'an, Ali's *The Holy Koran* is more than sixty pages long and is gnostic in theology. Much of it comes from Eliphas Levi's *The Aquarian Gospel of Jesus the Christ* and a Tibetan source called *Infinite Wisdom*. Since Ali, like all religious teachers in the West, must do *something* with Jesus, he taught that Jesus was black and denied Jesus' unique status as the God-man.

Finally, like Garvey and like the soon-to-come NOI, the Moors strove to be self-sufficient. They established The Moorish Industrial Group and operated various small businesses, including restaurants and barbershops.

THE THEOLOGY OF W. D. FARD AND THE NOI: 1930–1934

After the mysterious silk peddler gained a hearing in the homes of prospective members, he would tell them of their homeland and warn them of the diet to which they were accustomed. It was not long after that that Fard claimed he was the coming one foretold by the Bible, Marcus Garvey, and Noble Drew Ali.[5] Fard was captivating his then small audiences, and it was not long before home meetings began to multiply and Fard had to divide his time among several meetings each day. But this proved to be an unwise use of time, for attendance again mushroomed. For convenience, Fard's faithful secured a meeting hall, and Fard called it The Temple of Islam. Fard's "Lost-Found Nation of Islam" was born.[6]

The Bible, Qur'an, and Fard's Writings

The people who welcomed Fard into their homes were at least acquainted with the Bible. Fard therefore had to make use of it. Slowly but surely, though, as he commanded the respect of the householders, it was not long before he began to attack the veracity of the Bible. Brother Challar Sharrieff (Charles Peoples) tells of his first encounter with the teacher:

> The very first time I went to a meeting I heard him say: "The Bible tells you that the sun rises and sets. That is not so. The sun stands still. All your lives you have been thinking that the earth never moved. Stand and look toward the sun and know that it is the earth you are standing on which is moving." Up to that day I always went to the Baptist church. After I heard that sermon from the prophet, I was turned around completely. When I went home and heard that dinner was ready, I said: "I don't want to eat dinner. I just want to go back to the meetings. . . . Just to think that the sun above me never moved at all and that the earth we are on was doing all the moving. That changed everything for me.[7]

What were the people to do now that the Bible could not be trusted? Fard was quick to answer. For the time being he instituted a book that was completely authoritative and binding—the Qur'an. Now the people were dependent wholly upon Fard for spiritual leading. Given the facts that Fard used an Arabic version and that most people were not familiar with the Qur'an, he alone was able to translate it and hold monopoly on its interpretation.[8] Unlike Noble Drew Ali, who ousted the Bible, Fard still made use of it. The Bible served Fard's purposes when he cited it, offering the true and symbolic interpretation of certain passages in light of what he thought were the teachings of the Qur'an. The vast majority of people with whom Fard came into contact were not well versed in the Bible, and Fard worked this to his advantage. Later the teacher supplied English versions of the Qur'an to his people.

Though Fard's Islam is not that of traditional Islam, he nonetheless taught that the religion of the seventh-century prophet Muhammad is the true religion of the black people. In turn, Christianity is the white man's religion. Noble Drew Ali's influence here is unmistakable.

At some point Fard decided to leave with his followers authoritative texts of their own. Perhaps he thought this would guarantee a safe continuation of his movement once he was gone. At any rate, he created two manuals, the *Secret Ritual of the Nation of Islam* and *Teachings for the Lost-Found Nation of Islam*. The *Secret Ritual* is transmitted orally to members. It is likely that Fard was influenced by Freemasonry, as it has a secret ritual that members are to memorize. Also, its question-and-answer format resembles that of the Masonic Lodge. *Teachings* is an esoteric work given to members but which only Fard himself could interpret. Again, Fard's familiarity with books on Masonic symbolism may have played a part. Much of Freemasonry's symbolism has deeper levels of meaning reserved only for the elite.

Fard's use of theologically contradicting sources (the Qur'an, the Bible, Baptist theology, Jehovah's Witnesses' theology, and Freemasonry) evidences not only his attempt to meld all these into one but also Fard's unschooled theological mind leading other unschooled theological minds into believing his spiritual homogenization.

With Fard as the infallible interpreter of the Qur'an and the Bible and with his two theological manuals securely in place, Fard built his theological edifice. To his people he was God's chosen Messenger, Wallace D. Fard (or Farad), Master Fard Muhammad, born half original (black) and half white in the holy city of Mecca on February 26, 1877,[9] who arrived in the wilderness of North America on Independence Day, 1930. His teachings are as follows.

The Black Race

The black man (original man) is ontologically superior to the white man (the devil):

> The mental power of a real devil is nothing in comparison to that of the Original Man. He has only six ounces of brain while the Original Man has seven and one half ounces of brain. . . . The devil is weak-boned and weak-blooded because he was grafted from the Original. The devil's physical power is less than one-third that of the Original Man's.[10]

Statements like this served to solidify the members' attitude of superiority over whites, and they spilled over into everyday encounters with white devils. As E. D. Beynon observed, "When they meet Caucasians, they rejoice in the knowledge that they themselves are superiors meeting members of an inferior race."[11] They are the original race, the noblest and most glorious of all present races.

But Fard himself was half black, half white. Whether or not Fard admitted this to NOI members when he was in command is not certain, but his features should have at least hinted at the fact that he was not "pure." Later, Elijah Muhammad admitted that Fard was half white, but this was to make his divine mission more effective.

> He [Fard] told me that for 20 years, He came in and out without anyone knowing who He really was. And he went to school with the white people in their University, right out here in California.[12] Born to deliver you and me. But He must know how to do the job, so He goes and He looks like one of them.[13]

Apparently there was some discussion among followers about Fard's lack of black features, as the following account reveals, but Fard was quick to speak in his own defense:

> He said his father went often in the mountains there in their country where some Caucasians were living. . . . He said he got one of these women and took her for his wife so he could get a son to live more like this civilization of the whites so as to be able to get among them and they will not be able to distinguish him.[14]

Fard, like Noble Drew Ali, disliked the term "colored." Whites are colored because blacks are the original people of the earth. It was the whites who lost their original color.[15] And again, like Ali, Fard held that blacks are "actually a lost Asiatic tribe, wandering in the 'wilderness of North America.' "[16] They were lost because the "Caucasian cave man" had stolen their identity, enslaved them, and took them to North America.[17] This happened 379 years ago, when traders took them from the holy city of Mecca and took away their nation, language, and religion.[18] Once they were lost, but now Allah, working through his messenger Fard Muhammad, has found them.

Fard shared with Noble Drew Ali and Marcus Garvey the idea of an original homeland but differed with them as to place. For Ali and Garvey it was Morocco and Liberia, respectively. For Fard it was Mecca, the place of his birth. For this reason Fard taught his people that Arabic was their original tongue and Islam their true religion and that they did not belong to America: "They were citizens of the Holy City of Mecca and their only allegiance was to the Moslem Flag."[19] Fard also taught them that if they remain true to his teachings (the teachings of Allah), they would one day be brought to their original homeland and live as the "Original Man," the noble and virtuous black race of old, lived. This for Fard was "the resurrection of the dead" mentioned in the Bible. It is the resurrection of the mind of the "mentally dead" black man.

The White Race

The white race is an inferior race. Black Asiatics are superior to whites. The white man is by nature lower than the black man and cannot be trusted because his very essence is that of a deceiver. The devil is their father, and they, collectively, are the devil. White devils will be destroyed at the battle of Armageddon, the blacks restored to their original homeland of Mecca, and the earth purged of all the whites' evil. Things then will be as they once were.

Fard commanded the attention of his audience—an audience hungry for identity and social change. In the Depression, the vast majority of oppressed black people naturally tended to place existential needs over doctrinal beliefs. What was on the table to eat and how they were being treated came first. Fard took advantage of that, couching his message in the experience of his listeners, who were all too eager to respond and relate.

Fard's stabbing remarks about the whites are grounded not only in the influence of Noble Drew Ali and Marcus Garvey. There is an interesting "history" of the white race in the doctrinal annals of W. D. Fard that is the central myth of the NOI—the origin of the white race by the evil scientist Yakub.

Yakub Creates the White Race. According to Elijah Muhammad, Fard is responsible for bringing to him the truth of the origin of the white race.[20] I shall have more detail on this doctrine in chapter 8. For now it will suffice to merely outline it.

Sixty-six hundred years ago, Yakub was born. Yakub became an evil scientist who, in rebellion against his people, started a series of genetic experiments to "graft" a new man from the "Original" (the black man). From these experiments came the white man. Supposedly all originals have another nature along with their divine nature. This "lower nature" is in opposition to the divine nature and was grafted out from the black man to produce the white man. Because they come from the original black man, whites are a hybrid race and inferior in nature to blacks. (Fard, since he was black *and* white, is said to have "mastered the two natures that are in people."[21])

Despite his inferiority, the white man (devil) came to rule the original nation for six thousand years.[22] This he did by employing "tricknology," a term used to describe whites as tricksters who are out to lead the black man to doom and despair in order to be master over them.[23] For the NOI, this explains white supremacy in the world for the last six thousand years.

Destruction of Whites. After Fard won the trust of blacks, he began to prophesy the destruction of the devil white race—the white man.

According to Arthur J. Magida, Fard taught that the devils' domination of blacks ended in 1914.[24] At that time the lost-found nation began to come to its senses and began the process of rising up, both mentally and spiritually, to change the tyrannical reign of whites. Interestingly, this date generally coincides with the arrival of Noble Drew Ali and Marcus Garvey to the scene of black nationalism. Equally interesting is that this date is the same as that chosen by early Jehovah's Witnesses for a "biblically proven" apocalyptic event—the defeat of "the gentile nations." When that prophecy failed, the Witnesses said 1914 merely marked the invisible presence of Christ. Fard charged his followers to listen to the radio messages of Witnesses' leader Judge Joseph Rutherford. Much of Rutherford's message focused on Jehovah's destruction of the Gentile nations, something that Fard may have reinterpreted through his lens of black nationalism for the destruction of the devil race.[25] In later years, NOI members' acquaintance with Jehovah's Witness techniques of interpreting the Bible blossomed with denials of other essential Christian doctrines such as the deity of Christ and the doctrine of the Trinity.[26]

A tool for the destruction of whites, and apparently a taste of the ultimate judgment to come, was the horrid instruction for the murder of whites. As mentioned in the last chapter, "All Moslem[s] will murder the devil" and "by bringing and presenting four at one time his reward is . . . a free transportation to the Holy City of Mecca."[27] Mattias Gardell notes that the key to understanding this lesson is the biblical book of Daniel, chapter 7. He refers to the number four, the number of beasts mentioned in Daniel 7:3–7, and states that the NOI, in its "exoteric exegetic," gives "a specific role for each believer in the coming battle of Armageddon."[28]

Gardell may be correct. Elijah Muhammad, Fard's student, once commented on Daniel 7:7, which talks of the fourth beast, "dreadful and terrifying." A section of Muhammad's book, *Message to the Blackman in America,* is titled "The Beast, Part II, Who Is Able to Make War with Him?" The beast is, of course, Satan. Muhammad then proceeds to call the white race "the devil" and "the serpent" of Genesis 3:1. He then cites the Qur'an, where it talks of "a tree that grows in the bottom of hell . . . the shoots of its fruit stalks are like the heads of devils" (37:65). Muhammad then concludes that the forbidden tree of Genesis 2:17 is a person and that "the only one whom this tree could be is the devil."[29] Could it be that we have some cryptic command for the war of Armageddon, where the saints of God (the blacks) hew down the fruit stalks of "the tree"? It is logical to conclude that since Fard taught that Islam is the religion for blacks and Christianity is the white man's religion, then Fard's idea of Armageddon was indeed a battle between Islam and Christianity—a battle between blacks and whites.[30]

Fard's Doctrine of God

There are two phases to Fard's doctrine of God. At first Fard taught that God is Allah and that he was on a divine mission from Allah. There was no hint in his theology that he himself was God. In fact, he claimed less—he was the reincarnation of Noble Drew Ali. Later, with Elijah Muhammad's encouragement, Fard began to see himself as Allah in the flesh.

Early Fard. It is noteworthy to call attention to Fard's rejection of the "so-called mystery God" of Christianity. Fard's *Secret Ritual of the Nation of Islam* states,

> Me and my people who have been lost from home for 379 years have tried this so-called mystery God for bread, clothing and a home. And we receive nothing but hard times, hunger, naked and out of doors. Also was beat and killed by the ones that advocated that kind of God.[31]

Fard's rejection of Christianity's "mystery God," coupled with his belief that everything black is good and everything white is evil, led him to teach that Allah is black.[32] Further, God was not some "spook" in the sky (no doubt referring facetiously to Christianity's doctrine of God, in part)—not a spirit that is unexplainable to us. Rather, God is an embodied black man.[33]

Later Fard. In Fard's later teachings we see his direct claim to deity as well as Elijah Muhammad's recognition that he was God in the flesh. E. D. Beynon writes of Fard's followers coming to believe "that the prophet was more than a man."[34] Fard's follower Yussuf Mohammed recalls a police interrogation of Fard: "When the police asked him who he was, he said: 'I am the Supreme Ruler of the Universe.' He told those police more about himself than he would ever tell us."[35]

But Elijah Muhammad told him! After a lecture Fard gave in 1931, Elijah Muhammad (then Elijah Poole) approached Fard and declared, "I know who you are, you're God himself." Fard then softly said to Elijah, "That's right, but don't tell it now. It is not yet time for me to be known."[36] Elijah tells of another verbal exchange with Fard:

> When I got to him I shaked my hands with him and told him that I recognized who he is and he held his head down close to my face and he said to me, "Yes, Brother." I said to him: "You are that one we read in the Bible that he would come in the last day under the name Jesus." . . . finally he said; "Yes, I am the one that you have been looking for in the last two thousand years. . . ."[37]

Fard, it is reported, "had previously not promoted himself as Allah" and was "taken aback by Elijah's declaration."[38] But Fard quickly adapted to his new identity as savior. At the next NOI meeting he proclaimed that he was the long-awaited messiah.[39]

At his departure from his adoring disciples in 1934, Fard used words reminiscent of Christ's words to his disciples: "I am with you; I will be back to you in the near future to lead you out of this hell."[40] He also shared with Elijah Muhammad: "I love them [black people]. I will destroy the Nations of the Earth to save them and then die myself."[41] With these words of promise Elijah Muhammad, to whom Fard would give rule of the NOI, had his future proclamations of Fard as "God in flesh" firmly established.

Fard on Jesus

Fard's rejection of a white Jesus depicted in murals and paintings (reminiscent of the Garveyites), coupled with his belief that everything black is good and everything white is evil, led him to conclude that Jesus was a black Asiatic.

But Fard had more to say. Jesus was the son of a black Asiatic father named Joseph Al-Nejjar. Fard tainted the very core of Christian theology when he stated,

Mary's father was a rich man and therefore he refused to give Mary in marriage to her greatest lover, Joseph Al-Nejjar, because he was a poor man with nothing but a saw and a hammer, because he was a very poor carpenter. Being in love with Mary, hopeless of marrying her, Joseph had impregnated her with Jesus.[42]

Louis A. DeCaro Jr. notes that Fard's anti-incarnational theology not only violates Christianity but also violates Islam. Thus Fard was far removed from both Christianity and Islam.[43] The Qur'an states that Jesus was born of a virgin.[44] Fard's original doctrinal errors paved the way for further future NOI heresies concerning Jesus Christ.[45]

Naming

Fard had birthed in his people a new identity. (They would tell you that they always had this identity but it was stolen and they were made to think they never possessed it.) The black Asiatics were the chosen people of God. They were the "Original Man." The whites, through their "tricknology," had convinced them of the lie that they were inferior to whites and should therefore be subject to them in all aspects of life. These last 379 years of bondage at the hands of the white devils were enough! Allah now has come to rescue them. With Allah's help, Fard preached, they could experience the resurrection—the rising of the mind to an awareness of who they are by nature—and change their lifestyle. With that accomplished, Allah would lead them to the "Promised Land."

To complete the process of the recognition of the newly found identity, it was necessary to change one's name. Human beings are ritualistic by nature. The process of changing names, therefore, added a seal to the "resurrected" black Asiatic and served to further bond him to the group. In short, the new believer had something tangible to show the world that he recognized his true identity.

Before W. D. Fard arrived on the religious black nationalist scene, Noble Drew Ali established the practice of assigning new names to believers. For a fee they received the new name and a Moorish Science Temple member identification card. Fard did the same:

> To become a member, one had to complete a written application declaring one's intention to return to the holy original Nation. Enclosed normally would be a request for the Original name. . . . In return, he would be given his holy name printed on a national "Identification Card" that showed him to be a righteous Muslim, registered in the divine roll of Mecca.[46]

Along with the application and request, a registration fee, usually ten dollars,[47] was paid, and the original name secured. With eight thousand estimated converts, "this work must have been extremely profitable to the prophet."[48]

Fard then assigned a divine original Asiatic name to the convert "through the Spirit of Allah within him."[49] Upon reception of the new name, the "slave name" given to one's ancestors by the white devil slave masters was dropped. For example, "Joseph Shepard became Jam Sharrieff, Lindsey Garrett became Hazziez Allah, Henry Wells became Anwar Pasha, [and] William Blunt became Sharrieff Allah."[50] E. D. Beynon mentions a slip-up Fard made when he gave new names to Elijah Poole and his two brothers: "Despite his omniscience, the prophet once gave the surnames of Sharrieff, Karriem (given to Elijah[51]) and Mohammed to the three Poole brothers." Beynon then explains that Fard slipped out of this quandary by calling attention "to his divine knowledge of the different paternity of the three brothers."[52]

The new names were just about everything to the new converts: "I wouldn't give up my righteous name. That name is my life."[53] The new "Original name" signified not only a protest against white supremacy and oppression but also pride in their lost-found origin and submission to the will and laws of Allah.

Lifestyle

When W. D. Fard came to Detroit on July 4, 1930, he found many disillusioned black people. Many blacks in Detroit had migrated from the South and therefore had illnesses associated with the Michigan climate. Winters were especially harsh on those accustomed to above-freezing temperatures year round.[54] The migrants from the South came to blame the white man and the white man's city for their aches and pains "even before they met the prophet."[55]

Once again Fard rose to the occasion. After getting into the homes of blacks as a silk peddler, he began to tell them that they should not eat certain foods they were used to eating. "The people in your own country do not eat it," he said. Further, the new teacher exclaimed, "If you would live just like the people in your home country, you would never be sick any more."[56] It is difficult to say how Fard came to this knowledge. If he were a member of Noble Drew Ali's Moorish Science Temple, this would explain it.

Members of the NOI were told to eat once a day and abstain from "all meat of 'poison animals,' hogs, ducks, geese, possums and catfish."[57] Consequently their one meal per day was essentially vegetarian. Additionally, they were never to use alcohol and tobacco or commit adultery,[58] and they were to keep their houses and their bodies spotless.[59] Fard taught them that if they were faithful to these laws, Allah would bring them to the holy city of Mecca.[60]

Blacks under Fard's leadership no doubt benefited from such changes in lifestyle. They became much healthier. With these results, not to mention the pride associated with being a member, it was difficult to convince them that they should leave the NOI.

Education and Commerce

Like the Garveyites and the Moors before them, the NOI strove for economic and educational self-sufficiency. Though Fard's vision was to cure "social problems, lack of economic development, undisciplined family life and alcoholism,"[61] during the years of his leadership the NOI did not create individual commercial businesses. That they would do years later under the leadership of Elijah Muhammad. Perhaps Fard did not have the time. Four years can come and go quickly, especially when one is guiding a fledgling movement. Yet Fard, whether knowingly or not, surely did set the groundwork for Elijah's reign of power and the future establishment of NOI-owned businesses.

As the movement grew, it saw the need to form a University of Islam. This is not a university in the normal sense but rather an elementary and secondary school designed to teach children "higher mathematics, astronomy, and the general knowledge and ending of the spook civilization."[62] It was designed to replace public schools and to foster a "knowledge of our own" rather than the "civilization of the Caucasian devils."[63] Additionally, a Muslim Girls' Training and General Civilization Class was chartered to teach young NOI women how to cook food, clean their homes, and be effective wives and mothers.[64]

The Fruit of Islam

With the rapid growth of the movement, Fard became worried about physical persecution at the hands of unbelievers. Adding to this was a constant fear of the police, who saw the NOI as detrimental to the social well being of the city and, since the Smith murder,[65] capable of violence.

In response Fard formed a military-type protection unit and called it the Fruit of Islam (FOI). This designation was chosen because these young warriors were the "fruit" of Fard's teaching, and they were the ultimate example of strength and victory for the coming war of Armageddon. Captains were chosen to train NOI men in guard tactics and firearms. The FOI's main task was "to maintain order and decorum in the temple."[66] The reason for this was perhaps because the obvious time for an "attack" from "infidels" would be during a temple service. There attackers would be sure to find the greatest number of NOI believers in one place. Later, under the full control of Elijah Muhammad, the FOI would be given additional duties and more power.

SUMMARY

There is no NOI without Wallace D. Fard (Master Fard Muhammad). And there is no Wallace D. Fard without the social and religious environment that shaped him. Some people call him God; others call him a fraud. He certainly was a leader.

Master Fard Muhammad, says the NOI, was born on February 26, 1877.[67] To them he is Allah in person, God in the flesh, the Savior. To this day the NOI sets aside one day in February to celebrate the Savior's birth and his coming to his people on July 4, 1930. Saviour's Day is an ever-present reminder of the impact one man by the name of Wallace D. Fard had and still has upon millions of people.

The Rise of Elijah Muhammad

"I know who you are," said Elijah Poole to W. D. Fard, "You're God himself!" From that point on, Elijah Poole continued his undying commitment to Fard and his teachings and was later to become the fearless leader of the Lost-Found Nation of Islam (NOI) for more than forty years.

ELIJAH BEFORE FARD

Elijah Poole came into this world on October 7, 1897, in Sandersville, Georgia. He was one of thirteen children of William and Mariah Poole. William was a Baptist minister.

Elijah's Ancestry and His Early Years

According to Claude Andrew Clegg III, William Poole's grandparents on his mother's side were white and black (his grandfather was white, his grandmother was black). Thus William Poole's mother, Peggy (Elijah's grandmother), is mulatto. William's father, Irwin Pool (Elijah's grandfather), is listed in the census as black. As a youth, Irwin was "passed down to Jane Swint as a perpetual servant" by the slave owner Middleton Pool (1778–1861); thus his surname was that of his slave master.[1] In 1877 Elijah's father, William Poole, married Mariah Hall, who also had a white grandfather and black grandmother on her mother's side.[2]

Since Elijah's parents were also sharecroppers, he grew up in the oppression of blacks by whites.[3] His formal education was minimal. He learned "only the bare rudiments of reading, writing, and arithmetic before he had to go to the fields to help his family earn a living."[4] Some say Elijah never made it past the fourth grade, "but definitely not past the eighth."[5] Later his followers would call attention to his lack of formal education in order to heighten the sense of his divine calling.

Exposure to Christianity. Elijah Poole's Baptist upbringing was memorable in a positive way. Since he was "the preacher's son" he received special treatment from people in churches where his father preached. "This childhood experience of favor and recognition helped engender in the young Elijah a sense of calling and the belief that he was to be a great preacher some day."[6] Elijah came to love the Bible through his father's sermons and studied the Bible fervently, often to the point of despair for not being able to understand it as fully as he would have liked. Eventually he and his father engaged in theological tugs of war when Elijah discovered flaws in logic and biblical errors. "Something was missing from the presentations [his father's preaching], some hidden truth that had not been made clear."[7]

As a youth, Elijah exhibited a "tell it like it is" mentality when it came to Christianity. It was not necessarily because Elijah was a Christian himself. Indeed, he doubted he was because, as he said, "God had not told me anything."[8] Theological disagreements with his father resulted in his not wanting to become a member of the church unless he fully understood the church's doctrine, and he was quick to call to account those who insincerely professed Christianity.[9] Hypocrisy gnawed at him, and he often voiced opposition to the double standard of a confession of faith and lack of Christian lifestyle.

Enter the Violence. During this time Elijah grew up quickly—too quickly. Unfortunately he was exposed to the evils of white society and its violent treatment of blacks. He once saw the body of a black man who had been murdered for allegedly raping a white woman. Without a trial this man was hoisted up on a rope, hanged by the neck, and pummeled with bullets.[10] Elijah recalls:

> That event had impressed me so much that I cannot get over it; I did never forget it, not until this day. It was terrible

and horrible to see such things happening and all our grown men right there in the section allowing such things to happen. I returned to our house, which was about four miles away from the little town, grieving all the way. I wished I were a man so that I could try to do something about it. That scene hurt me very much.[11]

More violence followed Elijah as he grew up in rural Georgia, and it played an important role in his view of Christianity, the religion that these white murderers professed. He notes a former white boss of his who used to beat his employees at gunpoint. Elijah said later, "That man was a very cruel white man, as all the devils are."[12] These traumatic experiences produced wounds that left scars on Elijah and did much to buttress what his teacher, W. D. Fard, would later instill in him. He recalls another occasion of violence and intimidation by whites, this time in the context of his rejection of Christianity and the cross:

> Christianity is based upon the murder of a man 2,000 years ago. . . . On our blackboards his [the white man's] sign stands by a tree out of which he got his cross, then he places our brother on that same tree. . . . They ridicule the Righteous by making signs which they murder them on and handing the signs over to you to worship. . . . In the south I met a devil who had a piece of a Black Man's ear in his pocket, and he showed it to me, to try to make me fear him.[13]

Life as a Young Man

At sixteen years of age Elijah left home and went to Macon, Georgia. There he worked a variety of jobs, including sawmill laborer and foreman at a brick company.[14] He continued his life as a laborer through the war years, and in 1918 he just missed being drafted because the war ended "one day before they were calling up the group that I was in."[15] On March 17, 1919, he married Clara Evans in Cordele, Georgia.[16]

In 1920 or 1921, another episode of violence was forever imprinted on his mind and heart. As Elijah and one of his brothers went to Macon on a business trip, they saw the corpse of a black man. He had been hanged until dead, then dragged through the streets attached to a bumper of a truck.[17] Mattias Gardell writes, "As a symbol for white Christian order, a lynched Blackman dangling from a tree would be standard decoration in the NOI Temples Elijah would head as an adult."[18]

The struggles of everyday life and the many incidences of racist violence and threats proved to be too much for Elijah and Clara Poole. In April 1923, Elijah, his wife and two children, his parents, and his brothers and sisters left for Detroit. He was a bitter man, and rightly so. His bitterness was now deeply rooted. He was ready for a change, and that change would impact the rest of his life.

Life in the 1920s

Elijah and Clara Poole were among thousands of blacks who migrated from the South into Northern urban areas. Industrialization had lured many black agricultural workers to the North in the hope of a better life. For example, "Detroit's black population grew by 611 percent between the years 1910 and 1920."[19]

Elijah and his father struggled with employment once they moved to Detroit. To complicate matters, from 1923 to 1929 he and Clara had three more children.[20] After finding that selling firewood was only a seasonal occupation, he found employment with the American Nut Company, then with the American Wire and Brass Company, Detroit Copper Company, and the Briggs Body and Chevrolet Axle Company.[21] His employment struggles during this time caused Elijah great emotional turmoil. There are reports that Elijah took to drinking to quell his misery. Sometimes he would be found drunk in back alleys, and his wife would have to bring him home carrying him on her shoulders.[22] One can only imagine how the pressure on Elijah multiplied when the Great Depression hit.

Obviously the hopes of many Southern blacks that relocation to the urban industrial North would solve all their problems quickly faded. Life was not what the idealistic talk back home made it out to be. Further, the violence that plagued Elijah Poole in Georgia followed him to Detroit.

During his first year of residence in Michigan, Elijah Muhammad [then Poole] saw two blacks killed by policemen, which convinced him that "the difference [between the North and the South] is that they do not hang them up to the trees but they kill them right here on the streets!"[23]

Elijah Joins the UNIA and the Masons

The Northern cities' population boom between 1910 and 1930 afforded black religious and civil organizations the opportunity to fill certain voids. Blacks craved identity and fellowship, and certain groups helped to interpret the angst caused by relocation and the struggle with unemployment. In the 1920s one could find such groups as "black Hebrews, Daddy Grace, Father Divine, the Moorish Science Temple, Ethiopian churches, black Masons, Elks, and other fraternities."[24]

After the Pooles moved to Detroit, Elijah joined Marcus Garvey's UNIA.[25] For the emotionally beaten Elijah, this was much needed. In it he found identity, purpose, and an avenue through which he could interpret his experiences in Georgia and Detroit. This as well served to push Elijah to final separation from the Christian church with which he had earlier struggled during his days in the South.

Sometime in 1924, Poole joined the Prince Hall Masonic Lodge. Freemasonry started in England in 1717 and moved to the United States in the 1730s.[26] Because of inherent racism the lodge did not accept blacks into its fold. As a result, Prince Hall Freemasonry was established. Apparently many of the early converts to Fard's NOI were Masons.[27] In light of the toils and troubles that Detroit posed for the majority of Southern migrants, Freemasonry was yet another order that gave black men a sense of belonging and esoteric truth that only they were privileged to know. The Masonic Lodge met the sociological and spiritual needs that were void in the life of the average Detroit black. Additionally, perhaps there was an economic reason for Elijah's initiation into the rites of the lodge. Many men are known to join the local lodge in order to secure business connections. In the light of Poole's unemployment struggles, this is quite possible.[28]

The Real Issue

From Elijah Poole's perspective the UNIA and the Masonic Lodge had much to offer. But there was still something missing:

> I told my wife, when I was working on a job, that no matter how well I did, I wouldn't be satisfied until I was preaching. Sometimes the spirit in me to preach was so strong that I almost cried.[29]

It is obvious that from these words Elijah saw himself as a leader of men. Perhaps leading a congregation through preaching was branded in his heart through his father's example and the attention he received as the preacher's son. Second, though, is the dilemma of what to preach! Earlier, and by his own admission, he did not see himself as a Christian. At the very least he showed only a partial commitment to Christianity and its doctrines.

Something had to come along that would satisfy his yearning to preach. This something could never be Christianity. Already the seeds of hate for what he would later call the "white man's religion" were planted in his heart by whites who worshiped at the cross on Sundays but later in the week lynched blacks on branches of trees while a cross burned nearby. No, Christianity to Elijah was the friend of, and the excuse for, slavery and oppression.

Elijah was soon to meet the Master.

ELIJAH FINDS FARD

The man who would change Elijah Poole's life forever was virtually just around the corner. By 1931 W. D. Fard was almost a year into the founding of his Lost-Found Nation of Islam. That is when Elijah met the savior.

As was the case with the young Elijah, the Elijah who lived in Detroit was always game for theological debates, especially with his brother Billie.[30] Perhaps it was cathartic for him. One night their father, William, joined in. During the debate, he shared with them that he had met a man by the name of Brother Abdul Muhammad (formerly Mr. Brown). The elder Poole told his sons that Abdul had been a member of Noble Drew Ali's Moorish Science Temple of America but had now found the truth of Islam under a teacher named W. D. Fard. Abdul also told William, who in turn told his sons, that Fard had given him his new "Original" name.

Did Elijah's father, who was a Baptist preacher, not warn his sons about the anti-Christian theology of Islam? Did he attempt to find out more about Fard and his teachings so as to warn his sons of the differences? We can only speculate. Nevertheless, Elijah said to his brother and his father, "I like to hear that man! . . . That is good what Abdul Muhammad told you." The Poole brothers then visited the home of Abdul Muhammad, who gladly spelled out Fard's teachings to them.[31]

Elijah went to Fard's meeting at a rented hall a few months after William Poole's mention of Abdul Muhammad. In the interim, Elijah was meeting with Abdul. Why did he not go to a meeting right away? Perhaps it was the residue of Elijah's upbringing in a Christian home, where Islam was viewed as a heathen religion.[32] Whatever the case, when another of his brothers, Charlie, came home one evening spiritually high on the teachings of Fard, Elijah thought he would give it a try.[33]

The Meeting

Elijah went to the first meeting but was unable to get in due to the size of the crowd assembled in the basement. Apparently Poole had no idea of the popularity of Fard. As a result, he had to settle for "the few audible words that occasionally streamed through the basement's window."[34]

On his second attempt to hear the new teacher, Elijah was successful, at least enough so that this time he could hear more of Fard's words. Elijah was so impressed that he made an attempt to personally meet Fard right after the meeting. Elijah made his way through the excited crowd, went up to Fard, shook his hand, and said guardedly, "I know who you are; You're God himself." Fard whispered back, "That's right, but don't tell it now! It is not yet time for it to be known."[35] More than thirty years later Elijah stated in *Ebony*, "I recognized him. And right there I told him that he was the one the world had been looking for to come."[36]

Another account of the first meeting has Poole making his way through the crowd, shaking hands with Fard, and asking, "You are that one we read in the Bible that he would come in the last day under the name Jesus. . . . You are that one?" Fard seemed taken aback, as if surprised by the question. Fard paused, looked intently at Elijah, and whispered, "Yes, I am the One, but who knows that but yourself, and be quiet."[37] With all the commotion of the crowd, the excitement, and Fard's charisma, Elijah must have been chillingly astounded to meet the messiah.

Elijah adored his Master Fard Muhammad. Three decades later he would write of a subsequent dialogue with Fard,

> Allah came to us from the Holy City of Mecca, Arabia, in 1930. He used the name Wallace D. Fard, often signing it W. D. Fard. In the third year (1933), he signed his name W. F. Muhammad which stands for Wallace Fard Muhammad. He came alone. . . . He measured and weighed the earth and its water. . . . He declared that he would heal us and set us in heaven at once, if we would submit to Him. . . . And that He was able to force the whole world into submission to his will. He said that he loved us, (the so-called Negroes), his lost and found. . . . I asked him, "Who are you, and what is your real name?" He said, "I am the one that the world has been expecting for the past 2,000 years." I said to Him again, "What is your name?" He said, "My name is Mahdi; I am God."[38]

Fard came into Elijah Poole's life at the right time. From Poole's perspective all the previous years' horrors and struggles served wonderfully to prepare him to meet his savior. And the man at the podium, Allah himself, divinely arranged to meet him that evening in 1931. All the answers Elijah Poole needed were found in the person of W. D. Fard.

Elijah found that the biblical issues he had been struggling with ever since his youth were now answered. Fard had amazed him with the way he used the Bible and other books to drive home truths about the nature of the Original Man (black Asiatics), the nature of the white devils, and what the will of Allah was for his people. As far as Elijah Poole was concerned, years of personal study of the Bible added proof to his claim about Fard. Though a trained biblical scholar would be puzzled at how Elijah came to conclude the following, it nonetheless shows his deep-rooted love for Fard: "I was a student of the Bible. I recognized him to be the person the Bible predicted would come 2,000 years after Jesus' death. It came to me the first time I laid eyes on him."[39]

Elijah and Fard obviously were magnetized to each other immediately. Fard then began grooming Elijah for leadership in the Lost-Found Nation of Islam.

Elijah Rises in Status

Elijah Poole became a top official in Fard's NOI. His initial "recognition" of Fard must have impressed the savior, for after Elijah's confession Fard began to teach his converts that he was the promised messiah. To be sure, Fard said, he was not Jesus. Jesus was dead and gone. But Fard now proclaimed he was the "Mahdi," "the guided one," an eschatological person who will usher in righteousness for all the earth. At night Elijah would come home, hurry into his clothes closet, prostrate himself on the floor, and pray to Fard-Allah.[40] Also at his home he and other converts would discuss Fard's teachings.[41] This must have been an exciting time for Elijah Poole.

The Call and the Name. Elijah always wanted to preach, and soon his dream would be realized. After a little time had passed, the thrill of a lifetime came to Elijah. He received public recognition from Fard. Fard had just finished delivering a lesson when he asked the assembled crowd, "Anyone here in this hall know the little man who lives in Hamtramck?" Elijah's wife, Clara, was in the audience, and quickly responded, "Yes, he is my husband." Fard said to her in the presence of all the assembled faithful, "You tell him that he can go ahead . . . and start teaching [Islam], and I will back [him] up."[42] Elijah was not there, but he had been communicating with Fard previous to the "call." When Clara shared the news, Elijah was elated! Implying his disdain for Christianity, Elijah said to himself, "Now, we really have something to teach, and it is good."[43] This was the first part of two in Elijah's official calling by Fard and the beginning of his forty-four years in the NOI.[44]

Elijah, like everyone else, had to submit to the initiation rituals that Fard created and had to petition for his new name. He also had to study certain lessons that Fard wrote for prospective members.

The lessons ranged from geography to Fard's theology of the black Asiatics to Fard's mission to save the lost original people.[45]

Next on the agenda was to give Elijah Poole his new "Original" name. Fard gave him the name Karriem. From then on Elijah Poole was no longer Elijah Poole—he was Elijah Karriem. The new name signified identification with Allah, agreement to live a clean life, acceptance of the new original identity, and rejection of the old identity characterized by the slave name inherited from their ancestors, so named by their slave masters. With his new name Elijah forever blotted out the surname of the slave master Middleton Pool. Elijah detested his surname so much that he stated, "The name 'Poole' was never my name, nor was it my father's name. It was the name [of] the white slave-master of my grandfather."[46]

The second part of Fard's calling came at a meeting that Elijah Karriem attended. By this time he had already heard the news from his wife and was anticipating what might come next. Fard asked him to stand up and stand next to him in front of the audience. The two embraced, and Fard announced, "From now on, this is my minister." In fact, he then put an adjective in front of "minister"— "supreme."[47] "Supreme Minister Elijah Karriem." If we were to ask Elijah what he liked most about the title, he would undoubtedly say that the title was important to him because of the one who bestowed it upon him. Still, the reality was that Elijah was now in a powerful position. And this did not meet with the approval of everyone in Fard's NOI.

The Good and the Bad. Naming Elijah the Supreme Minister of the Lost-Found Nation of Islam brought both positive and negative effects. On the one hand, exciting times followed. Elijah became Fard's most loyal follower. He held meetings in his home, teaching the good news about Fard to all. He echoed Fard's theology about the true identity of blacks, the white devils, and the salvation that has come. Elijah's faith was now in something (or, rather, some*one*) tangible. In his first public sermon as Supreme Minister he reminded the people that Fard was the Promised One. Fard, impressed with his disciple, then sent him to Chicago to preach the message. Elijah gladly accepted. There, on a platform at 37 Wentworth Avenue, Elijah preached Fard. "Fard is Allah,"[48] he shouted, "who came to save the dark people." Fard later made "appearances before Chicago converts to show them what God looked like in person."[49] (Elijah would establish a second temple in Chicago in 1933.) It is reported that during one of his visits, the God-man proclaimed, "I am God Himself."[50] His past rejection of Christianity solidified. Now he chastised the white devils who believed in some "spook mystery god in the sky." He proclaimed that Christianity is the white man's religion. This religion, taught Elijah, only served the white man's oppression of the "so-called Negroes." It served to justify their brutality and violence toward Allah's people. Christianity, preached Elijah Karriem, must be rejected.

On the other hand, in the midst of the thrilling ministry with which Elijah had been entrusted came divisions. Some of the men vying for power in the movement did not take kindly to Fard's endearing embrace and calling of Elijah Karriem. This took place immediately after Fard's public stamp of approval. But Fard, even before calling Elijah, was facing competition within his own ranks. For example, the very man who once introduced Elijah to Fard, Abdul Muhammad, was among a few who were beginning to separate from the NOI.[51]

Before the appointment of Elijah Karriem to Supreme Minister (which made him Fard's closest confidant), Abdul Muhammad and Othman Ali were the closest to Fard and the most powerful under him. Abdul voiced his disgust at the selection of Elijah by causing dissention among the people. Abdul Muhammad, a former member of Noble Drew Ali's group, began to emphasize more his former teacher's theology and relegated Fard's teachings to second place. "Consequently, following Karriem's appointment, Fard's first assignment for the new minister was to take notes on what [Abdul] Muhammad preached and report back."[52]

Tensions caused by division, strife, and jealousy grew and grew and most likely would have reached the breaking point if it were not for the interruption of the murder of James Smith by Robert Harris.[53] With the police watching him, Fard continued to be the target of interrogations and was arrested on this and several other occasions. During this time he became less and less involved in guiding the movement and placed more and more authority into the hands of Elijah Karriem. He would meet secretly with Karriem to tie up loose theological ends, package Karriem in such a way that made him more acceptable to believers, and change his own name from W. D. Fard to Wallace Fard Muhammad.[54]

Fard again changed Elijah's name. He was going to give Elijah the name "Abdul," but Elijah protested the name because it reminded him of the troublemaker, traitor, and heretic Abdul Muhammad. Fard said in response, "I will give you a better name than Karriem. . . . You take Muhammad, My name."[55] Elijah Muhammad, Supreme Minister of the NOI, went to his family to share with them his new name that Allah gave to him. "Later," says Elijah, "my father and all our family accepted His Name."[56] Conversion to Fardian Islam encompassed the whole family of the former Christian preacher William Poole, now Wali Muhammad. Clara Poole was now Marie Muhammad.

FARD'S EXIT

With the NOI hanging by a thread in Detroit and with arrests and subsequent orders from the Detroit police to leave the city, Master Fard Muhammad sought peace in Chicago, where Elijah Muhammad had established Temple No. 2. As in Detroit, Fard was arrested in Chicago not long after his arrival. It soon became inevitable that he had to leave—for good. To secure matters as best he could he said to followers before he left Chicago, "You don't need me anymore; hear Elijah."[57]

With Fard gone it was most difficult for Elijah Muhammad to hold the Detroit-based NOI together (though he did). Some people were never convinced of Elijah's deification of Fard, while others were scared away by police investigations instigated by the Smith murder.[58] Still others returned to Christian churches, perhaps because Fard's banishment separated them from his mystique, giving them freedom to assess his claims to divinity. Abdul Muhammad drew followers away with a splinter group of his own. To differentiate his group from Fard's he called for loyalty to the American Constitution and removed himself from any deification of Fard.

Even Elijah Muhammad's brother, Kallatt Muhammad, Supreme

Captain of the NOI, turned against his brother. Ayman Muhammad, Elijah's eldest child, told of his Uncle Kallatt's jealousy of his father:

> Master Farad [Fard] first made my father minister. Later he made him the supreme minister of all the temples. He also made my uncle [Kallatt] the supreme captain of the Nation of Islam and also the head investigator. My uncle was envious of my father's position; he became an enemy of my father. He died because he began to be an alcoholic after he was expelled from the Nation of Islam under my father's leadership. [Kallatt] lost his mind. . . . My father said, "Allah put him in that condition," but at that time he meant Master Farad put him in that condition.[59]

With schisms and battles within the ranks of the NOI, threats were made against Elijah to the point that he now was risking death. He and his family thus made more and more visits to NOI Temple No. 2 in Chicago. "The hypocrites," as he called them, nauseated the Supreme Minister. To drive home their disagreement and protest of Elijah Muhammad's title and newest name, they would annoy him by referring to him as Elijah Karriem. In 1934, in Detroit's Temple No. 1, Elijah assembled all those loyal to him and the original teachings of Fard and broke off from his dissenters. He informed the faithful that they should stay in Detroit and carry on the work while he returned to Chicago to set up headquarters at Temple No. 2. He called his movement "The Temple People."[60] Elijah, now "the Messenger," was the only voice crying out in the wilderness, the only leader who was loyal to Allah in person. He was determined to carry on his savior's message.

SUMMARY

Elijah Muhammad is to all NOI members a human success story. He went from poor beginnings in Georgia to leading a mass movement in Chicago. He would lead this movement until his death in 1975. Slavery, white racist violence, and an inherent desire to seek for truth brought the young man from Sandersville, Georgia, into the loving embrace of Master Wallace Fard Muhammad, Allah in person. Does he *really* believe that Fard is God in the flesh? If words are the indication, he does.

> *God came to Me in 1931 in Detroit, Michigan. He taught Me for 3 years and 4 months. He taught Me night and day. . . . I am ready for you.*[61]

FIVE

Elijah Muhammad—
Struggles and Victories

Given the mysterious appearance and disappearance of W. D. Fard and his relatively short time of leadership, the name of Elijah Muhammad has, in the eyes of many outside the movement, become synonymous with the Lost-Found Nation of Islam (NOI). His long ministry as head of the organization and his forthright style of oratory combined to make him a staple of the movement and a flavorful news item for the media, all of which we shall examine in this chapter.

THE MESSENGER ELIJAH MUHAMMAD

When the Honorable Elijah Muhammad—the designation his disciples use to refer to him—assumed the seat of power and formed his Temple People (later he reclaimed the title NOI), he came under the watchful eye of law enforcement officials. To compound matters, other splinter groups competed for wandering converts from Fard's NOI. Trouble began immediately.

The "Running Years"

Elijah, settled in his Temple People's Chicago Temple No. 2, made visits to Detroit's Temple No. 1 in order to make sure of his group's maintenance of Fardian Islam. He also visited the followers in Detroit in order to maintain and solidify his role as Messenger of Allah.

Elijah, however, returned to Detroit only to witness battles with other groups seeking a place in this spiritually needy city. For example, Abdul Muhammad's organization, though short-lived, claimed to be the true expression of Allah's will on earth. Thus when Elijah Muhammad returned to Detroit, claimed his "Messenger of Allah" status, and further proclaimed the deity of W. D. Fard, he outraged his competitors. As part of the ammunition fired against the Temple People, rival groups referred to Elijah as "Elijah Karriem."[1] This was an implicit protest against his claim to be the Messenger and a denial of Fard's application of his own name to Elijah.

The law and other public officials were active in making life miserable for the Temple People. Overall, police saw Muslim black nationalist movements as a threat to the peace and safety of the city. Pressure tactics became standard in order to lower the morale of the Temple People. On one occasion police interrupted classes at the University of Islam, an elementary and secondary school, because of a complaint by the Michigan State Board of Education. It claimed that University of Islam students were being denied public education. As a result, it called for the arrest of teachers at the school. The police tried to board up the school, and the situation quickly deteriorated. No one was killed, but there were injuries on both sides.[2] The Messenger recalls:

> In Detroit, Michigan, where we were first attacked outright by the police Department in April, 1934, we were also unarmed. There were no deaths on the part of the Believers, however. They fought back against the policemen who attacked them for no just cause whatsoever but that they wanted our Muslim children to go to their schools. . . . It was said after the battle with my followers who had nothing to fight with but their hands, that there was hospitalization on both sides. . . . When the battle was over there were more of them hospitalized than there were of us.[3]

Muhammad eventually fully relocated in Chicago after an arrest on April 17, 1934, in Detroit. He was charged with "contributing to the delinquency of a minor child and voodooism."[4] Apparently the Smith murder[5] was still fresh in the minds of the Detroit police. Af-

ter the killing, rumors of a strange black voodoo cult that taught ritual sacrifices of humans began to spread. The NOI was tarnished by
this incident, despite the fact that the murder was never pinned on
the organization. Muhammad himself states that the charge was
"contributing to the delinquency of minors," but does not state that
he himself was arrested.[6] According to an FBI file dated August 9,
1957, "he was found guilty by Judge Gordon and sentenced to pay
$10.00 or to serve 10 days in the Detroit House of Correction." Fur-
ther, he was sentenced to six months of probation.[7] During this time
Muhammad was ordered to make sure that all the children of his
group attended public schools. He stood his ground, however, and
did not follow the court order. The court allowed his actions to go
unchecked. But more and more police pressure and a five-hundred-
dollar bounty put on his head by a rival organization pushed him to
make the decision to move to Chicago in September.[8]

Even in Chicago, trouble would follow Elijah Muhammad. In
1935, "in the Police Court on 11th and State Streets," someone
lodged a complaint against Muhammad's group. This issue once
again was the University of Islam. A parent was charged for allowing
his children to attend Muhammad's school. According to Muhammad, two court officials treated the women of his fold with disrespect. When Muhammad's male followers acted in their defense, a
battle ensued in the courtroom. When it was over, a police captain
was dead from a heart attack and others were wounded from court
officials' gunfire.[9]

Because of problems with law enforcement officials and threats
on his life, Muhammad traveled to several major East Coast cities.
For the next seven years he would be on the road "running from
not only black people but white people."[10] Indeed, 1935 to 1942
were the "running years" for Elijah Muhammad. Before heading to
the East he visited Milwaukee, Wisconsin, where there was already a
Temple No. 3. In these seven years he would make a few visits to
Clara and his children in Chicago, but he did not stay too long for
fear of his life.[11] These years were most taxing on Elijah Muhammad, for when he stayed for too long a time in any one place, the
law would be breathing down his neck. Often he went without food
and shelter. Additionally, men whom he put in charge of temples
began to secede and form new movements.[12] But Elijah would en-

dure because he was the Messenger of Allah in the flesh, Master Fard Muhammad. Allah, said Elijah, communicated annually with him during this difficult time in his life. These visits were not made in the flesh, but spiritually—Fard communicated with Elijah mentally.[13]

In 1939 Elijah Muhammad organized Temple No. 4 in the nation's capital.[14] Preaching and teaching under the names of Mr. Evans and Muhammad Rassoull (two of his aliases used because he was on the run), he made his first two converts—Benjamin and Clara Mitchell. Upon conversion their surname was changed to Muhammad. While in Washington Elijah spent some time in the Library of Congress trying to read more deeply the Qur'an and the 104 books Master Fard Muhammad commanded him to read,[15] a practice that convinced him all the more that Fard was Allah in the flesh.[16] Elijah Muhammad also preached his message in Philadelphia, Newark, Baltimore, Providence, Pittsburgh, Cleveland, and Atlanta.[17]

Now Elijah was teaching and preaching more than ever before. In 1942 in Washington he continued to scathe the white devils, but this time he added his hostility against the draft. To buttress this, the Messenger spoke of World War II in apocalyptic admonitions. The Japanese, he said, would invade America and be used by Allah to destroy the white devils. Muhammad, being forty-four years old, was at this time still eligible for the draft.[18] On February 16, 1942, his day to register, Elijah would not sign on. On May 8 he was arrested under another alias, this time Gulam Bogans, on charges of failing to register for the draft[19] and for teaching his disciples not to register for the draft.[20] Elijah claimed that Allah had instructed him so. Benjamin Muhammad later called Washington, D.C., the modern Jerusalem—Jerusalem was where they arrested Jesus.[21] Elijah was convicted and sentenced to serve five years in prison.[22] Scores of Muhammad's students followed suit during the war years and were also arrested,[23] and leaders from the temples in Detroit and Milwaukee were arrested for draft evasion when they visited Washington to speak with the Messenger.[24]

Since monies were hard to come by for the followers of Elijah, bail was not posted until July 23. On the bad advice of his lawyer, coupled with an alleged "spiritual" visit by Master Fard Muhammad wherein he told Elijah that the government's plans for him were "not pleasant,"[25] Muhammad and his wife (who came to bring him home) quickly left for Chicago. There, seven years since he left, he found less religious persecution and was able to cope much better, at least on that front. On another front, however, troubles were brewing. To put it bluntly, the FBI wanted him. His "anti-American" political preaching in Washington pushed buttons, as had his jumping bail. It became a mission, if not *the* mission, of the FBI to put Elijah behind bars for good.

Elijah Jailed

At this time the Chicago police and the FBI abruptly shut down Temple No. 2 on charges that Muhammad's group was connected with the Japanese.[26] (With the temple closed down, Elijah's wife, Clara, eventually led the Temple People to buy a former animal hospital and continued the group's activities from there.[27]) During wartime, government officials may have thought that the NOI was aiding the Japanese government to take over the United States, something not surprising given Elijah Muhammad's sermons in Washington and a possible NOI-Japanese connection in 1932.[28] On September 20, 1942, FBI agents raided Temple No. 2. They were looking for weapons but found none. They did, however, find plans on a blackboard for what the NOI called the "Mother Plane." This plane, said Muhammad, is "Ezekiel's Wheel" mentioned in the Bible. It is a half-mile-by-half-mile space vehicle twenty miles above the earth carrying fifteen hundred smaller planes with bombs fit for the destruction of the white devils. Allah (Fard), says Elijah, taught him about this Mother Plane.[29]

While the raid was carried out on Muhammad's temple, Elijah was hiding in his mother's house. The FBI went to the house, seized more materials, found Elijah under his mother's bed wrapped in a carpet and arrested him.[30] Conspiracy charges were brought against Muhammad, but the case, it seems, was weak. Still, they were interested somewhat in the Mother Plane and in other NOI teachings. According to Muhammad, the FBI told him,

> If you had come with this Teaching 20 years ago you would have been shot outright. Now it is time that your people should know this. We are not trying to stop you from your Teachings, but President Roosevelt doesn't want you out there in the public with that kind of Teaching while America is trying to prosecute the war between her, Germany

and Japan. That's all we are putting you in jail for, to keep you out of the public.[31]

From that day in 1942, Elijah Muhammad was incarcerated in the federal penitentiary in Milan, Michigan until August 24, 1946. He was admitted as Gulam Bogans, prisoner #10039-MM.[32] An unbearable and continuing battery of psychological tests highlighted his life in prison. He was classified as schizophrenic for claiming to have visits with Fard.[33] But he was not schizophrenic. He was convinced that Master Fard Muhammad was God himself and that his message would be carried to the far ends of the earth, no matter what the cost. He also asked prison officials for a copy of the Qur'an but was told to read the Bible.

When he was released, his parole officer told him,

Now, Elijah, you can go ahead and teach what you always have been teaching and nobody will bother you anymore. You teach whatever you have to teach. We didn't put you in jail for what you were teaching but just to keep you from teaching others while we were at war.[34]

Whatever one might think of his theology, Elijah's experience as a child and young boy at the hands of whites, his economic and emotional suffering as a young man, his distaste for Christianity, and his meeting W. D. Fard all contributed to his interpretation of the world around him. The war was no exception. Like any preacher would, he offered his running commentary on this world crisis. The trouble was that his commentary had as a base his hatred for the white devils of America. The government would not tolerate this during war years. But Elijah, whatever else he was, was a man of conviction, and his followers now viewed him as the prime example of what a martyr should be. The movement strengthened.

ELIJAH AFTER PRISON

When Elijah was released from prison, his NOI was still small, but this time he was the unquestioned leader. The Messenger's time in the penitentiary in Milan did much to bolster his authority. The people looked to his unselfish suffering at the hands of persecutors and were inspired to evangelism. Consequently his claims about the person of Master Fard Muhammad gained more validity in the eyes of those who were debating whether or not they should make the leap of faith and join the fold.

Growth and Prosperity

The years immediately following the Messenger's release from prison would be a time of growth, characterized by steps toward economic self-sufficiency. Muhammad encouraged his flock to take advantage of the boom in the economy produced by the war. In 1945, while he was still in prison, Muhammad instructed those on the outside to gather all their resources to buy a 140-acre farm in White Cloud, Michigan. In 1947 the NOI bought a grocery store, a restaurant (which they named Shabazz, referring to the original tribe of humanity), and a bakery. All these were examples to the black community that the Asiatics could rise up and command from the white devils the respect due them.[35] By the early 1950s Muhammad drew an annual income of around twenty-five thousand dollars.

Though membership at this time numbered only in the hundreds, the impact that the Messenger had upon NOI families was incredible. As was the case in the old days under Fard's leadership, members had to renounce their former lifestyles. This meant no extramarital sex, crime, smoking, bad diet, and slothfulness. They as a result gained a healthier outlook on life, a phenomenon that served to evidence Muhammad's claims about Fard and his Islam. Weekly studies in addition to temple services were offered, as well as recreational activities designed to keep people healthy.[36] As always, the Fruit of Islam was there to model Muhammad's teachings and to enforce any sentence pronounced for moral slips, failure to live up to meeting attendance, and theological error. Additionally, the University of Islam was in operation and producing stellar future leaders.

In the 1950s generally things were good, especially as compared with the terrible and trying time from 1932 to 1946. The few businesses that were started the decade before also increased. In Chicago the NOI added to its bakery and grocery store a car-repair shop, laundromat, cleaning plant, dress shop, haberdashery, and its own apartment building. Net profits reached as high as four hundred thousand dollars. At this time Muhammad and his wife were seen driving Cadillacs.[37] In sum, the NOI was showing the world what the original race was capable of accomplishing.

After his release from prison in 1946, Muhammad curtailed his polemics against the government. His time in prison perhaps softened him a bit. In the years to come his political activist methodology underwent significant modification, though his theology of white devils, Armageddon, separation, and disobedience to any laws of the United States that were contrary to the laws of Allah remained intact.

The FBI

For reasons related to civil disobedience and Armageddon, the FBI continued its surveillance of Elijah and his NOI throughout the 1950s and 1960s. An FBI file mentions the following:

> MUSLIM CULT OF ISLAM (MCI). A source, who has furnished reliable information in the past, advised on May 11, 1956 that the MCI is an organization composed entirely of Negroes, which was reportedly organized around 1930 in Detroit, Michigan. The national leader and founder is ELIJAH MOHAMMED, who claims to have been sent by Allah, the Supreme Being, to lead the Negroes out of slavery in the United States. Members fanatically follow the alleged teachings of Allah as interpreted by MOHAMMED and disavow allegiance to the United States. Members pledge allegiance only to Allah and Islam, and believe any civil law which conflicts with Muslim Law should be disobeyed. The Cult teaches that members of the dark-skinned race cannot be considered citizens of the United States . . . and . . . must free themselves by destroying non-Muslims and Christianity in the "War of Armageddon." . . . [They] believe that they are directly related to all Asiatic races and any conflict involving any Asiatic nation and a Western nation is considered a part of the "War of Armageddon," in which the Asiatic nation will be victorious.[38]

In 1957 surveillance taps were placed in Elijah Muhammad's 4847 South Woodlawn Avenue home in Chicago and in other residences of Muhammad. According to Mattias Gardell, in 1959 the FBI and the media combined to launch an offensive to inform the public of the NOI's "racist and hate type teachings." Magazines such as *Time, U.S. News & World Report,* and *Saturday Evening Post* and newspapers throughout the country were used in this campaign. In spite of this the NOI grew in membership and boosted its number of temples, a phenomenon that led the FBI to conclude that Muhammad and the NOI "thrived on publicity."[39]

The Mission Continues

By the late 1950s and into the early 1960s Elijah Muhammad was quite active in promoting his savior and the ideology of the NOI. As a result, membership rose from only several hundreds in the early part of the decade to several thousand by 1959. This was an intense growing time for the NOI, though it has always remained cryptic as to actual numbers of adherents. To quote Malcolm X, "Those who know aren't saying, and those who say don't know!" Consequently, estimates of the membership of the NOI by observers and critics ranged from only a few thousand to 250,000. Temples, however, were quite visible. A new Chicago Temple No. 2 was purchased, and by the end of the 1950s the NOI had as many as thirty temples in fifteen states and the District of Columbia.[40] This trend of growth continued into the 1960s.

Elijah Muhammad took every opportunity to reach blacks throughout the United States. His speaking engagements in many major cities drew impressive numbers. He also was a columnist for the *Pittsburgh Courier* and the weekly *Los Angeles Herald-Dispatch.* His articles in these media tools caused increasing support for his movement as well as widespread disdain from the white and black communities. For each of these newspapers Muhammad had an army of followers selling on street corners. Muhammad made an impact. On February 13, 1960, he was lauded by the *Herald-Dispatch* and given an award. It said of the Messenger:

> Mr. Muhammad has succeeded in organizing approximately one half million so-called Negroes. . . . He is uplifting fallen

humanity. . . . Because of his teachings, his program of positive action, the *Herald-Dispatch* will give him the highest Achievement Award ever given to an individual by this publication.[41]

CRITICS AND VINDICATION

Muhammad, again, was not without his critics in this time of growth. Orthodox Muslims such as Jamil Diab, Hamaas Abdul Khaalis, and Talib Ahmad Dawud were among the most vocal. The first two were once members of the NOI. When Diab joined the NOI he took it upon himself to school Elijah Muhammad in the tenets of Islam. Soon, though, differences arose and Diab was writing against Muhammad's movement, claiming that the NOI could never have any legitimacy in the true Islamic world. Khaalis also claimed he joined the NOI to bring Elijah and his followers closer to orthodox Islam. He shared the same view as Diab—the NOI was definitely not Islamic. Dawud, though never a part of the NOI, also attacked the legitimacy of the movement on traditional Islamic grounds, stating, "Neither Elijah Muhammad nor his followers can get into Mecca."[42]

Muhammad's critics had a point. There are significant differences between the doctrines of the NOI and those of traditional Islam, and Muhammad's enemies were quick to point them out. First and foremost is that Islam considers it blasphemy to call any man Allah in the flesh. Closely connected to this is Islam's doctrine of the incorporeal nature of Allah. Second, the Yakub myth can be found nowhere in the Qur'an or any related text of Islam. Third, Islam accepts all races into its fold.

As to whether or not Elijah could get into Mecca, he was determined to prove his critics wrong. On November 21, 1959, Elijah and his two sons, Herbert and Akbar, departed for the Middle East. They were on a trek to carry out *al-hajj,* "the greater pilgrimage" to the holy city of Mecca. All good and true Muslims are encouraged to make this trip. *Al-hajj* is a series of ritualistic actions taking several days to accomplish.[43] In reality, what Elijah Muhammad went through was considered *al-umrah,* "the lesser pilgrimage" to Mecca outside the *hajj* season, requiring only sixty to ninety minutes to complete.[44]

On their way Muhammad and his sons visited Islamic sights in Istanbul, Damascus, Beirut, Jerusalem, Cairo (where he was greeted by President Nasser and invited to stay in his palace[45]), and Khartoum. While in Africa, Elijah was exposed to the realities of human nature on the part of what he called Asiatics. What he found was not the history Fard taught him. Africans exploiting other Africans for wealth and power, the fruits of the Arab slave trade of the nineteenth century, and Ethiopia's slavery system all threatened Muhammad's idealistic views. Muhammad was also unaware of Saudi Arabia's enslavement of more than one hundred thousand Africans (a contradiction in light of Muhammad's picture of Arabs and blacks being from the same stock—the original man). Upon returning home he ridiculed the economic and social situation in the East, causing him to stress even more the economic self-sufficiency and freedom of his people.[46]

When they arrived in Mecca, Muhammad's possible vindication was near. Would he be allowed in to complete the *umrah?* To his delight, yes! Muhammad took part in the ritualistic washing of his hands and was given a guide to lead him to the Great Mosque. The guide directed Muhammad and his sons in prayer as they approached the center of the mosque. Then Muhammad circled the Kabah (a cube-shaped structure in the center) seven times, chanted in Arabic "Allah is the greatest," kissed the sacred Black Stone, drank water from the sacred well of Zamzam, and completed the one-thousand-foot run between the hills of Marwa and Al Safa. The pilgrimage was complete, and Muhammad had proved his rivals wrong. To him, the NOI was legitimate Islam.[47] Further, in Elijah's mind, Dawud's earlier statement, "Elijah Muhammad is not a Muslim; He is just plain Elijah Poole of Sandersville, Georgia,"[48] showed Dawud to be a liar.

Muhammad talked about his visit to Cairo. In addition to meeting President Nasser, he said,

> I met the Great Imam [spiritual leader]. He invited me to visit him, and I have experienced great happiness . . . with him. He is over all the Imams in . . . Egypt. He placed a kiss upon my head, and I placed a kiss on his hand.[49]

He later gloated about the backing he received from Muslims in the East: "The whole world of Islam is behind me. I was received as a brother and a leader. I did not ask for a visa to make the *hajj* to Mecca, the Holy City. They asked me to go."[50] Elijah made sure that major magazines and newspapers throughout the United States picked up on the successful trip, emphasizing his acceptance by the Muslim world.

One may wonder why the world of orthodox Islam would welcome someone whom it considers a blasphemer to make the sacred pilgrimage to the holy city. After all, a most central, if not the central tenet, of traditional Islam was treaded upon and kicked into the waste bucket by Elijah Muhammad. "Who is Allah?" is the question any orthodox Muslim needs to have answered before he will allow further inquiry as to whether or not one is a believer. Elijah Muhammad's answer to such a question is, "W. D. Fard is Allah in the flesh." With all the press Elijah attracted before his trip to Mecca, it is reasonable to say that Islamic officials knew of his beliefs. Why, then, was he allowed to complete this holy pilgrimage? Researchers have suggested the reason is more political than religious and that politics seems to have overruled the sacred.[51]

The Honorable Elijah Muhammad's Lost-Found Nation of Islam, despite acceptance from the East, continued to be the subject of scorn among many North American Islamic groups. Elijah did not believe in the Allah of the Qur'an. Additionally, Elijah wasted no time attacking Christianity. His temple speeches and books are laden with a mockery of basic Christian doctrinal teachings. They would have to be, given Elijah's replacing of the God-man Jesus Christ with the God-man W. D. Fard. When all was said and done, the NOI was neither Islam nor Christianity.

More from the FBI

A few months before Elijah Muhammad and his sons made their way to Mecca, another interesting event took place. Muhammad was scheduled to give a speech in Washington, D.C., and was once again greeted by police when he arrived. This time, though, they did not arrest him. Rather, ten police motorcyclists escorted him to the Roosevelt Hotel, where he was to stay. Years earlier he was a renegade seditious preacher; now he was treated like a visiting political dignitary. He later gave his speech before an audience of ten thousand people.[52] Muhammad reflects on the event: "The devil has great respect for Me. Did you hear about how they respected Me in 1959 when I visited Washington? They came out and met Me."[53]

But this did not mean that the FBI stopped its watch. Into the 1960s the FBI tried other means of discrediting the Messenger in the eyes of his disciples in the effort to prohibit the growth of the NOI. A campaign was undertaken to expose Muhammad's sexually illicit behavior. He is said to have had sexual relations with at least five NOI women.[54] Some became pregnant and eventually filed paternity suits against Muhammad,[55] but even this failed to break up his marriage or disrupt the growth of the movement.

Evidence of the reactions of the NOI community suggests several ways in which the faithful coped with Muhammad's infidelity, and researchers have offered a few theses. One option states that the black community at that time differed from the white middle-class community as to how infidelity was viewed. Whites saw it as a terrible thing, but many NOI adherents were from the inner-city ghettos. Consequently, being a "lady-killer" proved one's masculinity.[56] Perhaps this is substantiated in Malcolm X's somewhat comical yet serious words offered in the context of Elijah Muhammad's sexual exploits:

> You can't take nine teenaged women and seduce them and give them babies and not tell me you're—and then tell me you're moral. You do it if you admitted you did it and admitted that the babies were yours. I'd shake your hand and call you a man. A good one too. [Laughter.][57]

Second is to excuse one's behavior by mentioning the multiple wives of leaders in the Old Testament.[58] Elijah Muhammad reportedly told Malcolm X:

> I'm David. When you read about how David took another man's wife, I'm that David. You read about Noah, who got drunk—that's me. You read about Lot, who went and laid up with his own daughters. I had to fulfill all those things.[59]

Third is to overwrite Muhammad's actions in view of his divine mission and personal connection to Allah (Fard). According to the FBI, many of his followers adopted this view: "Muhammad's extracurricular escapades were accepted by his followers, their belief apparently being motivated by the fact Muhammad as the messenger of Allah was divinely inspired and missioned."[60]

All these theses may explain the varied responses of NOI members as a whole, but to Elijah and some of his faithful there still was something wrong with his extramarital relationships. Elijah's actions proved this. If one FBI file is accurate, "Muhammad," in the midst of the two paternity suits filed against him, "had tried to induce an assistant to assume responsibility for the paternity so that Muhammad could keep his spiritual image on a high plane in the eyes of his followers."[61] And Malcolm X, when told of Elijah's moral failings, reacted with vigor: "Adultery! Why, any Muslim guilty of adultery was summarily ousted in disgrace."[62] Malcolm's reaction to the news suggests his anger at his brother Reginald's earlier expulsion by Elijah Muhammad from the NOI on moral grounds. Malcolm X also stated that the thought of immorality on the part of Elijah Muhammad made him "shake with fear."[63] Finally, according to an FBI file on Elijah Muhammad, "AKBAR MUHAMMAD, Elijah's son, has 'disassociated himself' because of his father's immorality."[64]

None of the tactics used by the FBI were successful in stunting the growth of the NOI. Further, those who left the movement had little impact on stopping its growth. Even Clara overcame the difficulties his actions put on their marriage. She remained loyal to him until her death in 1972. The believers became all the more supportive of Elijah's divine mission, claiming persecution of Allah's chosen vessel.

Into the 1960s

With the civil rights movement in full swing and opting for integration, Elijah more than ever stressed his separate state ideology through public speaking, interviews, and a biweekly newspaper titled *Muhammad Speaks*. (Needless to say, Muhammad vehemently disagreed with Martin Luther King Jr., and vice versa. In August 1959, King struck at the heart of Muhammad's movement when he listed it among other black supremacist hate groups.[65]) Elijah claimed that the American government owed them a separate state and called for it to provide land where the NOI could live apart from the white devils, provide for itself, and protect itself with its own military force. The growth and economic well-being of the NOI in the 1950s had shown Elijah that this could be done. The Ku Klux Klan, though disagreeing immensely on who the superior race was, shared this vision with Muhammad. In order to facilitate this ideal, Muhammad, like W. D. Fard before him, organized meetings with the Klan to see how this might be accomplished.[66]

This was quite strange, considering that NOI sermons often contained mention of Allah's destruction of the white devils. Further, white supremacist hate mail (not only from the Klan) was constantly flowing into the mailboxes of NOI leaders. Yet even this did not stop Elijah from placing politics above doctrine and above his awful experiences as a young boy with racist lynchings, as is witnessed by his strange relationship with the white supremacist American Nazi Party head George Lincoln Rockwell. Rockwell often praised Muhammad's separation polity. Muhammad, brilliant as he was, made use of Rockwell's stamp of approval and allowed him (to the praise of the Klan) and his entourage to attend a temple service.[67] Perhaps he thought that Rockwell's presence would curb violence between white racists and his NOI and bear witness to the truth of Muhammad's separation agenda to the rest of the white world.[68]

As the NOI grew in membership and influence, it began to spread to other areas of the country. But this was to bring trouble. Social unrest and violence followed by arrests of NOI members were reported in Louisiana and California. The murder of NOI follower Ronald Stokes by police outside a Los Angeles mosque also grieved Elijah Muhammad. These events, coupled with his marital problems due to charges of infidelity, FBI investigations, and bronchial illnesses, took their toll on the Messenger.

MUHAMMAD'S LAST DECADE

Despite failing health, Muhammad summoned enough strength to make a second trip to Islamic countries in 1972, this time accompanied by boxing great Muhammad Ali[69] and several NOI dignitaries. The trip was highlighted by a personal invitation to visit with Libyan leader Muammar al-Gadhafi. Also, a few Islamic countries, including Libya, financed Muhammad's movement with millions of interest-free dollars. This stark contradiction—financial assistance in support of the NOI even with its unorthodox theology—did not seem to bother any Muslim politicians, who were on the side of the "anti-American" NOI. Muhammad was clearly an important figure for Eastern Muslim countries.

The Honorable Elijah Muhammad witnessed continued growth, expansion, and prosperity for his NOI in the 1970s. By 1975 there were seventy-six mosques, and although membership figures continued to be the subject of guessing games, hundreds attended temple services. It also was not uncommon for ten thousand people to attend annual Saviour's Day rallies, held each February to commemorate the savior Master Fard Muhammad (W. D. Fard).[70]

Financially the movement continued to rise even in the midst of increasing debt. The NOI was quite involved in self-owned retail industries and land consumption, and the newspaper *Muhammad Speaks* came out at an amazing clip that numbered into the hundreds of thousands.[71] Of course, this figure had as its reason the thousands of devoted followers of Muhammad who every day lined the streets of major cities to sell the periodical.

Elijah lived to enjoy more vindication. Muhammad must have praised Fard for the amazing change in the way his movement was viewed by some politicians. It had come a long way since the 1960s. Muhammad lived to see the 1973 Illinois State Legislature adopt a resolution praising Muhammad and his movement for contributing to the community. In 1974 Chicago mayor Richard Daley appointed March 29 as "Honorable Elijah Muhammad Day in Chicago."[72] Elijah had come a long way since his arrest by the FBI in 1942.

The Honorable Elijah Muhammad died from congestive heart failure on February 25, 1975.

SUMMARY

The life of Elijah Muhammad was indeed exciting. On the one hand there were terrible times of persecution from the outside and from within, poverty, no shelter, police and FBI investigations, arrests, intense suffering from bronchial illness for most of his life, and multiple threats on his life. On the other hand he lived to see himself vindicated several times. This must have given him great satisfaction as well as adoration in the eyes of his faithful followers. In the end, though, he would tell of his most precious possession—he was entrusted to spread the message that Allah in person has come to him for the salvation of his people. This, to Elijah Muhammad, was his only mission in life, his ultimate source of satisfaction. Indeed, it was not him but his God who allowed the growth of his Lost-Found Nation of Islam in spite of all the attacks of the enemy. For this reason he remains in the eyes of thousands The Messenger of Allah, and he continues to be a source of inspiration for those hungering for identity and religious meaning in their lives.

SIX

Malcolm and Louis: Groomed for the Task

Though he was still traveling extensively throughout the world in the late 1950s, the Honorable Elijah Muhammad was then more than sixty years of age. He knew that someone would soon have to fill the role of traveling spokesperson for the Lost-Found Nation of Islam (NOI), someone to carry the activist torch. Though he would without question remain the Messenger of Allah—*the* authority of the NOI—and his teachings remain the norm, he needed a national spokesperson to ignite the masses. These big shoes were filled profoundly by Malcolm Little, known as Malcolm X. Malcolm was esteemed by Elijah Muhammad, so much so that he allowed Malcolm to make a trip to visit the Islamic world in the Middle East even before he did.

Louis Farrakhan came into the limelight later than Malcolm did. We shall also briefly study events of his life in the NOI and his rise to the top. He was at the center of the battle for leadership after the death of Muhammad and eventually took leadership of a faction of Muhammad's following. Many people recognize Farrakhan, who leads the movement today, as the legitimate heir to Elijah Muhammad.

MALCOLM X

The man who was to become one of the most controversial black leaders in American history was born to Earl and Louise Little on May 19, 1925, in Omaha, Nebraska. At the time of Malcolm's birth, Elijah Muhammad was in Detroit struggling with life and was six years away from the turning point of his life.

Childhood

Like Elijah's father, Malcolm's father was a traveling Baptist preacher. The victim of a streetcar accident, Earl Little died in 1931. Earlier that year Malcolm became a kindergarten student at Pleasant Grove Elementary School in Michigan. The Great Depression placed a tremendous burden on Louise, who was faced with raising eight children. Eventually she suffered a mental breakdown, and the children were parceled out to foster homes.[1]

Earl Little was also a member of Marcus Garvey's Universal Negro Improvement Association (UNIA). He was the president of a local branch of the UNIA and took Malcolm with him to meetings.[2] The black nationalism of the Garveyites surely influenced Malcolm. Even though most adults cannot recall much from their lives as six year olds, the excitement of UNIA meetings engraved more than a few memories in Malcolm's mind.

But all was not peaceful in the life of Malcolm. Violence plagued the Little household, both inside and outside. His father and mother abused their eight[3] children. Further, after being driven away from Omaha, Nebraska, by the Ku Klux Klan, the family moved to Lansing, Michigan. In 1929 a white hate group known as the Black Legionnaires burned their house to the ground.[4]

Malcolm would later recall these events in his childhood as preparatory for his calling to black nationalism. He implicitly states that his father's death was no mere streetcar accident. Rather, he may have died because of a beating at the hands of white people, who then laid him on streetcar tracks to be run down by the next car. Further, four of his six brothers died violent deaths, three at the hands of white men.[5] He also tells of an incident when he was in the eighth grade at Mason Junior High School in Michigan. After sharing with a teacher that he wanted to become a lawyer, the teacher replied that that was not a realistic goal for "niggers."[6] Malcolm's childhood experiences surely played a profound part in shaping his ideology, thus preparing him for conversion to Elijah Muhammad's Lost-Found Nation of Islam.

On the Streets and in Prison

Troubled by his experience as a youth, Malcolm moved from foster home to foster home, finally ending up in Boston, Massachusetts, in 1941. There he became involved in underworld crime.[7] Another phenomenon shaped his general view of things. He became exposed to rich black Bostonians who were proud of themselves and playing the white man's game to get rich. This, thought Malcolm, was no way to achieve the liberation of the black race.[8]

Almost two full years in Boston made Malcolm Little streetwise. He learned the tricks of his trade well, living the life of a drug dealer, numbers runner, and thief.[9] At one point he left Boston and headed once again for Michigan, where he stayed only two months before bouncing between Harlem, Boston, Michigan, Harlem, and Boston. During this time Malcolm had not changed—he was still a criminal.

Ironically, the same year that Elijah Muhammad was released from prison, Malcolm, also known in the streets as "Big Red," was put in prison. In 1946 he was convicted of burglary and sentenced to six to ten years in Charlestown (Massachusetts) State Prison.

It was in prison in 1947 and 1948 that Malcolm Little came into contact with the teachings of the Honorable Elijah Muhammad. At this time he had been transferred to other jails in Concord and Norfolk, Massachusetts. In prison Malcolm read widely in philosophy, Christian theology, and world religions and was exposed to Jehovah's Witnesses' literature. Later he was introduced to the NOI by one of his brothers, who was at the time a member of the movement in Detroit.[10] Philbert had written Malcolm a letter stating that he had found the true religion of the black nation. Malcolm, however, was not impressed and quickly refused the invitation to seek this true religion.

His reading of theology, however, did not make Malcolm a Christian either. Rather, he became known as Satan to his cellmates because of his scathing remarks about all he had learned about religion to that point. "Religion to that point" was most likely all the above-mentioned religions. Adding fuel to this proverbial fire was the fact that Malcolm saw little Christianity in the lives of those who professed it.[11] He saw the hypocrisy plainly.

Preparing the Soil for Conversion. What Malcolm did not see was that his brother, Philbert, was not the only one in his family who had found Allah and the NOI—the whole family had found "the truth." Another brother, Reginald, later paid several visits to Malcolm and each time left the prisoner wondering if this was the truth.[12]

Malcolm's older sister, Hilda, then introduced Malcolm to Fard's Yakub theory. She also explained that Fard is God in the flesh who came to Detroit in 1930. Fard, she shared, was both black and white, enabling him to move about unnoticed in the midst of the white devils. At this point Malcolm began corresponding with Elijah Muhammad.[13] Muhammad showered Malcolm with attention, and Malcolm's experience with the Garvey movement solidified what he was hearing from the Messenger.

Conversion. Inmate Malcolm Little likens his spiritual journey to that of the apostle Paul. Claiming to have identified with the first-century apostle of Christianity, he always enjoyed patterning his religious efforts after those of Paul. Malcolm's conversion would also ring a similar tone with the man who encountered Christ on the road to Damascus.

While lying in bed in his cell one night, Malcolm had a vision. He suddenly became aware of a presence. Someone, he claims, was sitting beside him. This "man" had on a dark suit and was neither white nor black but had light brown skin and was "Asiatic" in appearance. The mysterious stranger did not frighten Malcolm, but the two stared at each other for several minutes. Malcolm was sure he was not dreaming. Suddenly, as quickly as the figure appeared, he disappeared. Malcolm would later call this his "pre-vision,"[14] but for now he remained agnostic as to the identity of the man that appeared in his cell that night.

Not too long after the vision, Malcolm was convinced that it was W. D. Fard that appeared to him. Time and more visits from family finally pushed Malcolm to conversion. Malcolm had become a believer.

A Star Is Born

For the next three to four years in prison the six-foot three-inch Malcolm Little grew in his faith and utilized prison-sanctioned debate competitions to hone his skills toward one day becoming the premier spokesperson and apologist for the NOI. He also was instrumental in converting fellow inmates to Fard's teachings. Even as a young convert he was receiving attention from the news media and press due to his demands as a follower of the Honorable Elijah Muhammad. His demands for books by black authors and for cell beds facing east were rejected, causing him to write ferocious letters to prison officials threatening the judgment of Almighty Allah.

In August 1952 Malcolm received his parole and traveled to Michigan to live with one of his brothers. He worked in a Detroit department store. Six weeks later, with permission from his parole officer, he traveled to Chicago to hear Elijah Muhammad preach. In a scene reminiscent of Fard's public "divine" calling of Elijah, Elijah called public attention to Malcolm. In a speech to his flock the Messenger likened Malcolm's sufferings to those of Job and stated that he would remain faithful.[15] This floored Malcolm. He was excited about the NOI to begin with, but this was an unexpected blessing he would cherish for a long time to come. Needless to say, he and Muhammad became quite close.

Malcolm Little then acquired the surname X, a one-letter statement that he no longer identified with his slave name. Saddling the charismatic preacher with responsibilities evidenced Elijah Muhammad's respect for his young disciple. Within a year the fired-up NOI evangelist was named assistant minister of Detroit Temple No. 1.[16] In 1954 he became the minister of Temple No. 12 in Philadelphia and Temple No. 7 in New York. As a temple speaker Malcolm was explosive. His offensive remarks about white devils and Christianity soon won him recognition as a leader, and one to be reckoned with. From Malcolm's perspective, his prison-time study of religious texts, especially the Bible, served him well. Jesus was a black man; Ezekiel's Wheel is the Mother Plane (a half-mile-by-half-mile space vehicle carrying bombs for Armageddon); the Book of Revelation tells of the total destruction of white devils through Fard's use of the Mother Plane.

All these were subjects of delight for this defender of the faith. The latter subject drew attention outside the camp. Malcolm X, like his leader, did not escape the scrutiny of the FBI. Early FBI files mention NOI beliefs such as allegiance only to Allah and not the United States and NOI remarks that the Korean war was futile in light of the coming Armageddon when Allah would destroy Christianity, North America, and Great Britain.[17] Before becoming the first minister of the Boston temple in the fall of 1953, Malcolm failed to register for the draft. His experience with draft officials was unlike his mentor's in that it did not end in his arrest. Rather, due to answering questions from his NOI perspective (claiming to be a citizen of Asia and citing Allah's will whenever possible) the draft board declared he was an "asocial personality with paranoid trends."[18]

The Middle Years

Malcolm X's social, political, and theological diatribes continued throughout the 1950s and early 1960s. He slammed integration, lambasted the white man's government, and attacked ferociously the central doctrines of Christianity. Likening the Honorable Elijah Muhammad to the biblical Moses, Malcolm X lauded him as the one who showed the people the way to freedom and deliverance and the one who led them away from integrating with the white system. The three gods of the Christian religion were an abomination in Allah's sight, and the Christian religion served only the white man's desire to enslave the original man, the Asiatic race. Malcolm X would consistently warn the white devils that pestilence and plagues of every sort awaited them. They were doomed to this fate by Allah in the flesh.[19]

On July 5, 1959, Malcolm X embarked on a Middle East tour of the Muslim world. Evidencing his importance and rise to power and influence within the NOI are the facts that he preceded Elijah Muhammad in making the trip (by Elijah's consent and appointment) and that he was treated as a dignitary while in Egypt. He was the guest of Anwar Sadat and his entourage at quite a few social gatherings.[20] Next Malcolm moved to Saudi Arabia but did not visit Mecca, probably because he thought that the first representative of the NOI to accomplish this sacred event should be Elijah.[21]

During this trip Malcolm experienced the unexpected. He was rudely awakened to the first seeds of contradiction. The doctrines and sociological ideologies of the Muslim world seemed to clash with those of Fardian Islam. He witnessed the enslavement (legally) of Africans by the Saudis. Moreover, although there was mention of

Allah by the Middle Eastern Muslims, there was not even a hint that W. D. Fard was Allah. Nonetheless, Malcolm X returned to America with glowing news from his excursion to the East. Despite the slavery in that land, he boasted about the lack of racial prejudice; instead of mentioning that the "Fard is Allah" doctrine would be considered blasphemous in the eyes of traditional Islam, he remained silent about the issue.

Why? A challenge to shift one's paradigm is not easily met. Several psychological and sociological phenomena contribute to initial resistance. One can only imagine the weight that was on Malcolm's shoulders. He not only represented thousands of his black brothers and sisters in the task of bringing the NOI to foreign soil but was specifically sent on this mission by the man who changed his life for the better. All these people were depending on him to bring Islamic validity and legitimacy to the NOI.

Adding to the pressure, a television documentary series produced by Mike Wallace and Louis Lomax, titled "The Hate That Hate Produced," aired while Malcolm was on his trip. The series focused on Malcolm in his role as spokesman for the NOI. Because Malcolm returned after the series aired, any mention of the contradictions he experienced in the Middle East would only fuel the fire started by the series. Therefore, a positive review of both the political and Islamic acceptance given Malcolm by the world of Islam was needed, despite what his conscience may have told him.

For the next few years Malcolm continued to fervently defend the Honorable Elijah Muhammad's teachings. He not only spoke out against the Wallace and Lomax documentary but also continued to battle United States–based Islamic groups as they consistently charged the NOI with unorthodoxy. In addition to his speaking, Malcolm X was the NOI's premier apologist.

Rumblings in the Latter Years

Like the haunting of the FBI, "The Hate That Hate Produced" failed to put the NOI off the map. In fact, even after the show aired there was an increase in membership and mosques (changed from "Temple" to "Mosque" sometime after the Middle East trips by Malcolm and Elijah).[22] The NOI, thanks to television, was more popular than ever.

And so was Malcolm X. This controversial, talented, outspoken, and charismatic soldier of the Star and Crescent of the Lost-Found Nation of Islam was thrust into the public's eye. Suddenly it was Malcolm, not so much Muhammad, who was looked to for opinions on social and political matters. In addition to his speaking engagements at mosques, he spent time debating on radio and television. He even challenged Martin Luther King Jr. to a debate, but King refused, stating that his time would be better spent in positive actions rather than in the negative atmosphere of debate. Malcolm was quite popular, and one found it difficult in the early 1960s to talk about anything black without raising the name Malcolm X.

But popularity breeds jealousy, even within the idealistic NOI. As Malcolm rose in fame, so did the egos of the upper echelon of Elijah Muhammad's power structure. In 1963 Elijah Muhammad, in a state of consistently failing health, appointed Malcolm as National Minister of the NOI. Elijah's bronchial problems had plagued him for many years, so there naturally was talk of who would succeed him as leader. There began to be in-house talk of how presumptuous a move this was on Elijah's part and how Malcolm did not have the goods to lead Allah's people.

Two more matters made things worse. First, when Elijah could not make the annual Saviour's Day celebration in February 1963, he appointed Malcolm to preside over the festivities. This witnessed to the entire body of the NOI that Malcolm X was, second to the Messenger himself, the most prominent figure of the movement.[23] Second, in March of that same year Malcolm was interviewed on *The Ben Hunter Show*. He was asked about being a Muslim. His response revealed three interesting phenomena. First, he did not preface his remarks with his usual formula, "The Honorable Elijah Muhammad says." Second, he stated that one becomes a Muslim only by accepting Islam. Third, one becomes a Muslim by believing in Allah and that *Jews know Allah as Jehovah and Christians know Allah as Christ.* Where was Elijah as the base of his answer? Why emphasize the acceptance of Islam rather than Elijah's doctrine of separation? And, finally, in light of Elijah's attacks and Malcolm's past attacks on the futility of the Christian doctrine of God and his belief in Fard as Allah, how can Christians know Allah as Jesus?[24]

The interview signaled that something was awry in Malcolm X's theological mind. In the first half of that year he fluctuated between defending Elijah's doctrines (after all, he said, it was Elijah who transformed him from inmate without a cause to believer with a mission) and yoking the NOI with traditional Islamic tenets. Malcolm wrestled with the contradictions, making it clear that he was in transition. In the meantime, Malcolm's enemies within the NOI were plotting ways in which they could cause the demise of their opponent. The transition would not move to completion, however, until late 1963.

Moving Out

By 1963 Malcolm became aware of Elijah Muhammad's sexual immorality. Despite the facts that he was at this time juggling the NOI with the views of traditional Islam and making out-of-line doctrinal statements on radio and television, the disillusioned Malcolm, with Muhammad, concocted a plan to rescue the Messenger from any accountability. They claimed biblical authority for his multiple affairs using the examples of Old Testament figures and citing Muhammad's escapades as examples of fulfilled prophecy.[25] However, Malcolm knew Elijah's behavior was out of line. This perhaps is evident in a statement made by Malcolm two years later. Speaking of Elijah Muhammad, he said, "Yes, he's immoral."[26] On the fence now, Malcolm was about to receive at the hand of his beloved mentor the final blow that knocked him out of the NOI for good.

On that awful day in November 1963, millions of Americans watched with tearful eyes the news programs announcing that President John F. Kennedy had been shot to death in Dallas, Texas.

Elijah Muhammad, knowing what he had taught his ministers concerning the destruction of white devils, instructed them not to editorialize on the assassination. Elijah was a careful politician. Further, Elijah was all too familiar with Malcolm X's comments to the press several months earlier regarding the crash of a commercial airliner killing 120 people. Malcolm happily stated that Allah was responsible for bringing 120 whites to the ground: "He gets rid of 120 of them in one whop. . . . We will continue to pray and we hope that every day another plane falls out of the sky."[27] Concerning the assassination, the order from the Messenger to his ministers was clear—stay out of it!

Sadly, Malcolm saw the need to break the order. Kennedy and he never saw eye to eye, the latter accusing the former of politicking for change in social conditions only because the world was watching. Further, Kennedy never pushed for separation, a key tenet in NOI beliefs. So when the time came for Malcolm to offer a few words on the assassination, the *New York Times* on December 2, 1963, quoted Malcolm as referring to the assassination as "the chickens coming home to roost. . . . Being an old farm boy myself, chickens coming home to roost never did make me sad; they've always made me glad."[28] Since Malcolm was already loosening the ties between himself and the NOI, there is every reason to believe that he broke Elijah's command with all intent.

Later, a furious Elijah Muhammad lashed out at the man he appointed as National Minister several months earlier. He issued a ninety-day suspension to Malcolm X on December 4, 1963. Malcolm made several reinstatement appeals to Muhammad, who rejected each in turn. During this time Malcolm spent time at Cassius Clay's fight camp and home. Malcolm was still hopeful about reinstatement, and it is possible Malcolm hoped Clay's influence would strengthen his plea. It did not. Things quickly soured between Malcolm and Elijah. In late February 1964, days after Clay won the heavyweight title, the suspended National Minister boasted, "If you think Cassius Clay was loud, wait until I start talking in March."[29] Clay soon formally converted to Elijah Muhammad's Islam, and Elijah Muhammad changed Clay's name to Muhammad Ali. After this Ali no longer met with Malcolm, probably due to his loyalty to Elijah Muhammad.

The New Malcolm

In March and April of 1964, Malcolm X was interviewed several times by the media. He never lost his flair, and this time turned it loose on the NOI. He told *Ebony* that the NOI has "got to kill me. They can't afford to let me live. . . . I know where the bodies are buried. And if they press me, I'll exhume some."[30] With this statement (if not meant figuratively to refer to the "dead bodies" that are hidden secrets of Elijah Muhammad—but see the quotation under "The End," below) Malcolm is admitting knowledge of persons that had been murdered by the NOI. If this was so, the NOI had every reason to fear Malcolm and the perfect reason to silence him. Obviously Elijah would now never revoke the suspension.

The combination of putting up with contradictions between traditional Islam and the NOI, fighting the turmoil caused by Muhammad's infidelity, his unsuccessful plea for reinstatement, and reports of threats on his life by the NOI[31] left Malcolm no choice but to leave the Lost-Found Nation of Islam. Though he earlier had tried his best to submit to his superior, a man he had respected to the utmost, Muhammad's constant no to his repenting plea was final.

In response, Malcolm formed two organizations of his own, The Muslim Mosque, Inc., and a secular expression of Malcolm's philosophy called the Organization of Afro-American Unity (OAAU).[32] Later Muhammad voiced his disapproval of Malcolm's two organizations. Referring to himself in the third person, he warned that only fools do not believe in the Honorable Elijah Muhammad's God and that if Malcolm really did believe that the Honorable Elijah Muhammad was the Messenger of Allah, he would fear the future.[33]

The Making of a Sunni. On April 13, 1964, Malcolm X set out to make the *hajj*, the sacred pilgrimage to Mecca. According to the FBI, Malcolm bought a one-way ticket under the name Malik El-Shabazz.[34] Unlike Elijah, who completed only the *umrah* and not the *hajj* (though Elijah said he made the *hajj*), Malcolm successfully completed the *hajj*, which involved several days of activities and ceremonies. Now he was El Hajj Malik Shabazz. My brevity in reporting Malcolm's pilgrimage should not be taken to portray the *hajj* as an easy undertaking. It is most difficult, requiring many major ceremonies and travel.[35]

Malcolm said this experience changed him. He therefore converted to Sunni Islam, which was far from the Fardian Islam he so dearly embraced and so fiercely defended. During his pilgrimage he found himself bowing in prayer with "blue-eyed devils." Malcolm also emphasized that Islam embraced all people of every race and color. Yet, in spite of this change, Malcolm still had to contend with racism when he returned to the United States and would at times be quoted rebuking the white man.

A Powerful Man. The break with Elijah was complete, and Malcolm would do everything he could to expose the self-proclaimed Messenger:

> Now, while I was in Mecca among the Muslims, I had a chance to meditate and think and see things with a great deal of clarity—with much greater clarity. . . . And I had made up my mind, yes, that I was going to tell the Black people in the Western Hemisphere, who I had played a great role in misleading into the hands of Elijah Muhammad, exactly what kind of man he was and what he was doing. And I might point out right here that it was not a case of my knowing all the time, because I didn't. I had blind faith in him.[36]

Elijah Muhammad had no cause to think Malcolm would not live up to his word. And Muhammad may have come to the slow realization that Malcolm was more powerful than he was. From October to November of 1964, Malcolm X had "visited eleven countries, talked with eleven heads of state, and addressed most of their parliaments." Threats were made, even one by Raymond Sharrieff, the Supreme Captain of the Fruit of Islam. According to Malcolm X, Sharrieff made public a statement to Malcolm that "the Muslims would not condone me making any statements about Elijah Muhammad."[37]

The End

On February 15, 1965, Malcolm X delivered a speech before six hundred people for his Organization of Afro-American Unity in New York City's Audubon Ballroom. As usual, he was hard-hitting:

> I wanted you to know that my house was bombed. It was bombed by the Black Muslim movement upon the orders of Elijah Muhammad. . . . One of the bombs was thrown at the rear window of my house where my three little baby girls sleep. . . . When you attack sleeping babies, why, you are lower than a god—*[Laughter and applause]*. . . . Elijah Muhammad could stop the whole thing tomorrow, just by raising his hand. . . . But he won't. He doesn't love Black

people. . . . They killed one in the Bronx. They shot another one in the Bronx. They tried to get six of us Sunday morning. . . . The man has gone insane, absolutely out of his mind. Besides, you can't be seventy years old and surround yourself by a handful of sixteen-, seventeen-, eighteen-year-old girls and keep your right mind *[Laughter and applause]*. So, from tonight on, there'll be a hot time in the old town *[laughter]* with regret. With great regret![38]

After the speech Malcolm took questions and stated that one of the leaders of the Fruit of Islam said that Malcolm "should have been killed" and that his tongue "should have been put in an envelope and sent back to Chicago."[39] Later, answering the same question, he mentioned that two Fruit of Islam members were sent to New York to kill him. When asked if Elijah Muhammad ordered the assassination, Malcolm answered, "Yes."[40] According to one researcher, the FBI, by tapping Elijah Muhammad's phone, was also aware of statements made by Muhammad to close Malcolm's eyes and chop off his head.[41]

One week later, on February 21, Malcolm X was murdered. The assassination took place at the same ballroom in which he spoke the week before. At 3:10 p.m. a man stormed the podium just seconds after Malcolm X was introduced and fired a shotgun blast into his body. Two other men with handguns fired at Malcolm. Malcolm hit the floor, and the men kept emptying their weapons in his direction. When it was over, Talmadge Hayer was arrested on the spot. The two other assassins, Thomas 15x Johnson and Norman 3x Butler of NOI Mosque No. 7, were apprehended some time later and convicted of murder.[42]

Elijah Muhammad was never convicted of ordering the assassination, stating over and over again to the press that the NOI does not condone violence and that he was "shocked and surprised" to hear of the murder. Muhammad also affirmed on numerous occasions that neither he nor his followers needed to kill Malcolm X— Malcolm merely decided his own future when he disassociated himself from Allah and his Messenger.[43]

To this day the force behind the order to murder Malcolm X has not been determined beyond reasonable doubt.

LOUIS FARRAKHAN

Malcolm X was assassinated when Louis X was minister of the Boston Mosque and a rising star in the movement. Louis was a most staunch defender of the Honorable Elijah Muhammad, as his words about Malcolm X revealed. Today, as Louis Farrakhan, he continues in that role as head of the Lost-Found Nation of Islam, claiming to be divinely chosen to carry on the work of W. D. Fard and Elijah Muhammad.

Birth

Born Louis Eugene Walcott in 1933, the young boy was raised in Roxbury, Massachusetts. His mother was a West Indian and kept good care of her family during the Depression. His father, whom Louis never knew, married Mae Clark and then left her. When he left, Mae lived with another man. Witnesses say that Mae was as black as one could be, and so was Louis's older brother, Alvan, whom Mae's lover fathered. But Farrakhan is not completely black. Louis's father came briefly into Mae's life again, and she became pregnant with Louis. Details are sketchy about the color of this man, but Farrakhan hinted that he was white. Referring to Mae's lover, Farrakhan said,

> She's with a man, but I'm not his child. She don't want to tell the man, "I've been unfaithful," so she's hoping, since my brother was here from this man, . . . she was hoping that I wouldn't be light . . . 'cause both my mother and the man she was living with were dark.[44]

A Struggling Talent

Louis's mother was an Episcopalian and had Louis baptized at a young age. He was a promising young musician who played the violin and at one point aspired to attend college for further musical training. In addition to appearing on *The Ted Mack Original Amateur Hour,* he was a high school track star. A high achiever, Louis was a born leader and was loved and respected in his community. Because he was reared in the highly family-oriented West Indian section of Roxbury and because of the discipline instilled in his mother when she was a child, Louis's childhood and his teenage years were vastly different from those of Malcolm X.

As a young boy Louis would overhear conversations his mother had with friends concerning the societal oppression black people were undergoing and would lament that God did not send a deliverer to the blacks, as he did in the past. Recalling these conversations and his active Christian church life, Louis said, "As a youngster, I loved Jesus and I loved scripture, but I just wanted answers."[45] The answers never came from Christianity. Like Elijah Muhammad and Malcolm X, Louis became disillusioned with the religion of "hypocrites" who talked the talk but did not walk the walk. Christianity, Louis lamented, did not do anything for blacks.

> I . . . knew that something was wrong with Christianity, the way that it was practiced, because I couldn't go to a white church, except to sit in the balcony, and I knew that that was not the teachings of Jesus.[46]

Poor finances eradicated the prospect of attending the prestigious Juilliard School of Music, so Louis attended a small college in North Carolina before dropping out after two years. Later he married Betsy Ross, whom he had made pregnant before their marriage. In 1955 a friend asked him and his wife to come to a Saviour's Day rally organized by the NOI. Since at that time Louis was a Garveyite, he was quite interested in what the NOI had to say.

Another Public Recognition

As was the case with Elijah Muhammad and Malcolm X, public recognition escorted Louis Walcott into the NOI. Elijah was publicly and directly called by W. D. Fard, God in the flesh, and Malcolm was publicly singled out by Elijah. Now it was Louis's turn.

During Elijah's speech at the Saviour's Day celebration, Louis sat in the balcony with his wife. Louis, who had a partial college education, noted in his own mind the inability of the Messenger to put sentences together. What happened just seconds later stunned the college-educated critic. Elijah called everyone's attention to Louis and stated that although he may not have the gift of putting words together eloquently, that does not detract from his message. If Walcott would accept the message, said Elijah, he could help Elijah save the black man. Louis sat there shocked at what he heard. A source suggests that Muhammad had been informed of Walcott's college education, where he was sitting, and that Walcott could be valuable to the NOI if he were to convert.[47] The 1955 Saviour's Day celebration was not Louis's first exposure to the NOI. Three years earlier Louis had a brief encounter with Malcolm X, and an NOI evangelist had briefly shared the truth with Louis that Allah had come and had chosen a Messenger to lead his people.[48]

But just as Malcolm was not immediately convinced by the apparition in his prison cell, Louis was not immediately convinced, not earlier when he met Malcolm and not even when Elijah had singled him out. His wife was, however, and quickly joined up. And even though Louis signed on when his wife did, he remained for two months not fully convinced—that is, until he heard Malcolm X speak.

A New Life

Malcolm this time left an impression. Louis Walcott was now Louis X, and he would later be named Louis Farrakhan. His life in the movement began in Temple No. 7 in New York, where Malcolm X was the head minister. He would later put his talent to use by producing NOI-based theatrical plays and recording a song titled "A White Man's Heaven Is a Black Man's Hell," a phrase that became a trademark for the NOI. Later, Elijah Muhammad put a stop to Louis's performance activities, probably because they conflicted with the movement's overall asceticism.

Farrakhan, discipled by Malcolm, became a lieutenant in the Fruit of Islam. Two years later Elijah Muhammad, recognizing the twenty-four-year-old's talent and commitment, appointed him as minister of Boston Temple No. 11.[49] Louis was a stellar leader, and under him the Boston temple, which was low in numbers compared with other temples in some major cities, began to find new life.

Rising Even Higher

Contributing greatly to Louis Farrakhan's rise to power was his undying loyalty to Elijah Muhammad. Before Elijah's son, Wallace Deen Muhammad, was imprisoned for draft evasion in 1961, he began to harbor doubts about the validity of his father's theology. Wallace, whom Fard decades earlier prophesied would succeed Elijah in leadership of the NOI, had trouble accepting Fard as Allah in the flesh. This was due to his study of traditional Islam. After his eighteen-month stint in prison, Wallace was convinced that Fard was a fraud.[50]

In addition to knowing that his father and Fard were not what they claimed to be, Wallace had to somehow react to the news of his father's infidelity. Would he keep it under wraps, as was the practice of the hierarchy of the NOI, or would he say something? His conscience bearing him witness, he decided to say something—to Malcolm X. Malcolm then confided in Louis Farrakhan. Farrakhan seemed unconcerned, saying, "All praise is due to Allah [Fard]."[51]

Later, Elijah suspended his son, which began a short series of reinstatements and subsequent suspensions over the next several years. In the meantime NOI leaders made threats on his life, and Malcolm had fallen from grace because he had referred to Kennedy's death as "the chickens coming home to roost." Also, Akbar, another of Elijah's son's, was suspended, and one of Elijah's grandsons, Hasan Sharrieff angrily withdrew from the movement, citing deep-rooted corruption, immorality, and stealing money from NOI members who had given donations to help the poor. Apparently Elijah's grandson was one of several NOI members who left the movement at this time.[52]

With numbers decreasing in Farrakhan's Boston mosque, he unleashed an offensive against the hypocrite apostates—especially Malcolm X. He accused Malcolm of being jealous, a liar, a hypocrite, and a fool. He added that Malcolm was "worthy of death."[53] Farrakhan drew the line on the field and squarely and firmly stepped into Elijah's side.

Farrakhan remained outspoken before, during, and after the murder of Malcolm X and roused many to the side of the Messenger. Before Malcolm's death, Farrakhan's speeches and sermons were characterized by the usual rhetoric about the white devils, their destruction in the coming war of Armageddon, the uselessness of the white man's religion, Allah and his chosen Messenger, and the need of all NOI followers to live healthy and clean lives. Now Farrakhan, though not neglecting these topics, spent a great deal of time denouncing those who would ever dare oppose Allah and his chosen vessel.

After Malcolm's assassination Elijah rewarded Farrakhan with an appointment as minister of the now infamous Mosque No. 7, where Malcolm had been minister. Two years later, in 1967, Muhammad made Farrakhan the national spokesman for the NOI.

It perhaps is safe to say that Muhammad's decision to promote Farrakhan did not rest solely on his loyalty to him during the war with Malcolm. Farrakhan's appeal to the educated black masses, due to his own college education, played a part in the decision, not to mention Farrakhan's inbred leadership qualities. Through Farrakhan Elijah campaigned to attract the upper echelons of black society. As the NOI rose in land holdings, commercial businesses, and even national-scale industries in the early 1970s, the image that Elijah Muhammad brought to his movement was even more stacked in the public eye than when the movement began to flourish from the middle 1940s into the 1950s. In short, with an articulate and higher educated national representative as the national spokesman, combined with economic boastings, the Lost-Found Nation of Islam was prospering.

Trouble

As is the case with any large organization, success comes with a price. Success draws powerful personalities, and there is never any guarantee that who it draws will be a model member.

In the early 1970s the NOI's beloved Messenger was becoming more and more fragile due to his bronchial problems. His moving to Phoenix for health reasons brought with it an ever-loosening grip on the movement than would have been the case had he remained in Chicago. Wallace's on-and-off relationship with his father, the struggle for power, and inter-NOI violence, as well as murders of members of splinter groups emerging from the NOI, plagued the organization. Farrakhan was even quoted as warning stool pigeons and traitors that although Elijah Muhammad is forgiving and will welcome them, there are younger members who would execute them. This threat by Farrakhan worked in the case of James Price, who was one of seven NOI members convicted of killing seven Hanafi Muslims, a splinter group from the NOI. Price decided to become an informant for the prosecution, but the day before his scheduled appearance in court he was found hanging by the neck in his jail cell. He had supposedly heard this statement by Farrakhan on the radio.[54] More threats by Farrakhan and more violence (even counterviolence by members of the splinter groups) made the lucrative early 1970s in some ways seem like a never-ending nightmare.

Elijah Muhammad was labeled "the most powerful black man in America." But in 1975, the powerful Messenger of Allah was dying. It is no surprise, then, to find out that there was competition for the throne.

Or was there? Elijah died on February 25, 1975, and the next day was Saviour's Day. To the applause of the crowd, Wallace Deen Muhammad was named leader of the NOI. Of course, there could be no Messenger again, but there had to be a leader. Farrakhan, in light of Wallace's stormy relationship with his father and the NOI, was the logical choice. But he was left out. True to the Messenger, Farrakhan stated publicly that he would do everything to support Wallace.

Wallace immediately began to change the NOI's doctrines. Within a relatively short time Fard was de-deified, whites were allowed to join, the Mother Plane did not exist, the Fruit of Islam was abolished, and the NOI's stand on racial separatism was a thing of the past.

In October 1976, Wallace D. Muhammad placed the last nail in the coffin of the NOI and renamed it the World Community of Islam in the West. Shortly thereafter his father's claim to be the Messenger of Allah was discarded.[55] Further, Wallace restructured the NOI's financial scheme. According to him the NOI was in debt in spite of its affluence. Wallace D. Muhammad therefore auctioned off the movement's newspaper, farming projects, and some other properties and made other financial moves to bring his father's organization out of debt. To many, Wallace's reforms were against all for which his father had worked—economic self-sufficiency and its own newspaper were trademarks of the NOI. Now they were gone.

Farrakhan was not pleased, especially with the doctrinal changes. To him Elijah Muhammad was still the Messenger and Fard was still Allah. To make things worse, Wallace transferred Farrakhan from robust New York to a down-and-out section of Chicago. The plan, it seems, was to make Farrakhan angry enough to leave on his own. He had far too much power to be suspended, and if he were "fired" many would follow him in protest against Wallace. A Chicago residence for Farrakhan also allowed the Chicago head-quarters to keep a closer watch on him, for there was fear he might organize a takeover. To make matters worse, Wallace renamed New York Mosque No. 7 after Malcolm X, whom Farrakhan had earlier called a liar and a traitor. The final move was to change Farrakhan's name to Abdul Haleem Farrakhan.

The Split

By the end of 1977, almost three years since the Messenger's death, Farrakhan's patience wore out. He broke with Wallace D. Muhammad's World Community of Islam in the West and set out to bring the Honorable Elijah Muhammad's God-sent teachings back to the world. Louis Farrakhan then reestablished the NOI.

Farrakhan claimed two years later that Elijah had chosen him to be the true leader of the NOI. He claimed that Elijah had warned him that the NOI would undergo a severe crisis (his son's takeover) but that he would rise to carry on Elijah's teachings once given him by Allah in the flesh in the 1930s. According to another source, on another occasion Elijah Muhammad, in plain sight of all at a mosque service, sat Louis Farrakhan in Elijah's seat and said, "Min-ister Farrakhan is one of the finest Ministers I have in North Amer-ica. If he tells you to go there, go there. If he tells you to stay from there, stay from there."[56] Further, according to this same source Eli-jah personally instructed Farrakhan "not to change the teachings while he was gone."[57]

Why, then, did Louis not speak up when Wallace D. Muhammad was given headship over the NOI? Perhaps Farrakhan waited be-cause Allah had instructed him to do so, waiting for the apostasy to reach its fullness before he moved Louis Farrakhan to resurrect the movement. One author states that Farrakhan interprets Elijah's giv-ing of power to someone other than himself as a test. For example, Elijah was grooming Malcolm X for headship of the NOI. But to test Malcolm, Elijah allowed others' bitterness and envy of Malcolm to continue. Malcolm was not up to the test, however, and attacked the

Messenger. Farrakhan, by contrast, went through the period of the transfer of power to Wallace to develop inner strength, something Malcolm failed to do.[58]

Someone else failed as well. When given the lead, Wallace D. Muhammad failed to continue in the teachings of the savior as taught by Elijah Muhammad. So Louis Farrakhan jumped in and did not allow those teachings to die. Thus, since 1978 the NOI has had a new leader—Louis Farrakhan. As one of his first steps, Farrakhan purchased a funeral home in Chicago and converted it into a mosque. He also reestablished the NOI newspaper and named it *The Final Call.* Farrakhan was diligent, starting home studies across the country and lecturing widely. When the new NOI celebrated Saviour's Day in 1981, six thousand people attended.[59] Farrakhan says,

> Elijah left and the nation [of Islam] went down and your brother, Louis Farrakhan, by the guidance of Allah, decided he was going to rebuild his father's[60] house in his name. I started off with just two or three people.[61]

Farrakhan would be the first to tell you that he is not the Messenger, nor does he have the status of Elijah Muhammad. He is simply the spokesman of Allah's (Fard's) Lost-Found Nation of Islam and the spokesman for the Honorable Messenger Elijah Muhammad. But Farrakhan is as active in spreading Allah's message as Elijah Muhammad was—maybe even more active. The Million Man March and his tour of eighteen African and Muslim nations in 1995 evidence this, and the latter is reminiscent of Elijah's and Malcolm X's tours in the 1950s and 1960s.[62]

Other Splits[63]

In the years when Elijah Muhammad was alive and following his death, several splinter sects formed. The leaders of these sects, for one reason or another, felt the need to break away from the Messenger's teachings or to restore the Messenger's teachings after his death.

I have already mentioned Wallace D. Muhammad's World Community of Islam in the West. Others include John Muhammad's Nation of Islam, which claims to be the original NOI. He states that since he is Elijah Muhammad's brother, he therefore is the lawful heir and leader of Fard's NOI. John Muhammad continues faithful to the Messenger's teachings and claims to have seen Fard, who continues to speak through him. The Lost Found Nation of Islam is led by Silas Muhammad. Located in Atlanta, Georgia, the group broke away from the NOI when Elijah Muhammad died. The Hanafi Muslims follow Sunni Islam, breaking away from Elijah Muhammad's teachings while Muhammad was still alive. Clarence 13X also broke away from the Messenger to form The Five Percenters. Finally, the United Nation of Islam, founded by a man named Solomon, continues the Allah in the flesh theology but instead names Solomon as Almighty God in person.

SUMMARY

Malcolm X and Louis Farrakhan were groomed to succeed Elijah Muhammad. One met an untimely death while in exile from the NOI. The other remains the leader of the Lost-Found Nation of Islam. To be sure, Malcolm's life witnessed more outer turmoil. With his mother dying while he was a teenager, his placement in several foster homes, and his early life as a criminal, Malcolm Little's upbringing was quite different from the sophisticated life of young Louis Walcott. But, like Malcolm, Louis struggled with inner philosophical turmoil. The plight of the black people into which they were born served to mold their distaste for the social conditions prevalent in American society in the 1930s, 1940s, and 1950s.

Influenced as they were by Marcus Garvey and other black nationalist leaders, these strong men could not stand to remain silent for long. As with Elijah Muhammad, the events in childhood, adolescence, and early manhood prepared them for conversion. Like Elijah, they found a leader who filled the vast hole left in their consciences by the oppressing social conditions.

Elijah Muhammad said, "I am raised up from among you by God, Himself, to teach you the Knowledge of God, the Devil, and the Day and Time in which we live."[64] We turn now to the theology of the NOI, a theology born from the depths of human misery, a theology that lashes out against white domination—a theology of its time.

SEVEN

The Bible, Qur'an, and the God(s) of the Nation of Islam

Theology is the study of God and in a wider sense the study of subjects related to the doctrine of God. Since one normally forms theology from a source other than oneself, it is wise to begin with the NOI's view of the Bible and the Qur'an and its doctrine of God.

In one sense all theology, no matter what the system or religion, starts with the doctrine of God. In another sense, with the Lost-Found Nation of Islam (NOI), theology starts with the social conditions in which its theology was birthed. The latter I have endeavored to outline in some detail in earlier chapters. Suffice it now to say that the doctrines of the NOI arose out of the social soil prepared by the black nationalist movements and leaders that preceded it.

Add to this the fact that human beings are religious and spiritual by nature. The inevitable result, therefore, is that certain theologies are created not only to explain the social maladies that plagued blacks in the nineteenth and twentieth centuries but also to serve as a tool for polemics against the white structure responsible for those maladies. For this reason one cannot truly understand the theology of the NOI without at least an awareness of the people, movements, and circumstances that paved the way for its existence. Thus the NOI's theology is an expression of protest. It protests against the white establishment.

Further, while we must not forget that NOI theology is a mixture mainly of Christianity and Islam, it is neither Christianity nor Islam. Though it utilizes Christian and Islamic terms and draws from the Bible and the Qur'an, its definitions of many of those terms are not those of the Bible or the Qur'an. For this reason it has drawn the protests of both Christians and orthodox Muslims. This phenomenon of "same terms, different definitions" arises immediately in the study of the NOI's doctrine of God.

In this and subsequent chapters I shall make mention of certain NOI doctrines that clash with those of traditional Islam. But I am also a Christian and believe that the historical and biblical Jesus is the only way of salvation. Therefore I shall reserve the last chapter for my objections to NOI doctrines.

THE BIBLE AND QUR'AN

NOI literature evidences a strange hermeneutic. Elijah Muhammad and his disciples have no regard for the historical contexts of either the Bible or the Qur'an, nor do they concern themselves with the meaning of words as explained in secondary scholarly works. Further, they say the Bible is a corrupt book, while the Qur'an is perfect. Yet the Bible and the Qur'an in practice are secondary in authority to W. D. Fard and Elijah Muhammad and will one day be replaced by "a new book."

Poison and Perfection

Most likely drawing upon his experiences of the actions of Christians who used the Bible to dominate blacks and to authorize slavery, Elijah Muhammad scorns,

> From the first day that the white race received the Divine Scripture they started tampering with its truth to make it to suit themselves and blind the black man. It is their nature to do evil and the book cannot be recognized as the pure and Holy Word of God. . . . The Bible is the graveyard of my people. . . . What a poison book![1]

Muhammad then admits that the Bible has "plenty of truth, *if understood*."[2]

The statement by Muhammad that the white race has tampered with its truth does not necessarily mean that translations themselves have changed the actual text. Muhammad's statement could be read to mean only that the interpretation offered by the white race is false. Further statements by the Messenger, however, reveal that the actual text is not what it originally was:

> The Bible is not all holy, nor is it all the word of God. . . . The second verse of the first chapter of Genesis reads: "And the earth was without form and void; darkness was upon the deep and the spirit of God moved upon the face of the waters." What was the water on, since there was no form of earth? As I see it, the Bible is very questionable.[3]

For the Qur'an it is a different story. The Qur'an is "very holy" and, unlike the Bible, comes directly from God:

> The Holy Quran—it is holy because it is the Word of Allah (God), who speaks directly to His servant ([the prophet] Muhammad). "Holy" means something that is PERFECTLY PURE, and this we just can't say of the poison Bible.[4]

A New Book to Come

Despite the fact that the NOI has the Qur'an and the Bible, Elijah Muhammad tells of a new book that will one day be revealed. This book will be written by Allah [Fard] and will be for the people of the black Asiatic race who have turned to Fard and his Messenger. It is known as the Last Book and will be used to escort NOI believers into the hereafter.[5] Muhammad says that even the Qur'an must eventually step aside (a view that is unorthodox in the eyes of traditional Islam) to make way for this new book that will take them into the afterlife:

> The Holy Quran, the Glorious Book, should be read and studied by us (the so-called Negroes). Both the present Bible and the Holy Quran must soon give way to that holy book which no man as yet but Allah has seen. The teachings (prophecies) of the present Bible and the Quran take us up to the resurrection and judgment of this world but not into the next life. That which is in that holy book is for the right-

eous and their future only, not for the mixed world of right-eous and evil.[6]

On Whose Authority?

How, then, should members of the NOI understand the Bible? They need to look to Elijah Muhammad, who sat under the tutelage of W. D. Fard from 1931 to 1934: "The Bible means good if you can rightly understand it. My interpretation of it is given to me from the Lord of the Worlds [Fard]."[7] We might also assume that the correct understanding of the perfectly holy Qur'an can come only through Elijah Muhammad, who was taught by Allah in the person of W. D. Fard.

But the Messenger of Allah portrays a strange understanding of many biblical texts and pays no attention to secondary scholarly works such as word studies, lexicons, historical background studies. For example, "Christ," says Elijah, means "Crusher." Thus Christ is the one coming in the last day to crush the wicked. The Christ could not be Jesus, because the wicked are still around. The Christ is W. D. Fard.[8]

Muhammad's practice of disregarding secondary sources and historical and cultural contexts seems strange to the serious student of the Bible, but the debate with him centers not around the text itself. Rather, the debate must begin with what Muhammad claims as his ultimate court of appeal—W. D. Fard, Allah in the flesh.

THE NATION OF ISLAM'S DOCTRINE OF GOD(S)

W. D. Fard taught the NOI doctrine of God to Elijah Muhammad. Elijah further claims that what he teaches is from the same source from which Moses and Jesus taught—Allah.[9] Elijah also affirms belief in one God, Allah, and that the one God is the God of the universe who created all things. On the surface, this seems to be in line with traditional Islam. Upon closer inspection, however, there are significant differences.

Contained in NOI literature is *What the Muslims Believe*, which is a twelve-point doctrinal statement. The first article reads, "We believe in One God whose proper name is Allah." However, in the discussion of the NOI's doctrine of God we encounter "on the one hand . . . on the other hand" several times. Therefore it is wise to look at the movement's doctrine of God in three areas—Allah in the beginning (as the original black man), Allah as the black man (collectively), and Allah as W. D. Fard. Though we shall see that the NOI's doctrine of God is confusing and contradictory, fluctuating between monotheism and polytheism, it nonetheless lives with the contradictions.

Allah in the Beginning

Straying very far away from traditional Islam, the NOI claims that God is a finite being. In the beginning the black God created himself out of total darkness. He came from darkness, and so he himself is dark. In the beginning he was the only being in the universe.[10] This God came from a single atom in total darkness.[11]

The first God was a man—he is the original black man, the first God and the first human being ever to exist. Alluding to Genesis 1:26, Elijah Muhammad reasons that since God created man in his own image and likeness, God must then be a man.[12] Muhammad reasons further that in the scriptures God acts with all five senses, and more—he talks, walks, stands, and sits. God, then, must be a human being.[13]

When was the first black man (God) created? Muhammad claims to be agnostic as to the question, but due to his cosmology, which has the earth created about seventy-six trillion years ago,[14] God would have to be older than that. But not by much, for Muhammad says that it was seventy-six trillion years ago when the first atom (that birthed God) moved in time. "The beginning of time," he says, "was the beginning of God."[15]

Muhammad claims to be in possession of a somewhat esoteric knowledge when it comes to knowing who God really is. Since man was created, only twelve men at each time have been in possession of the knowledge of God. They in turn have twelve men under them and are known as "scientists." The first twelve are the greater scientists, and the other twelve are the lesser scientists. Together they make up the twenty-four elders of the Book of Revelation (4:4). They pass this knowledge on to their sons, who pass it on to their sons, and so on. But there are never more than twelve adepts at any time in the whole history of the world possessing this knowledge. Men, therefore, have formed their opinions of God, but they are wrong because they have not been given the knowledge.[16] Elijah, the Messenger of God, has revealed this truth to the masses for the first time.[17]

What God Is Not. Elijah Muhammad has been given the knowledge of God, for God himself taught Muhammad. And when Muhammad teaches on the nature of God, he does so not only in the positive. He is quick to teach us what God is not. In doing so he attacks both the Christian and the traditional Islamic conceptions of God.

The vast majority of the Muslims in the world, says Muhammad, have a wrong theology. He states that "99% of the old world Muslims think that Allah is only a 'Spirit' and is not a man. . . . They too need to be taught today the reality of Allah."[18] As for Christianity, Muhammad builds a straw man (accusing Christians of believing something they do not believe) and then just as quickly dismisses it: "The devil's teaching is a division of gods—three gods into one god."[19]

A String of Gods. Fard taught the Messenger that no god lives forever. The first god is finite, not infinite. Thus there is in NOI thinking a string of finite gods who each exist for about one to two hundred years, though Muhammad says there is record of a god who lived for around a thousand years.[20]

How, then, can Muhammad claim belief in one God and further claim to fall in line with Islam? He can, if the phrase "at a time" is implied. Apparently there is some "essence" that continues from one god to another as they incarnate as finite, black men-gods. Speaking of the first god, Muhammad says, "We know again that from that God the person of God continued until today in His people."[21] This is how Muhammad can teach his modified monotheism, which is actually *finite* monotheism. In answer to the question "What is your concept of God?" Louis Farrakhan once stated, "Elijah Muhammad teaches us that God was a man, He is a man and shall always be a man."[22]

Moreover, these finite gods are also finite in knowledge. In other words, they are not omniscient. There are cycles of history, says Muhammad, that last for about twenty-five thousand years. Each god shows his wisdom for this time period (though paradoxically, each god does not live that long) and knows nothing of the knowledge or history of the god existing before him. Thus the theology each god creates is different from that of the preceding gods.[23] This has gone on for at least sixty-six trillion years, says Muhammad, when a great explosion caused by a black scientist severed the earth into two parts. The smaller part is our moon today.[24]

Allah as the Black Man

On the other hand, Allah is the "Black Man" in a collective sense; that is, the black race is Allah. The same may be said of the phrase "Original Man." On the one hand it refers to the first god, a black man who came into existence out of darkness. On the other hand, the original man is the black race. Elijah Muhammad further departs from orthodox Islam with this doctrine.

In 1959 a television news series titled "The Hate That Hate Produced" (produced by Mike Wallace and Louis Lomax) relates the following exchange:

> *Lomax:* Now if I have understood your teachings correctly, you teach that all of the members of Islam are God, and that one among you is supreme, and that that one is Allah. Now have I understood you correctly?
>
> *Elijah Muhammad:* That's right.[25]

Elijah Muhammad would later verify that answer. Speaking to the black man (collectively), he admonished, "You are walking around looking for a God to bow to and worship. You are the God!"[26]

To further confuse things, it seems that within this collective sense of God there is a hint of polytheism. NOI followers believe themselves to be gods.[27] Elijah Muhammad's loyal student, Louis Farrakhan, has taken Muhammad's teaching one step further than the "You are the God!" statement (unless, of course, Muhammad taught the following to Farrakhan). The current leader of the NOI has taught his people how the gods of the NOI are conceived. In a videotaped series titled "How to Give Birth to a God," Louis Farrakhan instructs his male disciples:

> How to produce a God has to be thought of in preconception times. Right now, before you have a baby, you must begin to prepare your body and your mind for what will ultimately become a reality in your life. Listen, now! As a young boy you must begin to prepare yourself to father a powerful sperm! The sperm is not fathered by the act of sexual intercourse alone. The sperm is fathered by the *thought* that is present in the brain that [makes repeated round and upward gestures with closed fist] empowers the sperm and becomes the *force* in the head of the sperm that will finally germinate and fertilize the egg. So, you can't walk around *mindless* and produce mental giants, though it happens accidentally! But if you *think* about what you are and who you are, you can do it every time. There ain't no missin'. And the condition that we're in—we don't want to hit and miss! We want to produce a giant! Every time the womb opens, let a *God* come forth![28]

As for the phrase "Original Man" meaning the black man, as well as the first god who "activated" himself out of darkness, Muhammad states, "The Original Man, Allah has declared, is none other than the black man."[29] The original man—the black race of the Asiatic tribe of Shabazz[30]—in this sense means that the blacks are the original race created directly out of God himself.[31]

Allah Is W. D. Fard

By far the most popular reference to Allah has to do with W. D. Fard (Master Fard Muhammad). Elijah Muhammad calls him "the present God."[32] Despite the fact that this doctrine is considered blasphemy in the eyes of orthodox Islam, Fard is nonetheless called the present god of this cycle, and we are in the sixteen thousandth year of this cycle.[33] His wisdom is infinite (another paradox, given that each god's knowledge is finite), and he came to end the six-thousand-year rule of the white race. Today's NOI worships "Almighty God, Allah, who appeared in the person of Master Fard Muhammad."[34] In *What the Muslims Believe,* article 12 in part reads,

> We believe that Allah (God) appeared in the Person of Master W. Fard Muhammad, July, 1930; the long-awaited "Messiah" of the Christians and the "Mahdi" of the Muslims. We believe further and lastly that Allah is God and besides HIM there is no God.

Though with the last part of this statement Muhammad sounds like he is in the fold of traditional Islam, what he means is that presently there is no God besides Allah. Muhammad cannot say that there are no gods before Fard, for he proclaims Fard as the superior god over all other gods who existed before him.[35]

God Is Born Incognito. God was born half original (black) and half white in the holy city of Mecca on February 26, 1877. "His father," says Louis Farrakhan, "was an original Black man and His mother was a woman from the Caucasus Mountains region."[36]

According to the NOI, the apostle Paul wrote of Fard coming "in the likeness of sinful flesh" (Rom. 8:3). He came this way for at least two reasons. First, his resulting color would allow him to walk among us unnoticed. This afforded him the opportunity to undergo preparation for his mission (he studied for forty years) and to teach without drawing attention to himself. Second, Fard, having the two natures in him, mastered the two and was victorious over the lower (white) nature. Fard was able to destroy the lower nature. This is vital to NOI soteriology, for Fard's victory gains for his people the knowledge that they can destroy their lower natures and bring the true nature to perfection, gaining heaven[37] on this earth. Consequently, the NOI's teachings on morality feature this doctrine as an example to admonish believers to a high standard of living.

Fard's Ministry and Jesus. The NOI draws parallels between W. D. Fard's ministry and Jesus' ministry. First on the list is the birth of Fard. Since in the eyes of the NOI Jesus was a prophet and only

a man (a black man[38]), any interpretations of Jesus being the ful-
fillment of Old Testament prophecies predicting his birth and ministry are removed and replaced with Fard. On Saviour's Day,
February 25, 1996, Louis Farrakhan preached,

> The Bible teaches that One would come in the last days. . . .
> Isaiah, the prophet, saw Him coming. . . . For unto us a child
> is born, and unto us a son is given, and a government shall
> be upon His shoulder; and He shall be called wonderful,
> counselor, the mighty God, the prince of peace, the ever-
> lasting Father; and of the increase of His government of
> peace there would be no end. Yet, He is a child born of a
> woman. . . . He was born February 26, 1877.[39]

The NOI does not believe that Jesus is God and Christ. Fard,
rather, is God and Christ. Because "Christ" means "Crusher," says
Muhammad, it means that someone must come in the last days to
crush the wicked. Jesus did not do this, so Jesus was not a Christ.[40]
For Muhammad, the phrase "God in the flesh" is reserved only for
W. D. Fard.

Additionally, Fard is the "Son of Man" of the New Testament,
who is to come like lightning from the east (Matt. 24:27).[41] Fifty-
three years after his birth Allah came to Detroit "from the East"—
Mecca. Elijah Muhammad states that after Allah's appearance his
ministry lasted for three and one-half years, a fact reminiscent of Jesus' ministry. Though he could have saved himself from suffering,
Allah (Fard) submitted humbly to his persecutors so that the scriptures could be fulfilled. Lastly, if people followed Fard, they too
would be persecuted but would wait for his return to bring them to
paradise,[42] heaven on the present earth.

But unlike Jesus—who, according to Elijah Muhammad, died
and stayed dead—Fard never died. To elevate Fard and devaluate
Christ, Elijah Muhammad writes,

> God is here in Person, so stop looking for a dead Jesus for
> help and pray to HIM whom Jesus prophesied that would
> come after him. My people pray to the One who is ALIVE
> and not a spook![43]

Since for the NOI there is no afterlife in the Christian sense of the term and Fard the present god for this cycle of time, Fard only disappeared in 1934. He is on the earth today[44] but apparently is walking around unnoticed "in the likeness of sinful flesh" waiting for his appointed time to destroy the white devils in the great war of Armageddon and usher in a new existence for his chosen black people.

Elijah Muhammad put succinctly into words much of what has been discussed regarding the NOI's doctrine of God(s):

> Allah is all of us. But we have a Supreme One. . . . He is Allah, The One over all of us; The Most Supreme One. . . . Every righteous person is a god. We are all God.[45]

SUMMARY

The Bible is a poison book, and the Qur'an is holy, but both can teach truth if interpreted by Elijah Muhammad, who in turn received proper interpretation from Allah (Fard). Somehow these books convey that there is an original, finite god, he being one of many culminating with the Supreme God (Fard). Further, the black race is collectively God, and at times many gods make up the black race. With these teachings of the "Original Man" comes the NOI's central myth and explanation of the scourge of blacks—Yakub and the white race. This is the subject of our next chapter.

EIGHT

Yakub and the White Race

The oppression of blacks in the early twentieth century afforded black leaders and black theologians the opportunity to offer spiritual teachings in the hope of comforting the oppressed. I have noted in earlier chapters the beliefs of Noble Drew Ali, Marcus Garvey, Garvey-related clergy, and others. W. D. Fard's Lost-Found Nation of Islam (NOI) is no exception. The central myth of the NOI is the story of Yakub. It explains the origin of the white race and offers the reason for its "hateful and domineering nature." Further, it provides theological ground for the NOI to state that Allah will one day destroy the whites in the battle of Armageddon.

Allah in the person of W. D. Fard taught the Messenger Elijah Muhammad that the history of the gods and the black man goes back about seventy-six trillion years and that blacks are the original man, coming directly from God. Throughout this history we find experiments performed by rebellious gods and other personages. For example, sixty-six trillion years ago one of the gods attempted to destroy the earth with a mighty explosion. The experiment failed to destroy all of the earth but did crack off a huge chunk, which became the moon. During this time, taught Fard, the Asian black nation called the tribe of Shabazz discovered the rich valley of the Nile River and settled there. In another example, Elijah Muhammad explains the "kinky hair" of the "Asiatics." Fifty thousand years ago another god wanted to make the Asiatics of Africa tougher in order to endure life in the jungle. The god could not get everyone to agree with him and so became dissatisfied and rebelled by giving the Asiatics kinky hair.[1]

YAKUB

The most popular character in the history of rebellious personages is the one responsible for the production of the white race—
the infamous evil scientist Yakub. As is the case with other NOI
doctrines, the Qur'an and other traditional orthodox Islamic literature will not substantiate the Yakub myth. This does not worry the
NOI. The fact that the source of the myth is W. D. Fard is proof
enough that it is true.

Prophecy and Birth

According to Master Fard Muhammad (Allah), Mr. Yakub was
born sixty-six hundred years ago. Approximately eighty-four hundred years before Yakub's birth the twenty-four scientists[2] of that
era[3] predicted the birth of Mr. Yakub. They were also aware that he
was going to create a new race of people out of the original black
man. He would be born twenty miles outside of Mecca.[4]

When Mr. Yakub was born, there was apparently some social unrest among the original race. A segment of the population, 30 percent to be exact, were "dissatisfied," while the other 70 percent were
"satisfied."[5] Yakub was not from good stock; his parents were among
the 30 percent. So as a boy he looked forward to the day when he
would make a people out of the original that would come to dominate the originals. One day he was playing with two pieces of steel
and noticed that one piece displayed magnetic power over the
other. Viciously, while holding the pieces, he told a family member
that he was going to make a people to rule the original race. There
is prophetic significance to the steel. It signifies an attraction between the two pieces—one attracting the other and placing it under
its power. Thus, by utilizing "tricknology," a term W. D. Fard gave to
Elijah Muhammad to describe the tricks and lies of the white race,[6]
the new race would come to dominate the originals.

Born with an unusually large head, Yakub had a special capacity
for learning, a trait not common among others of the tribe of
Shabazz. By eighteen years of age he had finished with all the
schools of higher learning the nation had to offer. Yakub was a great
scientist and learned that the originals had two people in them—
black and brown. He then realized through more experiments that

114

he could filter down the brown nature into white and that obviously the white, filtered-out nature would be weaker than the black.[7]

The Making of the White Race

To obtain people for his experiments, Yakub began preaching Islam in Mecca and drawing converts under the lie that he would make other people serve them. They became so huge in number that the authorities worried about his popularity. Persecutions set in, and Yakub's followers were put in prisons, but there were so many followers that the jails were unable to contain all of them. Finally the king visited Yakub's prison cell and made a bargain with him. Yakub said that he and his followers would leave Mecca if the government gave them twenty years' worth of supplies. The king agreed and sent Yakub and his 59,999 followers to Patmos in boats (some were found unworthy before departure and were thrown overboard).[8]

While in Patmos Yakub gathered up doctors to help him with his experiment. Yakub told the doctors (upon penalty of death if the doctors disobeyed him) to lie to an all-black couple when they came to have their blood tested in order to see if they could marry. The doctors pretended to test the blood but did not, and they told the couple that their blood did not mix well. The doctors' advice was that the couple should break up and find other mates. When two brown people came to be tested, the doctors told them they could marry (black and brown could not marry). The next step was infanticide of any black babies born to the brown couples. Hospital staffs were given strict orders to take a needle and prick the brains of black babies, while brown babies were allowed to live. Several generations of births and murders finally filtered the white race. After two hundred years all babies born were brown; another two hundred years witnessed yellow and red babies;[9] the final two hundred years brought an all-white, blue-eyed race into being. Through several generations of lying and murdering, lying and murdering were bred into the nature of all newborn infants, who in turn would grow up as liars and murderers to carry on the experiment.[10]

The Messenger once again proves himself an interesting exegete when he offers the interpretation of Genesis 1:26 ("Let Us make man in Our image"). Seeing the verse through the eyes of the

God-man W. D. Fard, who taught him the Yakub theory, Elijah believes that the "us" is the 59,999 followers of Yakub.[11]

Yakub lived for 150 years, but before he died he left orders to continue the experiment. The people followed the orders because Yakub told them there was a reward if they did so. Upon completion of the experiment they could return to Mecca.

THE RULE OF THE WHITE RACE

Little did Yakub know, he was a pawn in the hands of Allah, who allowed him to get the education needed to create a race of people that Allah ordained to rule the original race, including the brown, red, and yellow peoples. The rule of the new devil white race over the original and the intermediate peoples was to last six thousand years and was a testing period for the Asiatic tribe of Shabazz, the original race. After the six-thousand-year reign ended in 1914,[12] the most powerful and mighty god of them all came onto the scene to deliver the black race, the Asiatics. That was W. D. Fard.

In the eyes of the NOI the whites are simply no good. They are by nature inferior to the original black Asiatics because they are a hybrid and liars and murderers from the beginning of their existence. They would, however, use their evil-based inferiority to their advantage.

By using tricknology, the back-to-Mecca whites fooled the originals by causing disputes among them through gossip. Once the originals started killing each other, the whites offered to help them settle disputes. This allowed the whites to gain power over the originals. Elijah Muhammad says it is like this to this day. The blacks, he says, cannot agree among themselves for what is best for them and need the whites to help them with their disputes that were caused by the whites in the first place![13] (One now can interpret through Muhammad's eyes the disagreement between his philosophy of separation and the integration of Martin Luther King Jr.)

Eventually the originals caught on to the white devils' scheme and drove them away from the land into West Asia—to the hillside caves of the Caucasus Mountains (according to the NOI, the very region from which the savior's mother came). Once there the originals "roped" them in by placing border patrols around them to ensure that they would not come back to Mecca. This is Elijah Muhammad's explanation of Europe. "Eu" stands for the hills and caves of the continent, and "rope" signifies the roping in of the whites.[14]

Muhammad also uses verses in the Bible and the Qur'an as proof texts for his theology. In Genesis 3:23–24, the Lord sent "the Adam" (the whites) out of the garden of Eden (Mecca) and into present-day Europe. The flaming torch protecting from any reentry to the garden (Mecca) is the sword of Islam, and the cherubim guarding the entrance are the border patrols.[15] In Sura (chapter) 2:36 we read, "Then did Satan make them slip from the [Garden], and get them out of the state [of felicity] in which they had been."

For the next two thousand years the white Europeans (Caucasians) remained in caves, living like barbarians while the originals enjoyed the fruits of their advanced brains and civilization. The whites, recognizing their blunder and their bleak future, tried to reverse the Yakub grafting process from whence they came, but they could only produce a gorilla. In fact, Muhammad says Fard taught him that the monkey family originated in Europe during this two-thousand-year span.[16]

The two thousand years of caveman existence ended when God sent Moses, a black man, to bring whites back to civilization. But Moses admitted he had difficulty keeping the white devils in line. All along it was Allah's plan to allow the whites to once again slip into existence with the originals and dominate them. This is what the rest of Genesis 1:26 means. After the 59,999 made the white man in their image (to be sure, the image of the black man, but a lower form of the black man), they were allowed to "rule over all creation" for the next four thousand years.[17]

That whites were originally contained in Europe is evidenced, says Elijah Muhammad, by the fact that wherever the white man went he found black, brown, yellow, or red. Take, for example, Christopher Columbus, who was half original and half white. When he came to America he found the red man. So Muhammad states that since 1492 the devil white race has been allowed to disperse all over the earth.[18]

Any member of the NOI is quick to point out the truthfulness of the NOI's history of white rule by showing what the white man

THE NATION OF ISLAM

has done to the earth. He has polluted it, raped and murdered not only his own people but the originals as well, utilized his tricknology to harness blacks into submission with promises he intends not to keep, and uses religion to permit himself to perform all these acts. The white man is, in effect, a product of the 59,999 traitors who followed the arch-deceiver Yakub. In short, whites are in the business of continuing what Yakub intended from the beginning, coupled with the mission of systematically eliminating all blacks and replenishing the earth with their own kind.

THE DEMONOLOGY OF THE NOI

The six-thousand-year rule of the white devil should have ended in 1914 and with the coming of Allah in the person of Master Fard Muhammad (W. D. Fard). But it hasn't because the people are still asleep (ignorant and misled).[19] Unlike the times of Yakub, the end will come when there is 100 percent dissatisfaction. The whole world will then be ready for the full revealing of Fard in all his glory in the battle of Armageddon.

The Devil

In Elijah Muhammad's theology the scriptural devil and serpent of Genesis 3 refers to whites singularly or collectively, depending on context. They were made (grafted) from the original black race by the will of Allah, who desired to test his people and then destroy the wicked whites.

In Genesis we read of the devil (serpent) deceiving Adam and Eve. The devil white race caused Adam and Eve to disobey the will of Allah and follow their destructive teachings and ways.[20] Therefore Allah banished Adam and Eve from the garden. This occurred six thousand years ago—six hundred years after Yakub began his grafting process. The garden is the paradise of Mecca, and Adam and Eve are the first parents of the white, grafted offspring of the 59,999 traitors who were once exiled to Patmos.[21] These offspring and the first parents were thrown out of paradise and sent off to Europe. From then on this offspring would be bent on ruling the blacks and eventually killing all of them.

Additionally, the Book of Revelation (Muhammad, strangely, calls it "the first book of the Bible"[22]), says the Messenger, speaks of "the beast." Who is this beast? It as well is none other than the white race. It was not the apostle John who wrote of the beast while he was in exile on the island of Patmos. Rather, it was Yakub![23] Those who follow the beast are from all races. The blacks (any nonwhites such as brown, yellow, and red people) who follow the beast are ignorant of their divine heritage and the grafting of the white race from the original black man by the evil Yakub. They must be enlightened to these facts. They must embrace Fardian Islam and Fard's Messenger, the Honorable Elijah Muhammad. Those who do not follow the Messenger will be destroyed.

NOI Demonology at Work

W. D. Fard and the Messenger Elijah Muhammad have successfully and skillfully provided for thousands of blacks the explanation for all their social woes. The past and current oppression of slavery and the violence done against blacks can all be explained with one story—Mr. Yakub and his grafting of the white race. Yakub brought the devil into existence, and things have not been the same for the original man since then. With this basic demonological groundwork laid, one can begin to view the present social situation of blacks through the theological lens of Elijah Muhammad.

For example, what does Jesus mean when he says to the Jews, "You are of your father the devil. . . . He was a murderer from the beginning . . . because there is no truth in him" (John 8:44)? He means that they came from the white race that was made six thousand years ago. Perhaps this explains some of the reported statements made by NOI officials. For example, during the week preceding the Million Man March, held on Monday, October 16, 1995, the "Black Holocaust National Conference" was held. Anti-Jewish rhetoric characterized the conference. On one occasion NOI minister and keynote speaker Khalid Abdul Muhammad exclaimed, "We have lost over 600 million at the hands of the white man in the last 6,000 years."[24] Note his mention of six thousand years—a clear indication that he has absorbed Fard's making of the devil white race and his subsequent six-thousand-year murder-filled rule over the blacks. Khalid Muhammad continues, "That is 100 times worse than the so-called Holocaust of the so-called Jew, the imposter Jew."[25]

Or consider the account in Matthew where the devil tempts Jesus with all the kingdoms of the world and their glory (Matt. 4:8). The devil, once again, is the white race in the collective sense. Just as this devil tempted the black Jesus two thousand years ago, so he tempts blacks with all his wealth and collections: only "fall down and worship me" (Matt. 4:9). By this is meant that the devil white race promises the world to blacks, and those who want to be Uncle Toms give in and bow to their slave masters. But the promise is empty, for the devil has no intention of giving the black man anything except oppression. To be sure, the devil keeps a few token blacks (Uncle Toms) in position of authority, but this is only to lull the masses into thinking that they have a chance to make it in this world. This was the promise of the devil to Jesus, and it is his promise today. Jabril Muhammad, an NOI theologian and apologist, states,

> In *"The Fall of America,"* page 20, the Honorable Elijah Muhammad makes clear that our oppressor ". . . is the professional, the wisest of all deceivers." He continued that ". . . he has deceived all the civilization of the earth." He continues that the Bible teaches that these people deceived the whole world; not just Black people in America alone.[26]

Everything Louis Farrakhan and other NOI officials say regarding whites is grounded in the Yakub myth. "The white man," says Farrakhan, "was made to do evil; so when he does evil, we are not excited by it. . . . He is only acting out the nature in which he was made."[27]

The social evils carried out by whites against blacks were and are under the watchful eye of Allah (Fard) himself. Allah in the past allowed Yakub the opportunity to do his mischief. Little did Yakub know that he was simply being used by Allah to carry out his will. Allah allowed these events for important and providential reasons—testing his chosen people and waiting for the fullness of time (100 percent dissatisfied) before he unleashes upon the wicked white race-based government of the United

States the destruction promised them by Elijah Muhammad and his spokesmen:

> Oh, Washington, D.C., oh, government of America, you shall pay well for your evil done against the righteous, for there is a God on the scene, in The Person of Master Fard Muhammad, and He's anxious to kill you; He's anxious to destroy you. . . . He wants to get a chance to slay you, to prove that He is God and besides Him there is no other. So rush on with your plan, and rush on to your death.[28]

To be sure, the Yakub myth provides the explanation for the evil white devil race and the ills that that race has thrust upon blacks. But it has done something else. As the statement by Louis Farrakhan shows, it has provided thousands of oppressed and downtrodden blacks with identity and hope. As to identity, in the midst of the sufferings and struggles of life it has given them knowledge of their ontological superiority over whites. They are the superior race, the original man, God, from which the lowly whites came only six thousand years ago. Further attesting to their superiority is the fact that they are a "created" people, while the whites are merely a "made" people. As to hope, it has furnished them with faith not only in W. D. Fard as God, but also faith that he will come again to judge the wicked of this earth. Members of the NOI can only rejoice in the midst of persecution, for the time is soon coming when all will be made new and they will be vindicated, living in the paradise they once enjoyed before the evil Yakub turned everything around.

CHRISTIANITY–THE WHITE MAN'S RELIGION

The anthropology of the NOI arises from the basic premise that anything black is good and anything white is evil. This premise rests upon the foundation of the Yakub myth. The whites came from the originals. The originals had everything good and are by nature good and divine. Once one accepts the further premise that Christianity came from the white man, it then cannot be the original, true religion. Like the white man, it was a "made" religion. It was a religion born from the white race and a priori must be evil.

The Religion of Jesus

This is not to say that the religion of the real Jesus was evil. Jesus was black, says the NOI. The white man can only corrupt what is good, and so the Bible that we have now does not teach the religion of the black Moses, Abraham, Jesus, and other black Asiatic prophets of Allah. Their religion was Islam, not the Christianity of the white devil, who used this white religion to enslave blacks. As a matter of fact, Elijah Muhammad openly challenges anyone to prove to him that the Christianity of today is the religion of Jesus, Moses, David, Noah, and Abraham.[29] Muhammad says that if there is a true Christianity, a religion that follows the teachings of Jesus, it is Fardian Islam.[30]

Christianity is the white man's religion, and Islam belongs to the black Asiatics. Muhammad advocates that blacks cannot be Christians. One cannot be Christian unless one is white.[31] Despite the fact that millions of blacks are Christians, Muhammad is after something much deeper when he makes this claim. In the eyes of Allah, blacks are born from Allah. Allah is their true father. Allah was birthing them for scores of trillions of years. How, then, can they be of the religion of the grafted man, the unnatural man? It is simply a surface claim when a black man says he is a Christian. In reality—that is, in the eyes of Allah—he is not Christian. Allah's will, then, is that black brothers and sisters will awaken from their sleep and come to know who they truly are by nature.

Name Changing

As far as the NOI is concerned, four hundred years of slavery, violence, and oppression give Elijah Muhammad authority to state,

> Christianity is a religion organized and backed by the devils
> for the purpose of making slaves of black mankind. Freedom,
> Justice, Equality; money, good homes, etc.—these Christianity
> cannot give us (not the Christianity that has been taught us).
> He (Allah) said that Christianity was organized by the white
> race and they placed the name Jesus on it being the founder
> and author to deceive black people into accepting it.[32]

The first step, therefore, is to abolish anything Christian in title or name and establish a new identity. The designation Christianity, the names of its churches, and NOI members' individual slave names inherited from enslaved ancestors in the United States are forever banished.[33] Muhammad's religion is Islam; his movement is called the Lost-Found Nation of Islam; and his name has been changed, as have the names of all others who convert to Allah. The naming of individuals in part serves to ritualistically break them from the hold of Christianity, whether directly, if one once belonged to a Christian church, or indirectly, since blacks have inherited the names of their Christian slave masters.

Muhammad decries that since his God is not the "Spook God" of the Christians, believers in Allah are given one of the ninety-nine remaining names of Allah (Allah is the one hundredth).[34] This is also the "new name" that the Bible talks about in Isaiah 62:2 and Revelation 3:12. The practice, says Muhammad, is obedient to what the Bible says and identifies members of the NOI as the true and "original" people of Allah. "Everyone who is called by My name, and whom I have created for My glory, whom I have formed, even whom I have made" (Isa. 43:7), become followers of Allah and accept one of Allah's names. Those who do not accept Allah and take one of the names are servants of the devil and will be destroyed.[35]

Muhammad further reasons that all other peoples' names identify them with the nation to which they belong. "Lu Chin" immediately signals that a man is from China. Why is it, Muhammad asks, that a black man in America is called "Sam Jones"? This name has its roots in Europe; it cannot be the name of a man from Asia or Africa.[36] This is significant, for to Muhammad a European name identifies one with the European religion. To Muhammad this is the mark of the beast (of the Book of Revelation) that has been branded on the forehead of the original black nation.

SUMMARY

In this chapter I have explained in detail the central myth of the NOI, that of Yakub and the making of the white race. I have shown that this myth provides the basis for an explanation of blacks' woes at the hands of whites. Additionally, Christianity is the religion of whites and not the true religion of Allah. Muhammad's call to the black man, then, is to wake up from his sleep and recognize that the European white devil and his evil religion has them in chains and to "get out of her" before the coming battle of Armageddon, which is the subject of our next chapter.

NINE

Armageddon:
Who Will Survive?

The eschatology of the Lost-Found Nation of Islam (NOI) was born from the sociological issues of the day and in the wake of past black nationalist movements. The Universal Negro Improvement Association (UNIA) of Marcus Garvey, who influenced the leaders of the NOI more than any other black leader, and Noble Drew Ali's Moorish Science Temple of America passed on their ideologies and spiritual teachings to W. D. Fard for his taking and modification. Other leaders such as David Walker, Henry Highland Garnet, Alexander Crummell, Edward W. Blyden, Martin Delaney, Booker T. Washington, and W. E. B. Du Bois played an important part in shaping the thoughts and actions of millions of blacks in the United States. These men spoke to their current situations and offered a way for blacks to survive. They did not agree on all points, but they serve collectively as an ever-present reminder of the social ills plaguing blacks and whites.

Master Fard Muhammad knew how to embrace and excite the masses eager for change. His faithful know him as Allah in the flesh, and they are ready to believe what he says about the destiny of God's chosen people—the Asiatic blacks—through his Messenger, the Honorable Elijah Muhammad.

THE PLAYING FIELD

The NOI doctrine of Armageddon and the afterlife must be understood in the social milieu in which the NOI arose. The four-

hundred-year history of American slavery, other forms of white oppression of blacks, and countless examples of violence upon blacks
by whites mediated the movement's eschatological musings. Malcolm X, while he was in good standing with the Messenger of Allah,
wrote the following in the preface of the now out of print *Supreme
Wisdom* by Elijah Muhammad. His words serve to set the playing
field for the battle of Armageddon and serve to bring us into the
mindset of a people whose eschatology places the black man on the
throne of victory:

> The Slavemaster called our church the "NEGRO CHURCH"
> to let the world know that "ours" was a church separate, dis-
> tinct and apart from his own Christian Church which he had
> every intention of keeping Lily White. . . . The Negro Church
> [was] . . . even going so far as to parrot the Slavemaster's lying
> doctrine that the black people were cursed by God to work for
> white Christians. . . . [They] kept us confused and divided
> against each other. . . . We knew nothing of our own religious
> history, our religion, and our own God. . . . As "Negro Chris-
> tians" we idolized our Christian Slavemaster, and lived for the
> day when his plurality (trinity) of white gods would allow us
> to mingle and mix up with them. We worshipped the false
> beauty of the Slavemaster's leprous looking women. Our
> greatest desire was to have one of them even if it meant death.
> We regarded them with the utmost respect, courtesy and
> kindness, bowing and tipping our hats, showing our teeth. We
> perfected the art of humility and politness [*sic*] for their sake
> . . . but at the same time we treated our own women as if they
> were mere animals, with no love, respect or protection, beat-
> ing and abusing them even in public places, selling them
> from man to man, letting all the other races (even the Slave-
> master) mix freely with them. . . . In large numbers we be-
> came victims of drunkenness, drug addiction, reefer
> smoking. . . . Almighty God ALLAH has appeared in our
> midst and raised from among us a REFORMER in the person
> of the Honorable ELIJAH MUHAMMAD, the MESSENGER.
> . . . He has given us the desire not only to know ALLAH now,
> but to be with him in the hereafter.[1]

This is not only profound—much of it is true. What Malcolm X was speaking out against was the segregation of the masses within Christianity, something Jesus Christ and his apostles never taught. The Bible does not teach that blacks are cursed by God. Nor does it teach that white Christians must therefore enslave blacks because of the color of their skin. The sad truth is that white Christians did teach and practice these things in the name of Jesus and Christianity. Moreover, Malcolm X and the NOI directly link to the Christian doctrine of the Trinity the false hope of one day mixing and mingling with the white race. Though I am not sure why Malcolm X would say this, I sense in his words a deeply rooted anger at what he calls the religion of the white man.

As the quotation proceeds, Malcolm does not let his own people off the hook, either. Though he may cite as a reason for illicit[2] and illegal behavior the adverse conditions in which blacks were placed, he nonetheless holds them accountable. Malcolm has been there, and he knows there is a way out; he knows there is a way to escape. Allah, he says, has come in the person of W. D. Fard.

It was this God-man, you will recall, who visited Malcolm in his Massachusetts prison cell years after his so-called disappearance in 1934. And it is the Honorable Elijah Muhammad who preaches the truth of Fard for the salvation of blacks the world over. Malcolm X said that blacks once knew nothing of their own religious history, religion, and God. He was of course talking about W. D. Fard's and Elijah Muhammad's teaching that blacks are "the god," the original man who came from the first God that was created more than seventy-six trillion years ago. This is the cornerstone of the religion of the NOI. Blacks therefore can, like Malcolm, raise themselves out of their low condition and live in the hereafter with Allah, in the person of Master Fard Muhammad, if they come to believe in their true history, their true identity, and their true and only God and do what he commands.

NOI Lifestyle and Salvation

The NOI's doctrine of salvation and the afterlife differs from Christianity and traditional Islam in that it does not believe in the resurrection of the dead. Nor does it believe that the elect of God will live forever in their resurrected state. In this sense the NOI speaks of one continuous time line with a quite limited metaphysical change in believers and no metaphysical change of the earth.

Yet within this framework there is a sense of the already and the not yet. Theologically there are two aspects to the NOI's doctrine of salvation and two distinct time periods in which each aspect occurs. The line of separation, marking the step over to the "other side," is the war of Armageddon. Remember as well that salvation is obtained on either side of the Great Battle.

Salvation This Side of Armageddon

Allah commands a strict code of belief and behavior that will prepare NOI members for the life to come. In NOI theology, a strict moral code serves two basic purposes.

First, it shows the white devil, who thinks he is superior to blacks, that blacks are capable of being successful. It shows the white deceiver that blacks do not have to be criminals and drug addicts, unable to fend for themselves, making women pregnant and not providing for their offspring.

Second, it prepares blacks for the hereafter, that life to come when they will live in the presence of W. D. Fard. This is the grounds for the NOI doctrine of salvation.[3] Living the law of Allah gives the believer a taste of what the hereafter will be like and in turn pleases Allah. If Allah is pleased with you, he will receive you into his coming kingdom.

Blacks Can Live Righteously. In order to live righteously, one first has to "come to knowledge of self" and come to know Allah. These are the first components of salvation in NOI theology.

Salvation is "resurrection from the dead." By this is not meant the Christian definition of the bodily resurrection of the righteous after death. As far as the NOI is concerned, once you are dead, you are dead forever. Resurrection therefore is a resurrection of the mind—a resurrection of the "mentally dead." Article 5 in *What the Muslims Believe* states, "We believe in the resurrection of the dead—not in physical resurrection—but mental resurrection." Elijah Muhammad states that the "so-called Negroes" will be resurrected first. The Book of Revelation mentions the first resurrection, the resurrection of the righteous (20:5–6). This is what Elijah is interpreting as the first resurrection—the resurrection of mentally dead blacks who were "put to sleep" by Allah in order to allow the devil his six thousand years to wreak havoc as prophesied. The second resurrection (Rev. 20:11–15), the mental resurrection of the wicked, will occur when it is too late. This is the second resurrection of judgment. When Fard is revealed in all his glory, says the NOI, then the wicked of the earth will mourn.

Therefore, You Shall and Shall Not. If you are saved—mentally "resurrected"—then live like you are! "Stand up!" says Muhammad. This is another meaning of resurrection.[4] Further, blacks must understand that drugs and illicit behavior are merely symptoms. The root cause of unrighteous living is no respect for self. Elijah Muhammad, says Louis Farrakhan, goes right to the cause of the problem. When a black man comes to know who he truly is (an original man), he will come to respect himself. When he respects himself he will no longer act irresponsibly.[5] Does this abstract principle work in real lives? The NOI quickly answers yes and points to the ranks of the movement that are filled with reformed drug addicts, dope pushers, and pimps.

With the theology of self and Allah in place, imperatives now follow. Male members of the NOI are taught to respect their women, and women are taught the rules of righteous behavior. If a brother cannot take care of his woman, respect her, and treat her with dignity, he is a hypocrite who professes Islam but does not live Islam. Female members are to dress in a way that honors Allah and are not to look like the white man's woman. Elijah Muhammad commands his male followers to stop their women from bleaching their hair, painting their lips, cheeks, and eyebrows, and dressing half nude.[6] Further, no illegal use of narcotics is tolerated. Adultery,[7] failure to attend meetings, falling asleep during meetings, failing to evangelize blacks (whites are not counted worthy to be evangelized), eating pork (members are to avoid this and other "poison" foods and eat only one meal per day), failing to pay money for being overweight, drunkenness, and failing to be willing to die for Allah are punishable offenses.[8] The NOI means what it says. The NOI strong arm—the Fruit of Islam[9] (FOI)—investigates those who do not live up to this code of conduct. If people are found guilty they are required to perform some kind of service (similar to being sentenced to perform community service), placed under suspension, or expelled from the group permanently.[10]

In addition to preparing believers for the life to come, the external and internal witness of righteous living does wonders for the reputation of the NOI, even despite its caustic message about whites and the negative press that that message has inspired. One author writes that "Elijah Muhammad has been able to do what generations of welfare workers and committees and resolutions and reports and housing projects and playgrounds have failed to do."[11] Perhaps for this reason *Reader's Digest* once called Muhammad "the most powerful blackman in America."[12]

Pleasing Allah. Allah has not given rules and regulations to his people to burden them. Theologically and ethically these regulations serve a purpose.

Doing what Allah commands through the Honorable Elijah Muhammad pleases Allah. This is the simplest yet most powerful of all reasons for the strict moral code of the NOI. "Islam" means surrender, and surrender to Allah is the key tenet of Islam. Members of the NOI therefore are those who have surrendered themselves to W. D. Fard and his Messenger Elijah Muhammad.

Inward Moral Change. A black man must first come to know that he is an original man, a god, and that, unlike the white devils that were created from the original man six thousand years ago, he has no birth record.[13] Once the mind and spirit know this, a change begins to take place. He is morally able to accept outward rules to conform himself to Allah's will. Master Fard Muhammad is the example of perfection. Just as he mastered the two natures in him,[14] the believers are likewise to strive for that perfection.

Education leading to the knowledge of self leads to knowledge of Allah. For example, NOI children are taught knowledge of self in the movement's University of Islam. There they are taught reading, writing, and arithmetic as well as the history of the black nation (the NOI history of the black original man). The point is that education—not white education that leaves out knowledge of self and is "whitewashed"—is a focal point of the NOI.

Allah, through education (the mental resurrection), is the one who changes the believer, but the believer must do his part. When a person adheres to Allah's word of righteous living, Allah begins to change that person inwardly so that the desires of this white and wicked world no longer hold him in bondage. This prepares him for the world to come, a world in which Allah will reign supreme and maintain his imperatives for righteous living. In short, living righteously now enables the believer to make the transition into Allah's perfect world to come.

Separation—A Taste of the Future. Some of the movements that made up the black nationalism of the early part of the twentieth century desired to live in a separate state. The Back to Africa theme was popular among them (the Garveyites being the most visible) and gained many supporters even from the outside, including white supremacist groups that were all too eager to help blacks ship off to their original homeland.

The NOI, though not desiring specifically to go to Africa, demands from the United States government a separate state, a separate land, in which the saved of Allah may carry on in freedom and prosperity.

In addition to its doctrinal statement found in virtually all NOI publications (*What the Muslims Believe*), the NOI publishes a ten-point statement called *What the Muslims Want.* A portion follows:

> 4. We want our people in America whose parents or grand-parents were descendents from slaves, to be allowed to establish a separate state or territory of their own—either on this continent or elsewhere. We believe that our former slave masters are obligated to provide such land and that the area must be fertile and minerally rich. We believe that our former slave masters are obligated to maintain and supply our needs in this separate territory for the next 20 to 25 years until we are able to produce and supply our own needs.
>
> Since we cannot get along with them in peace and equality, after giving them 400 years of our sweat and blood receiving in return some of the worst treatment human beings have ever experienced, we believe our contribution to this

land and the suffering forced upon us by white America, jus-
tifies our demand for complete separation in a state or ter-
ritory of our own.

Theologically we may look at this appeal as prefiguring the life to
come on the other side of Armageddon and as a way to secure escape from Allah's (Fard's) destruction of the white world during Armageddon.[15]

ARMAGEDDON AND THE AFTERLIFE

We are living in the Days of Allah. The earth and its people
have been ruled by the evil race known as the white race. In
these days [of] Allah, the righteous (the Muslims) are now
gaining power over the wicked and will soon rule the earth
again as they did before the creation of the white race.[16]

In its simplest definition Armageddon is the final battle between the
righteous and the unrighteous. Though other religions will be involved, two religions will play the main roles—Islam and Christianity. The righteous will be victorious and the unrighteous destroyed.
The righteous are those who embrace Fardian Islam to the end.
Whites and apostates will not see the kingdom of Master Fard
Muhammad. The establishment of this kingdom—the afterlife—follows, which is the restoration of all things to their original state.
Only the originals will remain; whites will be killed off.

Fard Will Return

In order for Armageddon to take place, the savior must return.
W. D. Fard, Allah in person, is not dead. Nor did he ever die. Consequently there is no need for his resurrection. Fard is present in
the world today waiting for the fullness of time (100 percent dissatisfaction) so that he can unleash his divine wrath upon the unrighteous for their evils done against the originals for the last six
thousand years, especially the last four hundred years in America.
This, says Elijah Muhammad, is the return of the Son of Man prophesied in the Bible.

Perhaps Elijah Muhammad would draw our attention to the Qur'an, where the devil approaches Allah and asks, "O my Lord! Give me then respite till the day the dead are raised. [God] said: 'Respite is granted thee till the day of the time appointed' " (Sura 15:36–38). The "Lord," of course, is Fard, and the devil is the white race; and the "respite" lasts six thousand years, until the coming of Fard.

The Battle and the Mother Plane

While the original black nation was "asleep," Allah has been preparing for Armageddon. It is going to be the ultimate jihad, the holy war to end all holy wars. If the white devil would reform himself, there would be no Armageddon, says the NOI. However, it is virtually impossible for the devil to allow his mind to be resurrected. Thus he must be killed, and the black Asiatic nation, including brown, yellow, and red, will live on.

In the past, says Muhammad, Allah has shown his disfavor with his enemies and has destroyed them in a variety of ways—water in the days of Noah; fire in the days of Sodom and Gomorrah; fire, water, and hailstones in the days of Moses and Pharaoh. But the last battle will be fought with fire. Both the Bible and the Qur'an, explains Muhammad, mention and predict this great event. The Messenger further explains that the white race has been progressing toward this event for a long time. Guns and explosive bombs replaced the knives and swords of times past, and air battles have replaced the foot soldier. Slowly the white race has improved its technology to the point where battles take place from and in the air. This has been happening since 1914.[17]

The white race knows about the firepower of Allah and has been preparing to do battle with Allah (Fard) in the sky. But the white devils are not as smart as Allah. Fard in his divine wisdom long ago knew that the white devil was going to prepare for this final war. So at least as far back as the biblical prophet Ezekiel, Fard made known through the Hebrew prophet his divine plan. Of course, the whites do not have ears to hear or eyes to see and so missed the whole meaning of Ezekiel's famous prophecy. But Allah, after he appeared in Detroit in 1930, taught his premier disciple and Messenger the true meaning of Ezekiel's wheel within a wheel (Ezek. 1:16).

Ezekiel's vision of the wheel within a wheel is the central element to the great battle of Armageddon. According to the Messenger, the first mention of the wheel in the phrase refers to the contents of the larger wheel. The larger wheel is what the NOI refers to as the Mother Plane (or Ship) or the Mother of Planes.[18] According to Elijah Muhammad, nothing compares with this Mother Plane. It is a massive half-mile-by-half-mile ship, "a small human planet," capable of staying in space for up to a year without coming into the atmosphere of earth.[19]

When the FBI arrested Elijah Muhammad in 1942, it found in his Chicago temple a sketch of this Mother Plane.[20] The plane, says Muhammad, contains within it fifteen hundred smaller bombers (they may be the flying saucers people claim to have seen[21]). In his vision, Ezekiel saw one of these smaller wheels (bombers) within the Wheel (the Mother Ship). Each bomber is capable of carrying three motorized and timed steel bombs that can plunge into the earth a mile deep before exploding. Each interearth blast can create a one-mile-high mountain, killing people within fifty miles around the mountain. In fact, Allah taught the Messenger that God used these bombs to make the earth's current mountains.[22]

Elijah Muhammad says that the white man has gone to the moon to try to get a look at this Mother of Planes. The vehicle is so far beyond the white devil's present technology that it can move at speeds unintelligible to humans. America knows of the plane and has seen it (Muhammad has seen it). Muhammad boasts that when he was arrested in 1942, he sat down with the FBI and answered questions about the Mother Ship.[23]

The Messenger has instructed his people to run when they see the Mother Plane in the sky, for the battle is about to begin. Two original black scientists will be stationed every two blocks to guide Allah's chosen people to safety through supernatural telepathy. After all, Muhammad exclaims, original blacks are gods and are capable of such supernatural powers.[24]

The targets are the United States and England. From a height of forty miles, most of the bombs will be dropped on America, with three being reserved for England (three planes will go to England, and each will drop one bomb). Air force bases will be the first targets in order to prevent white devil air defense.[25] After this, the rest of the devil race will be wiped out along with any Uncle Toms (including black "Christians") and other Asiatics who willfully did not embrace Fard as Messiah,[26] including apostates.[27] Only Allah's chosen among the black Asiatic race will remain.[28]

Needless to say, all of this is far removed from traditional Islam. Although Elijah Muhammad's garden of Eden being Mecca is similar in some points to Islam's *al-Jannah,* which refers to the garden of Eden and is the future dwelling place of the righteous, there is for Elijah no physical resurrection that ushers believers to the garden. For Elijah, it is "once dead, always dead." No one who has already died will live in the hereafter.[29] He therefore holds that W. D. Fard never died. But did not Elijah Muhammad die in 1975? No, says the NOI. He merely "departed" and is "very alive"[30] and well living in different places on the earth or up in the Mother Ship.[31]

> The Honorable Elijah Muhammad said on another occasion before his departure, he said, "I am going away; the world will say and believe I am dead. But I will not be dead. I am going away to receive the new teachings."[32]

The Messenger also points to passages in the Qur'an that use apocalyptic language to speak of the heavens being torn apart before the end. However, one cannot find in Islamic literature any reference to a Mother Ship that carries fifteen hundred bombers armed with earth-drilling explosives that will put an end to the devil race, the United States, and England.

The Hereafter

In one sense the NOI says there is no hereafter, but when it states this it means to reject the "spook" Christian theology of the afterlife. "For my followers, hereafter is NOW," declares Muhammad.[33]

There is another sense to the word. The NOI explains that the word "hereafter" means "after the here and now." In other words, it means "after the rule of the white race." Allah has given the white devil six thousand years to rule over the original black nation. The Messenger teaches that this is the meaning of "six days you shall labor, and then you shall rest on the seventh day" (Ex. 20:9–10 NKJV). Each day represents one thousand years. Thus the white man was given six thousand years to do his work of ruling and deceiving, only to be killed (to rest) when the seventh thousand-year period begins.[34] Armageddon signals this final period when the "man of sin" (white race) is destroyed and thrown into the lake of fire.[35] When the Great War is over, things will be restored to the original, pristine condition from six thousand to more than sixty-six trillion years ago. Only Fard, Elijah Muhammad (both of whom never died), and the rest of the faithful original race will remain, and Allah's Islam (Fardian Islam) will alone be the people's religion.

Heaven. What will life be like at that time? In answering this question, the NOI first tells us what heaven is not. Speaking against the white man's religion, which is Christianity, Elijah Muhammad says that heaven is not going up to the sky or angels coming down out of the sky. To be sure, angels will come out of the sky, Muhammad teaches, but not in the way the devil has taught us to think. The angels are not, as he says, "spooks," but are men who will come in planes to take believers to safe places on the earth. The hereafter, Muhammad states, is a continuation of the present life of flesh and blood, not "spooks" being raised from their graves.[36]

Life for the original man will be the perfection of the lifestyle of the current NOI. There will be no sin or sickness. All who embrace the teachings of Elijah Muhammad will live in the presence of Allah. Allah's people will wear the finest clothes of silk interwoven with gold and will eat the finest food.[37]

Individual existence in Muhammad's hereafter, however, seems to be limited. At times his statements are confusing and can be taken to mean that the righteous will live "forever."[38] Other statements by Muhammad clearly communicate that the afterlife of the Asiatics is limited. No one lives forever. Even the gods, as we have seen, are limited to about two hundred years. Muhammad refers to heaven as a special but limited condition of life in which Allah will make his righteous undergo a "new growth" while continuing to observe the code of conduct practiced today, especially avoiding the poison foods and eating only one meal per day. In this condition, Allah will make his people feel like they are sixteen years old. This, says Muhammad, will make the chosen of God live two to three times longer than expected.[39]

Nor is heaven contained in one place on earth. After Armageddon rids the earth of the devil, the people of the new growth can live in America, on islands in the Pacific, in Asia, and on other continents.[40]

SUMMARY

These last three chapters have taken us from Creation (of the first god) to the end times. In the great battle of Armageddon Fard will descend upon the earth in the Mother Ship to destroy America, the white race, and all others who reject Fardian Islam. As has been stated many times throughout this book, the theology of the NOI cannot be comprehended contextually without an understanding of the situation and dilemma in which blacks who became NOI members found themselves. And this book is written to facilitate comprehension and understanding of the movement. But as Christians we must not limit ourselves to a mere understanding of the NOI. The biblical reality is that Christians are called to preach the gospel and to defend the faith against its attackers (Matt. 28:19; Jude 3). It is my prayer that the next chapter will serve to equip Christians to carry out these mandates by the grace of Jesus Christ, and that also by his grace souls may be truly saved through and by him.

TEN

A Christian Answer to the Nation of Islam

Some of Elijah Muhammad's sharp criticisms of whites' treatment of blacks for the last four hundred years are, sadly, accurate. Those who profess the name of Jesus while hanging people because they have dark skin are atrocities, and they always will be, no matter how many times they identify themselves with Jesus and at the same time perform these dreadful acts. The same may be said of those who enslave people with dark skin because dark skin evidences inferiority by nature. But one can also find sharp disagreement with Muhammad on several points, disagreements that arise from valid questions and observations.

First, one should hope to see from him and others in the NOI a more balanced and logical approach to what Christianity is. After that, if they must dismiss it, they have the freedom to do so.

Second, shouldn't there exist on the part of the NOI an acknowledgment that there were and still are Christians, black and white, who have vehemently spoken out against slavery and the violence done in the name of Jesus?

Third, there is ample evidence that biblical texts have been taken out of their contexts and interpreted in the context of W. D. Fard's claims. Closely allied to this, in many instances the NOI has misrepresented what Christianity teaches, only to proceed to tear down that misrepresented belief. Rather than this, one should expect to find an honest and worthwhile endeavor to interpret any literature in its historical and cultural setting, understand it in those settings, and then make criticisms.

Finally, the NOI has attacked the trustworthiness of the Bible without giving substantial, accurate evidence. For example, Elijah Muhammad says that the Bible is not the pure and holy Word of God because it begins in Genesis with the words of someone other than God.[1] But who says that the Bible has to open this way? Further, Muhammad here does not address what the apostle Paul may have had in mind when he wrote, "All Scripture is inspired by God" (2 Tim. 3:16). The claim by the NOI that the Bible is a "poison book" marks a foundational issue to be debated before we make any further Christian critique of the movement.

THE BIBLE

Elijah Muhammad makes a most revealing statement regarding his epistemology (the process by which he comes to understand something) and his statements about the Bible:

> If you desire to preach or teach that a certain religion is true or right, you should know all religions and their scriptures. The man that God chooseth for Himself from among the people as a warner to them, such a one does not need previous training and knowledge, for Allah is his teacher and trainer.[2]

Muhammad is this "warner" that W. D. Fard (Allah in the flesh) chose to teach and train the people. Thus we must accept that Fard is Allah, that he personally taught Elijah, and that Elijah does not need any previous training. Thus Elijah's epistemology rests solely on Fard. What Fard taught him is truth, and we are called to accept that truth on that premise.

Another illogical barricade that Muhammad has set up concerns one's claim that Christianity is true. In order to teach this, says Muhammad, one (except him) must know all religions and their scriptures. First, does this apply to NOI adherents as well? If so, do they know all religions and their scriptures in order to know that Fardian Islam is true? If not, why not? Is it because Fard taught Elijah, who in turn has taught adherents of the NOI? If so, why would this not be true of Jesus' disciples? They were taught directly by Jesus. Did they need to know all religions and their scriptures in order to know truth? Second, knowing all religions and their scriptures is impossible. One can spend a lifetime studying just one area of religion and never study other religions. It is impossible to know all religions and their scriptures. Third, what would Muhammad say to someone who claims to have had a personal revelation of God, and that God was not Fard? All he could do is answer with his experience, only to be countered once again by his opponent's experience. It would be a battle of subjective experiences.

These are problems for the NOI, and obviously the burden of proof rests upon Muhammad to objectively demonstrate his claims. Inquirers would expect to find these problems addressed by Muhammad and his disciples, but there seems to be a lack of objective evidence for support.

According to the premier disciple and Messenger of Allah, the Bible has been tampered with, commercialized, revised, and rewritten.[3] "What a poison book," says Muhammad.

Response

A reasoned response to Elijah Muhammad is twofold. First, does he have objective evidence for this? Second, if the Bible has been tampered with, revised, and rewritten, why does the NOI quote it so much?

Objective Evidence? One could argue with Muhammad on the basis of a subjective claim by saying, "No, the Bible has not been tampered with. I believe this." Would Muhammad then ask for evidence? Why is his claim any better than this response? It isn't, so the burden of proof rests upon him to back up his claim objectively. Otherwise it would revert to a battle of subjective experiences.

Why Quote It, Then? Throughout the movement's writings there is abundant use of the Bible. This is strange, given its "poison" nature. For example, in Muhammad's *Message to the Blackman in America,* more than 220 Bible verses are listed in the index. To be sure, Muhammad says that one has to understand the correct meaning of biblical texts and that he is the pipeline through which W. D.

Fard gives the true interpretations. But how does Muhammad know which verses have been tampered with, revised, or rewritten?

Would Muhammad answer, "Master Fard Muhammad told me"? If so, that would be a purely subjective argument, and on purely subjective grounds his subjectivity is no better than the subjectivity of someone else.

Would Muhammad answer, "that which I know to contradict the teachings of Master Fard Muhammad"? This answer would at least begin to be plausible if there is objective manuscript evidence showing that the verses clearly contradicting Fard are additions to the biblical text or have been tampered with in some way. But such evidence is lacking. A study of all the major existing Greek New Testament manuscripts reveal no tampering with the essential meaning of cardinal Christian doctrines such as the deity of Jesus Christ. For example, there are no textual variants existing that question Jesus' "I am" statement in John 8:58, a text that proves Jesus is God the Son. Or take John 20:28, where Thomas confesses Jesus as "my Lord and my God." There is no tampering there either.[4]

Of course, if one wants to and has the time, one could learn biblical Greek and take courses on New Testament interpretation, which includes the study of textual variants. One would then have the tools to find out that evidence for claims like Muhammad's does not exist. If one does not have time for this, one could read, for example, F. F. Bruce's *The New Testament Documents: Are They Reliable?* This book, written for laypeople by a renowned New Testament scholar, demonstrates that the New Testament text that exists today has been meticulously preserved.

Despite abundant evidence to the contrary, Muhammad's claims remain in print for his disciples to read. They of course take his claims at face value because they have accepted his presupposition—Fard is Allah and Fard taught Elijah Muhammad what has never before been revealed.

Another Question. Granting Elijah Muhammad's illogical acceptance of one biblical text over another and his presupposition of Fard's direct revelation to him,[5] another question is "On what objective evidence should we accept *that* meaning?" Consider the Messenger's interpretation of the word "Christ."

> According to the meanings of "Christ" that name means
> One coming in the Last Day or Crusher—He Crushes the
> wicked: Christ, the Crusher.[6]

According to what meanings? There is no standard Greek lexicon in existence today (nor has there ever been one) that states that Christ (Greek, *Christos*) means "crusher." In fact, all standard lexicons will tell you the word means "anointed one." Muhammad teaches that the word means "crusher" and that the Christ is anointed to crush the wicked. He then sets the stage for Fard to come in the last day to crush the wicked, for if the word means "crusher," he can tell us that Jesus did not crush the wicked—the wicked still remain.[7] Thus, in Muhammad's mind, Fard must be the Christ. Muhammad defies any theologian to dispute his claim that Christ means "Crusher" and that the Christ was born in 1877. "I have been taught by God," he says.[8]

Muhammad could argue that the Bible teaches that Christ will come to crush the wicked. This is true, but the word does not directly mean "crusher." It perhaps is an attribute of Christ, but the word in and of itself does not mean "crusher." Granting that Muhammad is indeed saying this, he still is faced with the difficulty of why he thinks Jesus does not fit the bill. His argument rests on the fact that Jesus did not crush the wicked. But where in the Bible does it say that Jesus' coming two thousand years ago meant that all evil and all the wicked would be destroyed? There is a sense that in his incarnation judgment has come, but the judgment will not be fully consummated until Jesus comes again. This is known in Christian theology as the "already, not yet." The sad thing—and this is the point—is that Muhammad makes no effort to understand the Christian position. He asserts an erroneous premise (Christ means crusher of the wicked; Jesus did not crush the wicked) and then makes an erroneous conclusion (Jesus therefore is not Christ).

Interpreting the Bible. Though the evidence proves that the Bible is historical and reliable and that no scholarly source supports his interpretations, Elijah Muhammad still rests on his hermeneutic of direct divine revelation from Allah in the person of Master Fard Muhammad. When all is said and done, his ultimate court of appeal is "Master Fard Muhammad told me so." This is the Messenger's hermeneutic, the method or process by which he arrives at the interpretation of biblical texts.

But it is not the process by which Christians or anyone should arrive at the meaning of the biblical texts. To interpret the Bible, one must first find out what the text says. Next, one must labor to find out what the text means. Doing the latter involves many steps, such as grammatical analysis, a study of the immediate and larger contexts, and consideration of the historical and cultural contexts.

Obviously, not all of us have the time to do this. But if one is going to set himself against Christianity, critique it, and utilize biblical passages to teach something other than what Christian orthodoxy has affirmed for two thousand years, one must be familiar with the issues and tools and secondary scholarly sources necessary to make a fair assessment.

Inspiration and Biblical Language

Working from the view of the inspiration of the Bible, we can in the next section begin to unravel the ball of logical, exegetical, and biblical flaws Elijah Muhammad models for his disciples. By "inspiration" is meant that God directly and in his sovereignty created the biblical authors and directly and in his sovereignty ordained their lives and circumstances. Further, God made use of these personalities and circumstances, inspiring the biblical authors by the Holy Spirit to communicate the truth he and he alone desires to be communicated. In this sense the Bible comes directly from God and is the word of God. Therefore, the Bible is the final word in determining whether or not Elijah Muhammad taught God's truth.

CONCLUSION

Elijah Muhammad and the NOI have been extremely careless in their assessment and refutation of Christian doctrine and in their interpretation of the Bible. Their carelessness occurs in two areas. First, after attacking the veracity of the Bible (offering no evidence for the attack) and warning others that it is a poison book, they pick and choose passages from this "tampered with" text without giving any reasons as to why they trust these passages. Second, when they interpret the passages, they do so without any consideration of the tools and steps needed to properly interpret the Bible.

The people of the NOI have learned an erroneous method of biblical interpretation from Elijah Muhammad, who learned it from W. D. Fard. Unless this changes, the NOI will always be stuck in Master Fard Muhammad's and his Messenger's subjective hermeneutic that keeps them from properly understanding the Bible and properly understanding Christianity.

Proceeding on the ground of the overwhelming evidence for the historicity, reliability, and meticulous preservation of the biblical text,[9] criticisms of the NOI's doctrine of God(s), Jesus, and salvation now follow.

GOD

Contrary to the NOI's finite "theism," which purports only one god existing at a time, the God of the Bible exists eternally.

Finite Godism?

There never was a time when God did not exist. "Before the mountains were born . . . from everlasting to everlasting, Thou art God" (Ps. 90:2). God is the "uncaused cause" and stands in direct contrast to the NOI's "birthed god" (the original black man) that arose from a single atom at the beginning of time.

Psalm 90:2 introduces the theme of contrast between the creation and God. It does so by the formula of the created order coming into existence as compared to the eternal existence of God. Before the mountains came into being God existed. This theme is found in John 1:1. John writes that Jesus "was,"[10] and the created order "came into being" (John 1:3).[11] The theme is further played out in John 8:58: "Before Abraham was born, I am." John is well aware of this theological theme and sees fit to apply it to Jesus Christ. Jesus as God the Son always existed, but the created order ("all things" in John 1:3, and "Abraham" in John 8:58) came into existence.[12]

Finitude in existence is not the only finite attribute of the gods of the NOI. They are finite in knowledge as well. Each god knows nothing of the previous gods' knowledge, teaching, or theology. Elijah Muhammad's theology of the first god coming into existence "in the beginning" puts him at odds with the prophet Isaiah, through whom the Lord spoke, saying, "I am God, and there is no other, . . . declaring the end from the beginning" (Isa. 46:9–10 NKJV). This not only implies that God's truth stands forever (see also Isa. 40:8) and is not replaced with another god's theology or teaching; it also implies one God throughout the whole process.

The historical context to which this portion of Isaiah speaks was one of compromise and idolatry. A rebellious Israel (v. 8), who claimed to worship Yahweh (God), was yoking itself to the gods of Babylon as well. They were guilty of syncretism. Here Yahweh, through the prophet Isaiah, tells the people that he alone is God and that he, unlike the idols they are worshiping (see vv. 1–2), knows all things from all eternity.[13]

God the Father

Muhammad warns that we should turn from believing in a "spook God." By this unnecessary choice of words he means to facetiously derail Christian theology. Perhaps the most direct contradiction to his theology comes from Jesus himself. In John 4:24 Jesus describes God the Father: "God is spirit, and those who worship Him must worship in spirit and truth." That Jesus is indeed describing the Father is clear from the preceding verse: "The true worshipers shall worship the Father in spirit and truth" (John 4:23). The parallel between verse 23 ("worship the Father in spirit and truth") and verse 24 ("worship Him [God] in spirit and truth") signals a synonymous parallelism—worshiping the Father equals worshiping God. Thus God equals the Father.[14] The Father, then, is not a black man but is spirit.

The Problem of Language. Elijah Muhammad first affirms W. D. Fard's theology that God the Father is a black man and then reasons that since the Bible tells of God hearing, seeing, speaking, smelling, touching, sitting, standing, and walking, Fard must be right. He does not appear to be familiar with the fact that the Bible uses phenomenological and anthropomorphic language to communicate truth. In other words, to communicate to humanity on the level of humanity, God has purposed to relate truth to us in ways we can understand. Another way to word it is that God did not reveal himself to his people in a vacuum but in their culture and in ways that are related to everyday existence. For example, in order to communicate that God is omnipresent, Proverbs 15:3 tells us that "the eyes of the LORD are in every place." If this is literal, as Muhammad might say, how many eyes would God have to have to be in every place?

To be sure, the Bible contains figurative, poetic language, but we must be careful to decide what is figurative and what is not. Proverbs 15:3 should be interpreted figuratively not only because the Hebrew of Proverbs is in the style of poetry, but first and foremost because to do so literally results in a nonsensical understanding of the text. God would have to have billions of eyes or have two enormous eyes.

What do we make, though, of other styles of writing in the Bible? There is, for example, biblical narrative. The Hebrew style of Genesis 29 is narration. Yet even Hebrew narrative can contain anthropomorphic language. Genesis 29:31 states that "the LORD saw that Leah was unloved, and He opened her womb" (NASB). Does this mean that God has eyes and is therefore a man? No. Christians do in fact believe that God sees, but does this mean he is a man? Why do we assume that since God sees he must be a man with eyes like all of us? Cannot God, who is spirit (John 4:24), see without the aid of human eyes? The fact is, God can see infinitely (can human eyes see infinitely?). One must conclude, then, that Genesis 29:31 employs anthropomorphic language that should not be taken to mean that God has human eyes and is therefore a man.

Obviously, space limitations do not allow for exhaustive treatment of the issue of anthropomorphic and phenomenological language, but one more example will suffice. You might recall the former Baptist who heard W. D. Fard teach, "The Bible tells you that the sun rises and sets. That is not so." After hearing Fard, the man became a former Baptist and a follower of Fard. This man was not aware that the Bible, when it speaks of the sun setting and rising, is using phenomenological language to make a point. It is utilizing the point of view of the author to drive home a point. It is not meant to be a scientific statement. For example, when the psalmist states, "From the rising of the sun to its setting the name of the LORD is to be praised" (Ps. 113:3), what is the intent? The intent is to communicate that God is worthy to be praised all the time. Its intent is not to give a short lesson in astronomy.

The Doctrine of the Trinity

Muhammad misunderstands the Christian doctrine of the Trinity and then rejects it. He accuses Christians of believing in three gods[15] and dividing three gods into one god.[16]

Neither the Bible nor the Christian church teaches what Muhammad says they do. The Christian doctrine of the Trinity states that there is one God and that the one God is the Father, the Son, and the Holy Spirit. The three distinct persons are the one God. That there is one God is shown in Isaiah 43:10 ("I am He. Before Me there was no God formed, and there will be none after Me" [Elijah Muhammad would disagree]). That there are three persons each called God is also clear—the Father is called God (2 Pet. 1:17), the Son is called God (John 20:28), and the Holy Spirit is equated with God (Acts 5:3–4). The one God is, therefore, the Father and the Son and the Holy Spirit (see Matt. 28:19, where the one "name" is the Father, Son, and Holy Spirit).

It is unfortunate that Muhammad did not understand the doctrine before offering his reasons of rejection. He could have gone to hundreds of sources to find out what Christians believe. For example, he could have consulted the Westminster Shorter Catechism of 1647. Part of this catechism reads,

> There is but one [God] only, the living and true God. . . .
> There are three persons in the Godhead: the Father, the
> Son, and the Holy Ghost; and these three are one God, the
> same in substance, equal in power and glory.[17]

As a result, thousands are under the impression that Christians believe in something they do not believe.[18]

JESUS CHRIST

The NOI has replaced Jesus with W. D. Fard in the belief systems of thousands of individuals. Since this doctrine is of vital importance, the NOI's denial of the biblical Christ must be answered with the witness of the Bible.

Why So Important?

Jesus said that what people thought of him was important. He asked, "Who do people say the Son of Man is?" The doctrine of the person and work of Jesus Christ is of vital importance to Christianity. Christianity stands or falls on this issue. Conversely, what people think of Christ immediately identifies them as either inside or outside the camp of Christianity.

Even though the NOI does not desire to be Christian (that is the white devil's religion), it does want to claim identity with the religion of Jesus, which they claim is not Christianity as it exists today. How does Muhammad come to know the religion of Jesus? Again, the evidence shows that he picks and chooses Bible verses to support his claim and reinterprets them but dismisses or erroneously interprets those verses that refute him, labeling them as "poison" and "tampered with."

One verse that evidences the importance of believing who Jesus is, and the awful consequences of rejecting who he claimed to be, is John 8:24. Here Muhammad would have to remain silent if he were familiar with the evidence, for there are no variants showing this claim to be "tampered with."[19] Jesus states, "Unless you believe that I am *He*, you shall die in your sins." "I am" must be read against its Old Testament background, where Yahweh, the true and living God, claims to be the "I AM" (see Deut. 32:39; Isa. 43:10 in the Septuagint,[20] and Ex. 3:14 in English translations). What Jesus is saying is that anyone who knowingly and intently denies that he is "I am" will reap judgment in the age to come. There is a price to pay for deliberate rejection of who Jesus is. In what follows, there is no question that the NOI intently rejects Jesus' identity as God the Son.

Rejection of Jesus

The Messenger holds the highest view of W. D. Fard but the lowest view of Christ:

> God is here in Person, so stop looking for a dead Jesus for help and pray to HIM whom Jesus prophesied would come

> after him. My people pray to the One who is ALIVE and not a spook![21]

> He (Jesus) was only a prophet like Moses and the other prophets[22] and had the same religion (Islam). He did his work and is dead like others of his time, and has no knowledge of their prayers to him.[23]

The NOI's statements in rejection of Jesus as God are in a few places much like the statements made by Jehovah's Witnesses, something not surprising given that W. D. Fard instructed his followers to listen to the radio broadcasts of Judge Joseph Rutherford, the Watchtower president.[24] Consider the following:

> Jesus never equated himself with the Father. In fact, one person in the Scripture said, "Good Master." Jesus said, "Why callest thou me good? There's none good but the Father." And then again, Jesus spoke onto his disciples and he told them, "That which I hear is that which I speak." He was depending on one greater than himself to guide him.[25]

> If Jesus said in his suffering "My God, My God, why hast thou forsaken me?" (Matt. 27:46) then most surely he did not recognize himself as being the equal of God, and no other scripture shows Jesus as the equal of God.[26]

Answering the Objection

Several issues arise.

The first one again concerns how the NOI chooses texts from a corrupt Bible. How is it that Louis Farrakhan and Elijah Muhammad find the above "Scripture" passages authentic? Is it merely because it suits their needs?

Second, in the case of the first quotation, Farrakhan misquotes Jesus. Jesus, in Mark 10:18 and Luke 18:19, responds to the rich young ruler, saying, "No one is good except God alone." When one looks at this passage in its context, Jesus ends up pointing the rich young ruler to himself. "Come, follow Me," Jesus says (Mark 10:21; Luke 18:22). After Jesus said, "No one is good except God alone," why did he not say, "Go, follow God"? Better yet, why did Jesus not say, "Follow the Father"? In pointing to himself as the ultimate satisfaction for the rich young ruler, Jesus' words ("No one is good except God alone") meant that the rich young ruler was rightly acknowledging him as good, and no one is good except God alone. Jesus' response to the ruler does not disprove his deity.

Farrakhan then quotes Jesus saying, "That which I hear is that which I speak." Farrakhan concludes that Jesus was dependent on God and therefore cannot be God. But the answer to Farrakhan's objection lies in the fact that he, like his mentor, does not understand the doctrine of the Trinity. Further, Farrakhan disregards the doctrine of the two natures of Christ. When the biblical doctrine of the Trinity is rightly understood, the distinctness of the persons is maintained, and thus God the Son can be dependent upon God the Father. When the doctrine of the two natures of Christ is understood, then one can see that Christ was fully human as well as fully deity. By virtue of his humanity, then, Christ was dependent upon the Father. Further, he was dependent upon the Father for a reason. In order to fulfill what humanity has failed to fulfill—perfect obedience to the Father—Christ was obedient to the Father. Thus those who are saved by grace through faith in Jesus Christ may be seen by the Father to fulfill all righteousness because they are in union with Christ and clothed with his righteousness. Farrakhan and thousands of others miss this wonderful truth.

Farrakhan is right in saying that Jesus was dependent on someone greater than himself. That is what the Bible says. In John 14:28 Jesus states, "The Father is greater than I." That is what it says. But what does it mean? Farrakhan's implied conclusion that Jesus therefore cannot be God is wrong because it does not keep to the context. Does it mean that the Father is greater by nature? Or does it mean that the Father is greater in function? It is not illogical when two distinct persons are equal in nature and one of them is greater than the other is. If by "greater" one means "greater by virtue of function," there is no problem. Take, for example, the president and vice president of the United States. The two persons are equal in nature— they are both human beings. However, the vice president can say, "The president is greater than I." Indeed, by virtue of his office, the president is greater. But again, the two are equal in nature.

151

All this is well and good, but what about Jesus' words in John 14:28? They as well must be interpreted in their context. We have the affirmation at the beginning of John's Gospel that "the Word was God" (1:1).[27] Further, Jesus was making himself equal with God (5:18).[28] Later we have Jesus' affirmation that he is "I Am" (8:58). Finally, Thomas's confession of Jesus as "My Lord and my God" (John 20:28)[29] shows that Jesus is God the Son. We must therefore interpret "greater" in John 14:28 to mean greater in function.[30]

In the second quote, Elijah Muhammad says that because Jesus cries out "My God, My God, why hast thou forsaken me," he cannot be God. But Jesus can be God the Son praying to God the Father. If Muhammad correctly represented the Christian and biblical doctrine of the Trinity, perhaps his problem would have been solved.

Lastly, Muhammad is incorrect to state that "no other scripture shows Jesus as the equal of God." John 5:18 certainly does,[31] as does Philippians 2:6. In John 5:18, John states that by the very fact that Jesus was calling God his own Father (see 5:17), Jesus was "making Himself equal with God." In Philippians 2:6, Paul states that though Jesus was existing "in the form of God, [he] did not regard equality with God [which he already possessed] a thing to be grasped." Verse 7 then states "but [he] emptied Himself, taking the form of a bond-servant." The meaning here is that the God-man Jesus was truly God the Son, equal with God the Father, but he did not consider that possessed equality something to assert. Rather, he went to the cross (see v. 8).[32]

Is Jesus the Christ?

For Elijah Muhammad, Louis Farrakhan, and the NOI, the answer is no. Fard is the Christ, for Christ means Crusher—one who will come in the last day to crush the wicked (the devil white race). Jesus, reasons Muhammad, did not crush the wicked. Jesus therefore is not the Christ. Nor is Jesus the Son of Man. Two biblical passages suffice to show that Jesus is both the Son of Man and the Christ.

Compare Elijah Muhammad's words with those of Matthew's Gospel. Muhammad states, "Jesus wasn't even a Christ back then."[33] Matthew states, "Jesus, who is called Christ" (1:16). As to Christ meaning "crusher," the standard Greek-English lexicon in New Testament studies nowhere mentions "crusher" under the entry of *Christos*.[34]

In Matthew 16:13, Jesus asks his disciples, "Who do people say that the Son of Man is?" The disciples respond that some say the Son of Man is Elijah, others say Jeremiah or one of the prophets (v. 14). Then Jesus asks, "But who do you say that I am?" (v. 15). Notice that Jesus does not once again use the phrase "Son of Man" but this time replaces it with "I," making himself the Son of Man. Peter then answers, "Thou art the Christ, the Son of the living God" (v. 16). Jesus responds by stating that Peter is blessed because the Father in heaven has revealed this to him.

Jesus Died and Rose Again

One of the interesting things about the contrasting of Jesus and W. D. Fard is the weakness of evidence that Fard is still alive (as the NOI claims for this 124-year-old man) and the abundance and strength of evidence that Jesus rose again from the dead.

For example, a few people in the NOI claimed to have seen Fard alive in the 1970s and 1980s. But where are the collaborating witnesses for each individual's sighting of Fard? Where is the evidence to substantiate the claims? Contrast this with Paul's words in 1 Corinthians 15:6, where five hundred eyewitnesses at the same time saw the resurrected Christ. The difference is this: Paul then says that many of these witnesses were alive when he wrote these words. He was in effect saying that eyewitnesses remain to verify the event.

Biblically we know that Jesus rose again from the dead. First, Jesus predicted he would rise again (John 2:19–22). Second, after his death Jesus appeared not only to the five hundred but on several occasions to his disciples and others (Matt. 28:16–20; Luke 24:15; 36–43; John 20:11–16, 25–27; 21:1–14).

Does the biblical resurrection mean a resurrection of the mind of the mentally dead? Again, no scholarly source supports this claim, nor does the context of any biblical passage that mentions resurrection.

Conclusion

Put simply, one cannot read the Bible without concluding that it testifies to Jesus being God the Son (Matt. 1:16, 23; 14:33; John 1:1; 8:58; 20:28), Christ (Matt. 16:16; John 20:31), and the Son of

Man (Matt. 9:6, 7; 16:13, 15) who was killed and after three days rose again from the dead (Mark 8:31).

Jesus, the Christ, warns his disciples, "See to it that no one misleads you. For many will come in My name, saying, 'I am the Christ,' and will mislead many" (Matt. 24:4–5).

SALVATION

It is true that Elijah Muhammad's teaching of a clean and healthy lifestyle coupled with pride and economic sufficiency is commendable. It has changed for the better the lives of thousands. But this is not the entire picture. Indeed, in the context of salvation the most important part of the picture is a biblical understanding of Jesus Christ and his view of salvation.

Created Equal

W. D. Fard, Elijah Muhammad, Malcolm X, and Louis Farrakhan have reason to be disgusted with so-called Christians who were bigots. Many racists claiming the name and love of Christ sat in pews, occupied pulpits, and used biblical verses as proof texts for the ontological inferiority of blacks. And they still do! Theirs is a disgusting and distasteful legacy, a legacy that Christ himself one day will look upon with shame and judgment.

People in the NOI should know that the Bible nowhere teaches the inferiority of any people group. All people come from the first human beings created—Adam and Eve (Paul calls Adam "the first man" [1 Cor. 15:45 NIV]). All people are by nature equal and deserve to know it.

While no one should excuse the behavior of racist whites, at the same time one should not excuse the NOI's counterracist anthropology. Seeing the white race as the devil race grafted from the original black man's lower nature six thousand years ago by the evil scientist Yakub sets the NOI in the racist camp. It views whites as ontologically inferior to black, brown, red, and yellow. With this the NOI is not in company with true Christianity and traditional Islam. The Bible knows nothing of the Yakub myth and its vicious racist theme.

Equality in the New Birth

Christianity as taught in the Bible not only emphasizes the ontological equality of all peoples in Adam (thus all are created equal) but also emphasizes the ontological equality of all people who are in Christ. The apostle Paul wrote, "There is neither Jew nor Greek, there is neither slave nor free man, there is neither male nor female; for you are all one in Christ Jesus" (Gal. 3:28).

The Christian should lovingly inform those of the NOI what true Christianity is and that Paul, guided by God the Holy Spirit, is going against the grain of his culture.[35] He mentions first that there is no distinction of races. "There is neither Jew nor Greek." In Paul's day the Jews saw themselves as the only children of Abraham. The Greeks, in the Jews' minds, were among the Gentiles, the uncircumcised heathen who did not belong to God. Paul cuts across racial barriers and says there is no distinction. There must be neither black, white, yellow, red, nor brown.

Second, Paul speaks against the dividing lines of social status. "There is neither slave nor free man," he says. He means that with Christians these things are of no concern—all should be treated as if one in Christ. As a matter of fact, then, Christianity can change the ungodly social distinctions that exist in our culture!

Finally, true Christianity wages war on this ancient culture's sexist view of women, something the NOI should appreciate since it as well honors women. Paul says, "there is neither male nor female." Elijah Muhammad should have appreciated the apostle's stand against the tide of sexism so entrenched in his day. For example, male Jews prayed, "I thank God that thou hast not made me a woman." The Jewish historian Josephus wrote, "Woman is inferior to man in every way."

This is the Christianity of the Jesus of the Bible and his followers. What's more, these followers exist today and are black, white, brown, yellow, and red. This is the message the NOI needs to hear.

Salvation Only in Christ

The historical and reliable Bible preaches Jesus the Christ, God the Son. It joyfully proclaims that Jesus Christ has come for the salvation of all who call upon his name. Jesus was indeed a historical person. There is no doubt of that even from Elijah Muhammad and the NOI. But Jesus made claims that would at the very least be boisterous if he were not God the Son. He made claims that made W. D. Fard and Elijah Muhammad question the very integrity of the Bible. That is how powerful Jesus' claims were.

For all times and for all cultures, Jesus is the only way of salvation. He said, "I am the way, and the truth, and the life; no one comes to the Father, but through Me" (John 14:6). Peter as well leaves no room for doubt: "And there is salvation in no one else; for there is no other name under heaven that has been given among men, by which we must be saved" (Acts 4:12).

Of course, all who call upon Jesus' name will be saved (Rom. 10:13). This includes black, brown, red, yellow, and white. The Jesus of the Bible saves everyone who confesses him as Lord and Savior. This should be the witness of Christianity to the NOI, which sees the whites as devils and not worthy of salvation.

Heaven

Elijah Muhammad seems confused over the Christian doctrine of heaven. He thinks that heaven is "pie in the sky" in the presence of a "spook God." It is not as simple as this.

When the Bible speaks of heaven or the heavens, it can mean different things depending on context. In one sense, heaven refers to the sky and all the created order of the universe (Gen. 1:1). In another sense, it refers to the dwelling place of God. Jesus commands his disciples to pray, "Our Father, who art in heaven" (Matt. 6:9). Finally, heaven is the new Eden, a physical paradise that will one day be restored to all who have believed on Christ and who have been physically resurrected from the dead. In the new Eden (the new heaven and new earth of Rev. 21:1[36]) these people of God will live forever in his presence.

Thus the members of the NOI should know that Christianity's heaven as described by Elijah Muhammad is not the heaven described in the Bible and that once again the Messenger has simplified and misrepresented Christian doctrine before proceeding to tear it down.

WITNESSING TIPS (WITH JERRY BUCKNER)

In order to provide an effective witness of the gospel in any culture, Christians must familiarize themselves with that culture. The NOI is a subculture within the larger culture of the United States and is no less a mission field than an island tribe ten thousand miles away.

This book was written to provide Christians with knowledge of the black nationalist soil in which the NOI was planted and from which it grew. It was written to aid Christians to become familiar with the mindset of the movement as a whole and the mindset of individuals belonging to the NOI. Possessing this insight is invaluable to understanding NOI doctrine and lends sensitivity to our apologetic and evangelism that would otherwise be absent had we not taken the time to study what makes the NOI click. It now remains to offer a few suggestions relative to presenting the truth of Christ to members of the NOI.

Responsibilities of the Church

Christians the world over must be sensitive to the need of the church to address racism and to stand against it.

The NOI is popular because, in part, it addresses the wrongs of racism and has a leader, a role model, namely, Louis Farrakhan. If black Christians were more aggressive on the issue of racism, we would see a substantial decrease of the percentage of blacks, especially youths, entering the NOI. Rather than being drawn to the NOI, blacks would then be drawn to the Christian church with Christ as its leader and have the opportunity to hear the gospel of Christ. Similarly, white Christians standing with black Christians against the evils of racism would manifest a loud voice of protest to the public at large. How can this be done?

Black churches and white churches need to join hands in evangelistic fervor to reach with the gospel of Christ people of every color. Pulpit exchanges between white and black churches, church events in which both black and white participate, co-laboring in the effort to reach inner-city black youths with the gospel, concentrated efforts in prison ministry, and offering mentoring and surrogate father programs can produce marvelous effects. For example, a pilot project in Houston where white churches worked with black churches in the mission of curbing crime in the black community yielded astounding results. These churches provided substitute fathers for troubled black youths, and crime dropped significantly.[37] The fact that these young people were provided with positive role models made all the difference. Moreover, the church can develop economic empowerment programs in which blacks can be given economic education and care. This is one of the top drawing points of the Nation of Islam. The Christian church, if it is willing, is able to do far more in this area than the NOI.

The Encounter

Obviously, if you are a friend of an NOI member, go on to the next section. If not, the "initial encounter" is important.

If you are white, it will be difficult for you to establish contact. Trust God. He is bigger than racial and racist barriers. Be genuine, be what God has made you, and be courteous! Try to ask questions about the person. This allows you to be to some extent involved in his or her life, if only for a few moments. Ask questions about the person's involvement with the NOI. Ask questions about Marcus Garvey, Noble Drew Ali, and W. D. Fard. This will be a witness in and of itself. In the mind of the NOI, white people know little if nothing about black history because American history is whitewashed to exclude blacks and their importance. Knowing about W. D. Fard should impress them as well. Just imagine yourself in a part of the world that knows little about Jesus and a person coming up to you that knows about him!

Doctrine

Once you have demonstrated your familiarity with the NOI and its history, move to doctrine. The theology of the NOI is somewhat complicated, and individual encounters vary (personalities, time restraints, etc., all play a part), so there is no formula to follow. The goal is to be sensitive to the person to whom you are speaking, and pray for an opportunity, a window into a discussion of NOI beliefs.

Remember that if you are white, the person thinks you are a devil. He or she will no doubt be impressed that you know of Yakub and his grafting the white race, W. D. Fard as Allah in the flesh, and the Mother Plane's role in Armageddon, but devils use knowledge to deceive. So ask for the Holy Spirit's guidance.

Presenting the Gospel

During your discussion of NOI doctrine, the person might interject scathing remarks about Christian doctrine. Much of your time, then, might be spent in pre-evangelism—apologetics, or defending the Christian faith. Remember that because of the horrid examples of so-called Christians, the NOI is partially justified in its view of Christianity. It is therefore vitally important to gently correct any misrepresentations of the teachings of Jesus and his apostles and use this opportunity to show NOI people that a true Christian is talking with them. As much as is possible, reiterate the point that in Christ there is neither black nor white, slave nor free, male nor female (Gal. 3:28). And there is nothing wrong with showing your disgust at the behavior of those who in the past have defiled Christ by their racist actions.

Pray as well for the Lord to open a window to present the gospel. All people—black, brown, red, yellow, and white—are sinners. Christ Jesus came to save sinners. That is the great truth of the gospel. Remember as well two basic yet all-important blessings. First, Jesus is with you. He promised us that his divine presence will never leave us, including when we preach the gospel (Matt. 28:20). Second, the gospel is the power of God for salvation to every one who believes (Rom. 1:16).

Some Do's and Don'ts

Do know why you believe what you believe. Know the essentials of the Christian faith. This is a must and will equip you in sharing the truth of Christ with members of the NOI.

Do pray. Pray that the Holy Spirit will open the eyes and ears of your NOI contact.

Do show love. Scripture commands us to love our neighbor. Based on the supreme example of Christ, this is giving to others in sacrificial service. Of course, how and what one gives is different in every situation. The best advice we can give you is to be sensitive to the Spirit's leading of how you might show Christ's love to your contact.

Do listen. If you are not genuinely interested in what your contact has to say, you should seriously question your motive. For the sake of Christ and his work on the cross to save sinners we should be interested! So listen. When it's your turn to speak, ask that the favor be returned to you.

Do share the uniqueness of Christ. Jesus is uniquely God in the flesh (John 1:14, 18). This, obviously, means that no one else is, including W. D. Fard. Additionally, Jesus is the only way of salvation (John 14:6). Remind your NOI contact that according to the Qur'an, "No true prophet of God can lie." If, as they say, Jesus is a prophet, why do they not believe Jesus who said, "No one comes to the Father, except through Me"?[38]

Do share that righteousness comes only through Christ. Righteousness does not come through our own works but only through Christ's righteousness being declared by God upon those who believe in Christ (Rom. 3:21–22).

Don't play the role of the Spirit. We cannot convert members of the NOI with our own strength. But the Holy Spirit can! Our job is to share the gospel. It is God who converts sinners into a relationship with Christ.

Don't overwhelm with Scripture. In other words, don't use Scripture like a machine gun. Use Scripture intelligently, carefully explaining it as you progress in conversation.

Don't use a King James Bible. If you do, NOI members will not listen. Rather, we recommend using the New International Version or the New American Standard Bible.

Don't use a marked Bible. Members of the NOI consider it degrading to the Bible and a mark of disrespect on the Christian's part if the Bible has been marked with personal notes and highlighting.

Don't unwittingly use the word "Trinity." To the NOI this word connotes the worship of three gods. We recommend stating that God is one Being existing eternally in three persons. If you must use the word, be careful to define it as so.

Don't offend—let the cross offend. In telling the truth in love, we must not be the offense. If anything should offend, let it be the message of the cross of Christ.

Appendix:
Is Louis Farrakhan Changing?

In late February 2000 I was walking on the campus of Harvard University when I noticed a gentleman holding up a newspaper to passers-by. As I drew closer I noticed the title of the publication, *Muslim Journal*. I greeted the man, he greeted me, and I asked, "What do you have here?" He told me that the *Muslim Journal* was a Sunni Muslim publication promoting orthodox Islam in the West, and that his teacher was Imam (leader) W. Deen Mohammed. I recognized immediately that this was Elijah Muhammad's son, Wallace, who had in 1975 been appointed leader of the NOI upon his father's death.

You might recall that it was W. Deen Mohammed who at that time instituted changes in the NOI, discarding the "Fard as Allah in the flesh" doctrine and accepting people of all colors into the fold of the NOI. It was W. Deen Mohammed's desire to reform the NOI so that it would be in line with orthodox Islamic thinking. As a result Louis Farrakhan would a few years later lead a group of Elijah Muhammad's followers (those desiring to maintain and preserve the teachings of the Messenger) away from the reformed NOI and claim true lineage with the Messenger.

I was struck that while my new acquaintance placed much emphasis on the differences between Mohammed's and Farrakhan's doctrines of God and race, he saw these differences as a thing of the past. Louis Farrakhan had changed his views! Indeed, the publication featured a front-page quotation from Imam W. Deen Mohammed: "Min. Louis Farrakhan has been a good leader for the Nation of Islam, and we recognize the changes and improvements."[1]

161

I eagerly bought the newspaper and read the article inside titled "Imam W. Deen Mohammed Speaks on the Hon. Elijah Muhammad, Min. Louis Farrakhan and the Nation of Islam."[2] The article was a reproduction of an interview between Mohammed and Nathaniel Omar that took place on January 6, 2000. In it Omar mentions that Farrakhan, at a recent news conference, "announced his recovery from a bout with cancer." Omar continues, "At this news conference, Min. Farrakhan also announced conceptual changes, whereby he apologized for his past racial statements and philosophy."[3] Mohammed responded that this would indeed improve the chance for unity between the two religious groups, and that "we were already feeling a sense of a fraternal bond with Min. Farrakhan and the members of the Nation of Islam."[4]

Unfortunately, no specific details were given in the article, such as what news conference this was or what specific words Farrakhan uttered concerning race. I was puzzled. Compounding my puzzlement was no mention at all of Farrakhan reversing his position of Fard as Allah, a doctrine that should be considered high on the blasphemy list of orthodox Muslims. Instead, Mohammed stated that he participated in praying with members of the NOI, and throughout the article emphasized Farrakhan's and Elijah Muhammad's leadership qualities in the context of social reform.

Given Imam Mohammed's failure to address the NOI's doctrine of Fard, I was left wondering how this unity could be genuine. Perhaps Imam Mohammed defines unity differently than I. But regardless of the article in the *Muslim Journal* it is clear that prior to that time there was little agreement between the Imam and Farrakhan in matters of religion. "Q: 'What is your [i.e. Imam Mohammed's] relationship with Farrakhan?' A: 'He's a great friend of mine. He's been friends with me all my life. I differ with him on religion, but I never stopped thinking of him as a close friend.' "[5]

The question rises, Has Farrakhan changed his views on race and Fard? Having read the NOI's newspaper, *The Final Call*, since 1994, I must admit that Louis Farrakhan has been paradoxical in his words. The January 4, 2000, issue of *The Final Call* quotes Farrakhan expressing thanks at a press conference for those who prayed for him during his illness. "Prayers were sent up for me from my Muslim family, from my Hebrew Israelite family and there were people of good will praying for me who were Black, brown, red, yellow and white."[6] Another example is Farrakhan's use of "Jesus" at this press conference. Farrakhan states, "Santa Claus is a falsehood. Jesus Christ is the truth and came into the world. . . . We are asking that Santa Claus does not take the place of the meaning of the birth, life, ministry, and death of Jesus the Christ."[7]

Though at first glance one could rejoice with these words, I must admit that they left me just as bewildered as did the *Muslim Journal*. Specific questions must be addressed before we can draw conclusions: Has Louis Farrakhan really changed? Do current issues of *The Final Call* reflect changes?

Regarding the statement about Jesus, if we consider other of Farrakhan's public statements about Jesus, we find him expressing different if not conflicting views, at times totally redefining the title "Jesus the Christ." For example, in *The Final Call*, March 15, 1995, Farrakhan mentions "one who comes at the end of the world, who is called Messiah, or Jesus the Christ." But in this article the Messiah (Jesus the Christ) is Fard. First, the article states that the Messiah is to come "in the duality of the nature of man."[8] We have seen that it is Fard who purportedly mastered the lower nature to conform with his higher nature. Second, in NOI theology Jesus is forever dead and cannot come again. That is reserved only for Fard.

We must be aware, then, that Farrakhan, while using the name "Jesus" or the titles "Messiah" and "Jesus the Christ," may mean something entirely different than what the name and titles historically mean.

Have Farrakhan's and the NOI's views of the white race and Fard changed? Though public statements by Farrakhan may seem contrary to long-held NOI beliefs, it appears that neither his nor the NOI's views have changed at the core. The following evidence bears consideration.

As I write this appendix, it is February 24, 2001, a full year after my encounter with the Sunni Muslim selling *Muslim World*. I found on the NOI's Web site its "Final Call On-Line Edition." The article is titled "Farrakhan Meets the Press." Here Tim Russert (TR) and David Broder interview Minister Louis Farrakhan

(MLF) on NBC television's *Meet the Press* (April 13, 1997). Russert comes quite to the point:

TR: Last year you gave an interview to Henry Louis Gates, a professor from Harvard, in *New Yorker* magazine where he asked you whether you still subscribe to the teachings of Elijah Muhammad on Yakub, a black scientist who 6,600 years ago created the white man, and that by the end of the 20th century, a spaceship will come and rain down upon white people and people who don't embrace Islam. Do you subscribe to the teachings of Yakub, that Yakub, the black scientist, created the white man?

MLF: I subscribe to every word that the Honorable Elijah Muhammad taught us.[9]

It is significant that even though this interview took place in April 1997, the NOI still posts it on its Web site. Likewise *The Final Call*, well after my encounter with that follower of Imam W. Deen Mohammed, still contains diatribes against the white race and "Uncle Toms" of the clergy class, as well as the proclamation of Fard as Allah. Speaking of the "two people," "Black and white," Elijah Muhammad states, "The two people are not brothers. They are alien to each other. God did not make them brothers to each other."[10] Current issues of *The Final Call* reprint Muhammad's words of the past. In these issues he calls the white race "Yakub's grafted people"[11] and "arch-deceivers."[12] Further, Muhammad, referring to America as "she," exclaims, "She deceives them [the "American Negro"] through a few of what we call 'Uncle Toms' in the political circle, clergy class and all professional classes."[13] Lastly, Fard is once again labeled "Almighty God Allah, in the Person of Master Fard Muhammad."[14]

Has Minister Louis Farrakhan changed? If Farrakhan oversees the publication of *The Final Call*, recent issues of which have printed the above teachings of Elijah Muhammad, it appears that Farrakhan still holds to the teachings of the Messenger. But the Minister himself erases all doubt:

This is why the Teachings of the Honorable Elijah Muhammad are so vital and valuable to our people. And if our teachers do not study His Teachings and administer them properly, our people are lost forever. . . . The Honorable Elijah Muhammad has healing in his wings.[15]

I am praying for Louis Farrakhan and the members of the NOI. I pray that there would truly be a change in Louis Farrakhan, but not a change toward a more orthodox expression of Islam. Rather, I pray that he and the NOI will come to recognize and know the true and living Lord of Glory, the historic Jesus that walked the earth two thousand years ago, the Jesus that truly has healing in his wings (Matt. 23:37).

Notes

CHAPTER ONE: SOCIOLOGICAL AND RELIGIOUS SOIL

1 Martha F. Lee, *The Nation of Islam, An American Millenarian Movement* (Lewiston, N.Y.: Edwin Mellen Press, 1988), 1.

2 Ibid., 2.

3 I use the term without negative connotations. Black nationalism exhibits certain characteristics: a sense of who blacks are as a people; a sense of their true origin; a sense of ultimate purpose and destiny; in some cases a desire to set up an independent state in Africa for the emigration of African Americans, with independent economy, commerce, and political power. Henry Highland Garnet, a black nationalist leader of the nineteenth century, was president of the African Civilization Society in 1858. He desired the latter for African Americans (see Clifton E. Marsh, *From Black Muslims to Muslims: The Resurrection, Transformation, and Change of the Lost-Found Nation of Islam in America, 1930–1995,* 2d ed. [Lanham, Md.: Scarecrow Press, 1996], 86). On the negative side, black nationalism has been criticized on a wide front. All the preceding characteristics can be espoused by black leaders in the context of the inherent racial superiority of blacks. On this point, C. Eric Lincoln strongly criticizes black nationalism, charging that it goes well beyond racial pride and courage and crosses over into the arena of racism to battle the racism of whites (see C. Eric Lincoln, *The Black Muslims in America* [Grand Rapids: Eerdmans, 1994], 41–42). He states, "From the soil of hostility and repression grow bitter fruits, and black nationalism is one of the most bitter" (33).

4 "Rationally speaking, 'We must accept the fact that White racism was responsible for Black Nationalist teaching.' " (Marsh, *From Black Muslims to Muslims,* 80). Marsh quotes Adib Rashad, *The History of Islam and Black Nationalism in the Americas* (Beltsville, Md.: Writers Inc., 1991), 79.

5 Wilson Jeremiah Moses, *Black Messiahs and Uncle Toms: Social and Literary Manipulations of a Religious Myth,* rev. ed. (University Park: Pennsylvania State University Press, 1993), xii. On page 50 Moses lists Robert Breckin-

ridge, another nineteenth-century white author who saw blacks as having a "redemptive destiny."

6 Ibid., 1.

7 Ibid. "Mahdi" in Islamic thought refers to a "guided one," an eschatological person who will usher in righteousness for all the earth.

8 Walker and Garnet had at least one predecessor. Marsh lists Paul Cuffee (1815) as a promoter of African-American nationalism who called for emigration back to Africa (*From Black Muslims to Muslims*, 80).

9 Moses, *Black Messiahs and Uncle Toms*, 41.

10 Moses quotes Thomas Jefferson's statement regarding black men and their preference for white mates "as uniformly as in the preference of the Oranootan for the black woman over those of his own species" (*Black Messiahs and Uncle Toms*, 40).

11 Moses, *Black Messiahs and Uncle Toms*, 39.

12 Ibid. Moses notes on the same page that Robert Alexander Young made this prediction earlier in his *Ethiopian Manifesto* of 1829.

13 Moses, *Black Messiahs and Uncle Toms*, 229.

14 "As early as 1852, the year *Uncle Tom's Cabin* appeared, the Reverend J. B. Smith, a black minister, protested against Uncle Tom's conception of Christian virtue because it made him submit to tyranny" (Moses, *Black Messiahs and Uncle Toms*, 51).

15 Cited in Moses, *Black Messiahs and Uncle Toms*, 45.

16 Ibid., 44.

17 Ibid., xii.

18 Ibid.

19 This basic message had varying degrees of difference among other nineteenth-century black nationalist leaders. Prominent leaders include Edward W. Blyden, Martin Delaney, Alexander Crummell, W. E. B. Du Bois, and Henry Sylvester Williams (the latter two near the turn of the twentieth century).

20 Lincoln, *Black Muslims in America*, 47.

21 Claude Andrew Clegg III states that Garveyism "was as much a religious movement as it was a political force" (Claude Andrew Clegg III, *An Original Man: The Life and Times of Elijah Muhammad* [New York: St. Martin's Press, 1997], 70).

22 As later mentioned by Lincoln, *Black Muslims in America*, 57–58.

23 As we shall see, Garvey did have a theology, though it may not have been as intricate as that of other movements.

24 Lincoln, *Black Muslims in America*, 54.

25 Lincoln, *Black Muslims in America*, 52, quoting George W. Bagnall in Bagnall's "The Madness of Marcus Garvey".

26 Lincoln, *Black Muslims in America*, 53.

27 Ibid. Lincoln says that black leaders came to despise Garvey as well, because of Garvey's "extreme black nationalism" (*Black Muslims in America*, 53–54).

28 Quoted in Lincoln, *Black Muslims in America*, 53.

29 Marsh, *From Black Muslims to Muslims*, 89.

30 Lincoln, *Black Muslims in America,* 54.

31 Arthur J. Magida, *Prophet of Rage: A Life of Louis Farrakhan and His Nation* (New York: HarperCollins, 1996), 15.

32 Elijah Muhammad and the NOI employ the phrase "so-called Negroes," evidencing further a Garvey influence upon the NOI.

33 Lincoln, *Black Muslims in America,* 54.

34 Ibid.

35 Ibid.

36 Moses, *Black Messiahs and Uncle Toms,* 140. Garvey was inconsistent, however, for mulattoes were among UNIA leadership (see 135). As Moses said, "inconsistency did not bother him" (140).

37 See Mary Lefkowitz, *Not Out of Africa: How Afrocentrism Became an Excuse to Teach Myth as History* (New York: Basic Books, 1997), 132. As is obvious from her book's title, Lefkowitz challenges Afrocentrists on their assertion that, for example, "Socrates and Cleopatra were of African descent, and that Greek philosophy had been stolen from Egypt" (xi).

38 Ibid., 129.

39 Ibid., 128.

40 Ibid., 130.

41 Ibid., 131.

42 Ibid., 129. As a source for this thesis, Lefkowitz cites Loretta J. Williams, *Black Freemasonry and Middle-Class Realities,* University of Missouri Studies, vol. 20 (Columbia: University of Missouri Press, 1980).

43 Lefkowitz, *Not Out of Africa,* 129–130.

44 See William A. Muraskin, *Middle-Class Blacks in a White Society: Prince Hall Freemasonry in America* (Berkeley: University of California Press, 1975). I am indebted to Mary Lefkowitz for calling my attention to this source.

45 Marsh, *From Black Muslims to Muslims,* 89.

46 Ibid., 90.

47 Dinesh D'Souza, *The End of Racism: Principles for a Multiracial Society* (New York: The Free Press, 1995), 398.

48 Quoted in Lincoln, *Black Muslims in America,* 55.

49 Lee mentions that this slogan was to be "a rallying cry frequently used by the Muslims' Messenger Elijah Muhammad" (*The Nation of Islam,* 30).

50 Quoted in Lincoln, *Black Muslims in America,* 57.

51 Lincoln, *Black Muslims in America,* 56.

52 Ibid., 56. Add to this list factories and publishing houses; see Marsh, *From Black Muslims to Muslims,* 89.

53 Magida, *Prophet of Rage,* 16.

54 Marsh, *From Black Muslims to Muslims,* 90.

55 Clegg, *An Original Man,* 71.

56 Among the several protestant groups were adherents of black Jewish sects. One was Beth B'nai Abraham, a black Hebrew congregation led by J. Arnold Ford (see Moses, *Black Messiahs and Uncle Toms,* 137).

57 Perhaps for this reason Garveyism is said to have been a civil religion, adopting nonsectarian religious practices and theological statements. See Moses, *Black Messiahs and Uncle Toms,* 137–38. Note, though, that Magida states that "the 'structure' Garvey assigned to God was traditionally Christian: an omniscient, omnipotent trinity, 'not a person,' but 'a spirit' " (*Prophet of Rage,* 17).

58 Lincoln, *Black Muslims in America,* 57. McGuire was most likely "former" because, as Lincoln points out, he was a long-time critic of the denomination, seeking with no success to establish independent black congregations (58). It should be noted that McGuire's relationship with Garvey was not without its difficulties (see Moses, *Black Messiah's and Uncle Toms,* 136), most probably due to differing emphases on the part of both men. McGuire's was religious; Garvey's was mainly political.

59 Quoted in Lincoln, *Black Muslims in America,* 58.

60 Lincoln, *Black Muslims in America,* 58.

61 Moses mentions a "sizeable amount of support for the UNIA among clergy." Of the ministers active in the UNIA, one-third were Baptist, approximately one-third were Methodist, and the remainder were from other denominations (see *Black Messiahs and Uncle Toms,* 135).

62 Quoted in Lincoln, *Black Muslims in America,* 58. To keep a balance, it should be noted that Garvey once stated, "Whilst our God has no color, yet it is human to see everything through one's own spectacles, and since the white people have seen their God through white spectacles, we have only now started out (late though it be) to see our God through our own spectacles" (Amy Jacques Garvey, ed., *Philosophy and Opinions of Marcus Garvey,* 2 vols. [New York: Atheneum, 1969], 1:44; quoted in Moses, *Black Messiahs and Uncle Toms,* 134). This was not original with Garvey. As early as the 1890s Bishop Turner held this view (see Moses, *Black Messiahs and Uncle Toms,* 134).

63 The slight difference being that Garvey (see the previous note) was not concerned primarily with the ontological nature of God. He was more concerned with the social dynamic. The Nation of Islam under Elijah Muhammad spoke on ontological grounds in its claim that God was black.

64 Lincoln, *Black Muslims in America,* 58–59.

65 For all these observations I thank Lincoln, *Black Muslims in America.* For more details, see pages 60–61.

66 Lincoln, *Black Muslims in America,* 61.

67 Moses, *Black Messiahs and Uncle Toms,* 138.

68 Some researchers place the founding of the Moorish Science Temple one year later. It is more important to note that its founding was quite close to the beginnings of the Garveyite movement.

69 Clegg, *An Original Man,* 19; Marsh, *From Black Muslims to Muslims,* 33; Lincoln, *Black Muslims in America,* 48.

70 But, as we shall see, in many ways Ali's Islam was not orthodox. Further, Ali was not the first to see in Islam an answer to the plight of the black people. Edward W. Blyden was a mid-nineteenth-century black nationalist leader who

advocated Islam and repudiated Christianity (see Marsh, *From Black Muslims to Muslims*, 9). As for the history of Islam in America, Clegg notes that Islam arrived in Spanish Florida and French Louisiana by way of the slave trade before colonization by the British. Also, in the first decade of the nineteenth century "possibly tens of thousands of Muslims from Senegambia and other Islamic parts of West Africa were transported to North America as slaves" (*An Original Man*, 18).

71 Marsh, *From Black Muslims to Muslims*, 29.

72 Ibid.

73 Marsh, *From Black Muslims to Muslims*, 93, quoting Imam Warith Deen Muhammad.

74 Marsh, *From Black Muslims to Muslims*, 31, quoting Arthur Huff Fauset, *Black Gods of the Metropolis* (1944; Philadelphia: University of Pennsylvania Press, 1971), 41.

75 "Members of the Moorish Science Temple believe that Marcus Garvey 'was a forerunner to plant the seed in the people and prepare them to be received by Noble Drew Ali' " (Marsh, *From Black Muslims to Muslims*, 30, quoting Moorish Science Temple minister George Bey, interview held on August 4, 1976).

76 Moses, *Black Messiahs and Uncle Toms*, 186.

77 Marsh, *From Black Muslims to Muslims*, 31.

78 Arthur Huff Fauset, "Moorish Science Temple of America," in *Religion, Society, and the Individual*, ed. J. Milton Yinger (New York: Macmillan, 1957), 504.

79 Scholars have noted the influence of Freemasonry upon the NOI. See Mattias Gardell, *In the Name of Elijah Muhammad: Louis Farrakhan and the Nation of Islam* (Durham, N.C.: Duke University Press, 1996), 149, 151–52; Clegg, *An Original Man*, 71–72; Erdmann Doane Beynon, "The Voodoo Cult among Negro Migrants in Detroit," *American Journal of Sociology* 43 (May 1938): 900.

80 Gardell, *In the Name of Elijah Muhammad*, 39–42.

81 Louis A. DeCaro Jr., *On the Side of My People: A Religious Life of Malcolm X* (New York: New York University Press, 1996), 19.

82 Marsh, *From Black Muslims to Muslims*, 32, 33.

83 Not to be confused with Islam's Qur'an. See the body text.

84 Cited in Marsh, *From Black Muslims to Muslims*, 34.

85 Lincoln, *Black Muslims in America*, 49.

86 Ibid.

87 Ibid.

88 DeCaro, *On the Side of My People*, 19.

89 Gardell, *In the Name of Elijah Muhammad*, 39.

90 Ibid., 40, noting Abbie Whyte, "Christian Elements in Negro American Muslim Religious Beliefs," in *Phylon: The Atlanta University Review of Race and Culture* 25.4 (winter 1964): 384.

91 For a brief synopsis of Ali's theology, see Gardell, *In the Name of Elijah Muhammad*, 37–46.

92 Ibid., 37.

93 DeCaro, *On the Side of My People*, 18.

94 Gardell, *In the Name of Elijah Muhammad*, 38.

95 Ibid.

96 Ibid., 44–45.

97 Ali reportedly taught Father Divine and passed on to him his mission (see Marsh, *From Black Muslims to Muslims*, 35).

98 Gardell, *In the Name of Elijah Muhammad*, 45.

99 Marsh interviewed one follower of Ali, who stated, "His health went bad on him; as far as I know he died a natural death" (Marsh, *From Black Muslims to Muslims*, 35). Others cite the police and their harassment as the cause for Ali's death (see Gardell, *In the Name of Elijah Muhammad*, 45).

100 Marsh, *From Black Muslims to Muslims*, 35.

101 Ibid. Marsh quotes from an interview with a follower of Ali.

102 This is not to say that all black nationalist groups agree with all the men listed here. Nor do I mean to say that all these men agreed with one another in all aspects. For example, Dinesh D'Souza mentions that Booker T. Washington and W. E. B. Du Bois differed in their approaches. "Washington," he says, "is respected in two camps today: black conservatives and black nationalists." On the other hand, "For many mainstream black scholars and civil rights activists, however, Booker T. Washington is an embarrassment." For a detailed analysis, see D'Souza, *The End of Racism*, 184–89.

CHAPTER TWO: W. D. FARD: THE STRANGER FROM THE EAST

1 According to the NOI this was the exact day when Fard came to Detroit. Independence Day has taken on a new meaning for the NOI, symbolizing the beginning of blacks' independence from the rule of the white man.

2 See Claude Andrew Clegg III, *An Original Man: The Life and Times of Elijah Muhammad* (New York: St. Martin's Press, 1997), 21. Clifton E. Marsh, in *From Black Muslims to Muslims: The Resurrection, Transformation, and Change of the Lost-Found Nation of Islam in America, 1930–1995*, 2d ed. (Lanham, Md.: Scarecrow Press, 1996), 93, states positively that "Master Fard Muhammad was influenced by Marcus Garvey [and] Noble Drew Ali."

3 Erdmann Doane Beynon, "The Voodoo Cult among Negro Migrants in Detroit," *American Journal of Sociology* 43 (May 1938): 894.

4 Beynon writes, "Accustomed as these people were to the cottage prayer meeting of the Negro Methodist and Baptist churches they found no difficulty in holding informal meetings in their homes" ("The Voodoo Cult among Negro Migrants in Detroit," 895).

5 Quoted in Beynon, "The Voodoo Cult among Negro Migrants in Detroit," 895.

6 Beynon, "The Voodoo Cult among Negro Migrants in Detroit," 896.

7 Louis E. Lomax, *When the Word Is Given* (1963; Westport, Conn.: Greenwood Press, 1979), 42.

8 Quoted in Beynon, "The Voodoo Cult among Negro Migrants in Detroit," 896.

9 Beynon, "The Voodoo Cult among Negro Migrants in Detroit," 896–97; Arthur J. Magida, *Prophet of Rage: A Life of Louis Farrakhan and His Nation* (New York: HarperCollins, 1996), 45.

10 Magida, *Prophet of Rage,* 40.

11 Quoted in Beynon, "The Voodoo Cult among Negro Migrants in Detroit," 897.

12 Marsh, *From Black Muslims to Muslims,* 38, quoting from a 1979 interview with Wallace D. Muhammad.

13 Ibid.

14 Interview with Elijah Muhammad in Hatim A. Sahib, *The Nation of Islam* (master's thesis, University of Chicago, 1951), 94, cited in Martha F. Lee, *The Nation of Islam, An American Millenarian Movement* (Lewiston, N.Y.: Edwin Mellen Press, 1988), 31.

15 Magida, *Prophet of Rage,* 48, emphasis original. Magida lists two newspapers that contain information on Fard's birth stories. See "Black Muslims' Founder a Fake; Posed as Negro," *Seattle Post-Intelligencer,* July 28, 1963, 1, and "Prophet of Muslims Afoul of Law in L.A.," *Los Angeles Herald-Examiner,* July 29, 1963, 1.

16 C. Eric Lincoln, *The Black Muslims in America* (Grand Rapids: Eerdmans, 1994), 12.

17 Ibid.

18 Ibid., 12–13. See also Beynon, "The Voodoo Cult among Negro Migrants in Detroit," 897.

19 Quoted in Lincoln, *Black Muslims in America,* 13. See *The New Crusader,* August 15, 1959, 1.

20 Mattias Gardell, *In the Name of Elijah Muhammad: Louis Farrakhan and the Nation of Islam* (Durham, N.C.: Duke University Press, 1996), 51.

21 Ibid. Gardell lists Arna Bontemps, Jack Conroy, E. U. Essien-Udom, and Clifton Marsh as promoting this theory. Gardell then states that he has not found substantial evidence supporting this theory.

22 Ibid., 51.

23 Ibid., 52. See Howard Brotz, *The Black Jews of Harlem* (London: Macmillan, 1964), 11–12.

24 Gardell, *In the Name of Elijah Muhammad,* 52.

25 Ibid.

26 Ibid.

27 Ibid.

28 Cited in Gardell, *In the Name of Elijah Muhammad,* 52. See Robert A. Hill and Barbara Bair, "Glossary of Names and Terms," in *Garvey, Marcus, Life and Lessons,* ed. Robert A. Hill and Barbara Bair (Berkeley: University of California Press, 1987), 383.

29 Fard renamed his converts, taking away their "slave name" and replacing it with a name that reflected their true origin.

30 Beynon uses the term "roomer."

31 Beynon, "The Voodoo Cult among Negro Migrants in Detroit," 903.

32 These details are taken from Clegg, *An Original Man,* 30.

33 Beynon, "The Voodoo Cult among Negro Migrants in Detroit," 903.

34 Gardell, *In the Name of Elijah Muhammad*, 55.

35 Ibid., 31–32.

36 Ibid., 32.

37 Lomax, *When the Word Is Given*, 46.

38 This word most likely comes from Fard's Yakub myth. This myth is the NOI's explanation for the white race. Yakub, an evil scientist, "grafted" the white race from the original black race six thousand years ago. See chapter 8 for more details.

39 Master Fard Muhammad, *Lesson #1* (n.d.), quoted in Gardell, *In the Name of Elijah Muhammad*, 56. Gardell later offers his understanding of this teaching (see chapter 3 of this book under the subheading "Destruction of Whites"). Magida notes, "In later years, Nation of Islam leaders would argue that the section in the lost-found lessons about murdering devils was only a metaphor designed to rally NOI members to 'slay' whites' psychological and social grip on them" (*Prophet of Rage*, 52).

40 However, Clegg quotes from an interview in which Elijah Karriem (Elijah Muhammad) said that Fard indeed taught Black Muslims to kill four whites. This would "take the fear of the white man out of the hearts of the followers" (*An Original Man*, 32).

41 Gardell, *In the Name of Elijah Muhammad*, 55.

42 Clegg, *An Original Man*, 31.

43 Clegg recounts the event another way: Ugan Ali alone promised to do all he could to disband the NOI. Thus he was released. Fard, writes Clegg, was released from detention only after hundreds of angry Fard supporters protested in front of First Precinct (*An Original Man*, 32–33).

44 Gardell, *In the Name of Elijah Muhammad*, 56.

45 The X is used to show that Charles is no longer his name. Charles is a slave name inherited from white slave masters.

46 Ali K. Muslim never let the man enter. The police were notified, and the man was arrested.

47 Steven Barboza, *American Jihad: Islam after Malcolm X* (New York: Doubleday, 1993), 115–16.

48 Cited in Gardell, *In the Name of Elijah Muhammad*, 53.

49 Gardell, *In the Name of Elijah Muhammad*, 53. Gardell says that the FBI files on Fard/Ford classify him as white.

50 Ibid. In his notes Gardell lists FBI file 100–43165–15 and Los Angeles FBI file 105–4805 (356 n. 31).

51 Ibid., 356 n. 32. Gardell lists FBI files 100–43165–15; 100–43165–1; 100–43165; 105–63642.

52 Ibid., 53.

53 Ibid. Gardell cites FBI file 100–43165–15 (357 n. 36).

54 Clegg, *An Original Man*, 20–21. Gardell is not convinced. He says, "The FBI files' picture of Ford . . . has . . . only a remote resemblance to the one of Master Farad [Fard] Muhammad printed in the NOI papers." He states further that

"in the light of the FBI's counterintelligence activities directed against the NOI, the evidence presented above very well could be fabricated" (see *In the Name of Elijah Muhammad,* 53). Gardell then tells us, "During the 1950s and 1960s, the FBI frequently furnished what they called 'derogatory information' to selected reporters in hopes of disrupting the growth of the NOI" (ibid.). Gardell, in chapter 4 of his book, supplies more information to support his claim.

55 Gardell, *In the Name of Elijah Muhammad,* 58.

56 Elijah Muhammad, *The Supreme Wisdom: Solution to the So-Called Negroes' Problem* (Chicago: University of Islam, 1957), 15.

57 Clegg, *An Original Man,* 33.

58 Ibid.

59 Ibid.

60 Ibid., 34.

61 Ibid.

62 Gardell, *In the Name of Elijah Muhammad,* 58. See FBI file 105–63642–28.

63 Clegg, *An Original Man,* 34.

64 Ibid.

65 Ibid., 35.

66 Ibid.

67 Lee, *The Nation of Islam,* 35.

68 Lincoln, *Black Muslims in America,* 15.

69 Ibid.

70 Ibid.

71 Magida, *Prophet of Rage,* 51, quoting "Black Muslims' Founder a Fake; Posed as Negro," *Seattle Post-Intelligencer,* July 28, 1963, 4.

72 Ibid.

73 Gardell, *In the Name of Elijah Muhammad,* 101. Wallace D. Muhammad then began to reform NOI doctrine and polity. Some followers of Elijah Muhammad did not react positively to the changes and formed splinter groups considered to be the true continuation of Fard's and Elijah Muhammad's religion. One of these persons was Louis Farrakhan.

74 In the early 1960s Elijah Muhammad put a ban on Wallace; Wallace defected and returned to the fold a year later. Then, on two other occasions in the late 1960s and early 1970s, Wallace was suspended from the NOI. For more details, see Gardell, *In the Name of Elijah Muhammad,* 102.

75 Wallace D. Muhammad, quoted in Gardell, *In the Name of Elijah Muhammad,* 106–7.

76 Gardell, *In the Name of Elijah Muhammad,* 107.

CHAPTER THREE: THE TEACHINGS OF W. D. FARD

1 Erdmann Doane Beynon, "The Voodoo Cult among Negro Migrants in Detroit," *American Journal of Sociology* 43 (May 1938): 900.

2 Ibid.

3 For a more thorough treatment of the Garveyite movement, see chapter 1.

4 See chapter 1 for an in-depth discussion of Noble Drew Ali and his Moorish Science Temple of America.

5 Beynon, "The Voodoo Cult among Negro Migrants in Detroit," 900.

6 The term "Lost-Found" means that blacks had lost the knowledge of who they truly are as a people and that they were rescued from this ignorance by W. D. Fard.

7 Beynon, "The Voodoo Cult among Negro Migrants in Detroit," 896. Louis A. DeCaro Jr. writes that when Christian clergy baffled Fard with their questions, he still was able to hold the respect of his followers with claims of supernatural powers and knowledge (see *On the Side of My People: A Religious Life of Malcolm X* [New York: New York University Press, 1996], 24).

8 Beynon, "The Voodoo Cult among Negro Migrants in Detroit," 896.

9 Martha F. Lee mentions two contradictory stories of Fard's origin: "To Elijah Muhammad . . . [Fard] declared himself a member of the royal dynasty of the Hashemide Sheriffs of Mecca, while to Elijah's wife Clara, he apparently stated he was a member of the tribe of Koreish" (the prophet Mohammad's tribe). See Martha F. Lee, *The Nation of Islam, An American Millenarian Movement* (Lewiston, N.Y.: Edwin Mellen Press, 1988), 31.

10 Quoted in Arthur J. Magida, *Prophet of Rage* (New York: HarperCollins, 1996), 50.

11 Beynon, "The Voodoo Cult among Negro Migrants in Detroit," 905.

12 Beynon mentions that "Sister Carrie Mohammed and certain others claim that the prophet graduated from the University of Southern California in Los Angeles" ("The Voodoo Cult among Negro Migrants in Detroit," 897).

13 Mattias Gardell, *In the Name of Elijah Muhammad: Louis Farrakhan and the Nation of Islam* (Durham, N.C.: Duke University Press, 1996), 357 n. 39.

14 Interview with Elijah Muhammad in Hatim A. Sahib, *The Nation of Islam* (master's thesis, University of Chicago, 1951), 94; cited in Lee, *The Nation of Islam*, 31.

15 Beynon, "The Voodoo Cult among Negro Migrants in Detroit," 901.

16 DeCaro, *On the Side of My People*, 23.

17 Gardell, *In the Name of Elijah Muhammad*, 51.

18 Beynon, "The Voodoo Cult among Negro Migrants in Detroit," 901.

19 Ibid., 903.

20 Elijah Muhammad, *Message to the Blackman in America* (Chicago: Muhammad's Temple No. 2, 1965), 110.

21 Clifton E. Marsh, *From Black Muslims to Muslims: The Resurrection, Transformation, and Change of the Lost-Found Nation of Islam in America, 1930–1995*, 2d ed. (Lanham, Md.: Scarecrow Press, 1996), 93.

22 Muhammad, *Message to the Blackman in America*, 110–11.

23 Beynon, "The Voodoo Cult among Negro Migrants in Detroit," 898.

24 Magida, *Prophet of Rage*, 49–50.

25 As noted at the beginning of this chapter, Baptist preacher Frank Norris influenced Fard. According to Louis A. DeCaro Jr., Norris was dispensationalist

in theology. Consequently his dispensationalist views of eschatology played a large part in Fard's eschatology. See DeCaro's *Malcolm and the Cross: The Nation of Islam, Malcolm X, and Christianity* (New York: New York University Press, 1998), 16–18.

26 William A. Maesen, "Watchtower Influences on Black Muslim Eschatology: An Exploratory Story," *Journal for the Scientific Study of Religion* (winter 1970): 324. Some of the stock arguments by NOI leaders reflect this influence. They claim that Jesus never claimed to be God, that Jesus never claimed to be equal to God, and that the Christian Trinity has three gods.

27 Master Fard Muhammad, *Lesson #1* (n.d.), quoted in Gardell, *In the Name of Elijah Muhammad*, 56.

28 Gardell, *In the Name of Elijah Muhammad*, 56.

29 Muhammad, *Message to the Blackman in America*, 126–27.

30 Marsh, *From Black Muslims to Muslims*, 38.

31 Beynon, "The Voodoo Cult among Negro Migrants in Detroit," 898.

32 DeCaro, *On the Side of My People*, 24.

33 Magida, *Prophet of Rage*, 40.

34 Beynon, "The Voodoo Cult among Negro Migrants in Detroit," 897.

35 Ibid.

36 Quoted in Marsh, *From Black Muslims to Muslims*, 39. Marsh's source for the quote is the newspaper *Muhammad Speaks,* special issue, April 1972.

37 Lee, *The Nation of Islam*, 33.

38 Ibid.

39 Ibid.

40 Claude Andrew Clegg III, *An Original Man: The Life and Times of Elijah Muhammad* (New York: St. Martin's Press, 1997), 34.

41 Ibid.

42 DeCaro, *Malcolm and the Cross*, 15. DeCaro quotes from Hatim A. Sahib, "The Nation of Islam" (master's thesis, University of Chicago, 1951), 70.

43 DeCaro, *Malcolm and the Cross*, 15. DeCaro mentions that Sahib, a traditional Muslim, scathes Fard for denying Islam's doctrine of the virgin birth of Jesus. Hatim states, "[The Qur'an] considers such accusing individuals as being atheists and non-Moslems and states that they will be punished in the after life by being put in Jehenna [hades]" (cited in *Malcolm and the Cross*, 241 n. 10).

44 I do not mean to suggest that Islam and the Qur'an affirm the biblical doctrine of the virgin birth. Though affirming that Jesus was born of a virgin, it denies other central doctrines of the person of Christ, such as Christ's deity. This makes its virgin birth unbiblical, because the incarnation (marking Jesus as the God-man) is directly tied to the virgin birth. For further information, see Steven Tsoukalas, *Knowing Christ in the Challenge of Heresy: A Christology of the Cults, a Christology of the Bible* (Lanham, Md.: University Press of America, 1999), 174. Along these lines, DeCaro rightly notes that Christianity's virgin birth is an incarnational miracle, while Islam's is a creational miracle (*Malcolm and the Cross*, 15).

45 DeCaro, *Malcolm and the Cross,* 15.

46 Gardell, *In the Name of Elijah Muhammad,* 54. See also C. Eric Lincoln, *The Black Muslims in America* (Grand Rapids: Eerdmans, 1994), 15.

47 Beynon, "The Voodoo Cult among Negro Migrants in Detroit," 901.

48 Ibid.

49 Ibid.

50 Ibid.

51 Elijah Karriem later was named Elijah Muhammad.

52 Beynon, "The Voodoo Cult among Negro Migrants in Detroit," 901.

53 Ibid., 902. Here Beynon quotes Mrs. William McCoy, named Rosa Karriem.

54 Beynon, "The Voodoo Cult among Negro Migrants in Detroit," 899.

55 Ibid.

56 Ibid., 895.

57 Ibid., 901.

58 Beynon states that extramarital relations were forbidden, "except with ministers of Islam" ("The Voodoo Cult among Negro Migrants in Detroit," 902).

59 Keeping themselves and their homes clean would show that they had rid themselves of the marks of slavery (see Beynon, "The Voodoo Cult among Negro Migrants in Detroit," 902).

60 Ibid., 901.

61 Marsh, *From Black Muslims to Muslims,* 37.

62 Beynon, "The Voodoo Cult among Negro Migrants in Detroit," 902. See also Lincoln, *Black Muslims in America,* 14.

63 Beynon, "The Voodoo Cult among Negro Migrants in Detroit," 902.

64 Lincoln, *Black Muslims in America,* 14, and Beynon, "The Voodoo Cult among Negro Migrants in Detroit," 902.

65 See chapter 2 of this book under the subheading "Fard a Fraud."

66 Clegg, *An Original Man,* 28.

67 Minister Louis Farrakhan, "After the Million Man March, Now What? Guidance and Instruction to the Year 2000," *The Final Call,* March 20, 1996, 20.

CHAPTER FOUR: THE RISE OF ELIJAH MUHAMMAD

1 Middleton Pool, according to the 1850 census, owned twenty-two slaves. At one point the Poole family changed their name from Pool to Poole to distinguish themselves from the white Pools. See Claude Andrew Clegg III, *An Original Man: The Life and Times of Elijah Muhammad* (New York: St. Martin's Press, 1997), 4, 291 n. 9.

2 Ibid., vii, 3–4.

3 Louis A. DeCaro Jr., *Malcolm and the Cross: The Nation of Islam, Malcolm X, and Christianity* (New York: New York University Press, 1998), 23.

4 Elijah Muhammad, *Message to the Blackman in America* (Chicago: Muhammad's Temple No. 2, 1965), xiii.

5 Clegg, *An Original Man,* 9.

6 DeCaro, *Malcolm and the Cross,* 23–24.

7 Clegg, *An Original Man,* 8.

8 Ibid.

9 Ibid.

10 Ibid., 10.

11 DeCaro, *Malcolm and the Cross,* 25.

12 Ibid.

13 Abass Rassoull, *The Theology of Time: By the Honorable Elijah Muhammad, the Messenger of Allah* (Hampton, Va.: UBUS Communications Systems, 1992), 227.

14 Clegg, *An Original Man,* 10–11.

15 Ibid., 12.

16 Ibid.

17 Ibid., 13.

18 Mattias Gardell, *In the Name of Elijah Muhammad: Louis Farrakhan and the Nation of Islam* (Durham, N.C.: Duke University Press, 1996), 47–48.

19 Ibid., 48.

20 Clegg, *An Original Man,* 16.

21 Ibid.

22 Ibid., 17. Elijah's grandson, Wali Farad Muhammad, recalls this time in his grandfather's life: "At that time, him not having a religion, he did a lot of drinking" (Steven Barboza, *American Jihad: Islam after Malcolm X* [New York: Doubleday, 1993], 272).

23 Clegg, *An Original Man,* 294 n. 8.

24 Gardell, *In the Name of Elijah Muhammad,* 49.

25 Ibid.

26 For a Christian theological critique of the doctrines of Freemasonry, see Steven Tsoukalas, *Masonic Rites and Wrongs: An Examination of Freemasonry* (Phillipsburg, N.J.: Presbyterian and Reformed Publishing, 1995).

27 Clegg, *An Original Man,* 71.

28 Elijah Muhammad (Poole) admits he joined the Masonic Lodge. See Rassoul, *The Theology of Time,* 282.

29 DeCaro, *Malcolm and the Cross,* 27.

30 Clegg, *An Original Man,* 17.

31 Ibid.

32 Ibid., 17–18.

33 Ibid., 18.

34 Clegg, *An Original Man,* 21.

35 Gardell, *In the Name of Elijah Muhammad,* 50. According to Gardell, this account comes from Muhammad University of Islam, "History," Year Book no. 2, 1973, 24ff. According to Clifton E. Marsh, the account of the exchange comes from a special issue of the newspaper *Muhammad Speaks,* April 1972 (see Clifton E. Marsh, *From Black Muslims to Muslims: The Resurrection, Transformation, and Change of the Lost-Found Nation of Islam in America, 1930–1995,* 2d

ed. [Lanham, Md.: Scarecrow Press, 1996], 48 n. 10). Arthur J. Magida lists as a reference *History of the Nation of Islam,* as discussed by Elijah Muhammad (Cleveland: Secretarius Publication, 1993), 2. See Arthur J. Magida, *Prophet of Rage: A Life of Louis Farrakhan and His Nation* (New York: HarperCollins, 1996), 217 n. 51.

36 DeCaro, *Malcolm and the Cross,* 29.

37 Clegg, *An Original Man,* 22.

38 Muhammad, *Message to the Blackman in America,* 16, 17.

39 DeCaro, *Malcolm and the Cross,* 29.

40 "Mahdi" in Islam does not refer to one who is God in the flesh. The mahdi is a man who is divinely guided by Allah (see DeCaro, *Malcolm and the Cross,* 30). Elijah at that time was not aware of Islamic doctrine and therefore did not pick up on the Fard-Allah contradiction. But he was aware of Christian doctrine, which views Christ as both God and man. With his unawareness of traditional Islam's tenets, coupled with his knowledge of Christianity, Elijah proclaimed Fard as God in the flesh.

41 Clegg, *An Original Man,* 22, 23.

42 Ibid., 23.

43 DeCaro, *Malcolm and the Cross,* 32.

44 Clegg, *An Original Man,* 23.

45 Ibid., 26–27.

46 Muhammad, *Message to the Blackman in America,* 179.

47 Clegg, *An Original Man,* 23.

48 Clegg states that some in the NOI did not take kindly to Elijah's deification of Fard. Fard then cautioned Elijah to "give them a little milk. . . . You cannot give babies meat!" Fard later said, "When I am gone . . . then you can say whatever you want about me" (*An Original Man,* 26, 296 n. 29).

49 Clegg, *An Original Man,* 25. Clegg here quotes from Hatim A. Sahib, *Nation of Islam* (master's thesis, University of Chicago, 1951), 96.

50 DeCaro, *Malcolm and the Cross,* 35.

51 Ibid., 33.

52 Clegg, *An Original Man,* 29.

53 See chapter 2 in this book under the subheading "Fard a Fraud."

54 Clegg, *An Original Man,* 33.

55 Ibid., 33.

56 Muhammad, *Message to the Blackman in America,* 179.

57 Gardell, *In the Name of Elijah Muhammad,* 58.

58 Not all blacks were supportive of the NOI. Black leaders from other organizations saw Fard as a cult leader who was dangerous to the well-being of society. They encouraged the Detroit police to keep pressure on the movement (see Erdmann Doane Beynon, "The Voodoo Cult among Negro Migrants in Detroit," *American Journal of Sociology* 43 [May 1938]: 903–4).

59 Barboza, *American Jihad,* 269. In 1935 Kallatt was murdered (Gardell, *In the Name of Elijah Muhammad,* 358 n. 69).

60 Beynon, "The Voodoo Cult among Negro Migrants in Detroit," 906.

61 Rassoull, *The Theology of Time*, 84.

CHAPTER FIVE: ELIJAH MUHAMMAD– STRUGGLES AND VICTORIES

1 Claude Andrew Clegg III, *An Original Man: The Life and Times of Elijah Muhammad* (New York: St. Martin's Press, 1997), 36.

2 Ibid., 36–37.

3 Elijah Muhammad, *Message to the Blackman in America* (Chicago: Muhammad's Temple No. 2, 1965), 212–13. Muhammad states that they refused to let their children take their first courses in public schools. Young people in their upper teens could take public school classes, "but let us shape our children first" (213).

4 August 9, 1957, FBI file.

5 See chapter 2 of this book under the subtitle "Fard a Fraud."

6 Muhammad, *Message to the Blackman in America*, 213.

7 August 9, 1957, FBI file.

8 Clegg, *An Original Man*, 37.

9 Muhammad, *Message to the Blackman in America*, 213.

10 Steven Barboza, *American Jihad: Islam after Malcolm X* (New York: Doubleday, 1993), 80.

11 Clegg, *An Original Man*, 79.

12 Erdmann Doane Beynon, "The Voodoo Cult among Negro Migrants in Detroit," *American Journal of Sociology* 43 (May 1938): 907.

13 Clegg, *An Original Man*, 79.

14 Louis A. DeCaro Jr., *Malcolm and the Cross: The Nation of Islam, Malcolm X, and Christianity* (New York: New York University Press, 1998), 36.

15 Clegg, *An Original Man*, 80. Hatim A. Sahib puts the number at 150 (see DeCaro, *Malcolm and the Cross*, 38).

16 DeCaro, *Malcolm and the Cross*, 38.

17 Clegg, *An Original Man*, 80.

18 Elijah Muhammad claims that at forty-four years old he was not eligible for the draft (see *Message to the Blackman in America*, 179). Clegg, however, cites the Selective Training and Service Act of 1940, which calls for induction of men between the ages of eighteen and forty-five. According to Clegg, Elijah Muhammad began a fast in order to be too thin to fight (see *An Original Man*, 82).

19 Clegg, *An Original Man*, 84.

20 DeCaro, *Malcolm and the Cross*, 36–37.

21 Barboza, *American Jihad*, 80.

22 Louis A. DeCaro Jr. *On the Side of My People: A Religious Life of Malcolm X* (New York: New York University Press, 1996), 26.

23 "In September 1942, the FBI arrested eighty-five African Americans from three organizations, the Peace Movement of Ethiopia, the Brotherhood of

Liberty for Black People of America, and the Nation of Islam. The vast majority, sixty-five defendants, were [NOI] Muslims." See Mattias Gardell, *In the Name of Elijah Muhammad: Louis Farrakhan and the Nation of Islam* (Durham, N.C.: Duke University Press, 1996), 70.

24 Clegg, *An Original Man*, 85.

25 Ibid., 86.

26 DeCaro, *Malcolm and the Cross*, 37; Clegg, *An Original Man*, 89.

27 DeCaro, *Malcolm and the Cross*, 37.

28 In 1932 a Japanese propagandist named Satokata Takahashi capitalized on the NOI's view of Asiatics and tried to convince them that Imperial Japan was the champion of all races. The FBI was aware of this, and the media were as well. *Time* (October 5, 1942) carried an article titled "Takahashi's Blacks." For more information, see Clegg, *An Original Man*, 29, 89, 307 n. 5.

29 See Abass Rassoull, *The Theology of Time: By the Honorable Elijah Muhammad, the Messenger of Allah* (Hampton, Va.: UBUS Communications Systems, 1992), 509–14.

30 Clegg, *An Original Man*, 89.

31 Rassoull, *The Theology of Time*, 18.

32 Clegg, *An Original Man*, 95.

33 Ibid.

34 Rassoull, *The Theology of Time*, 18.

35 Clegg, *An Original Man*, 99.

36 Ibid., 101.

37 Ibid., 111, 113.

38 Appendix, page 50A, on Elijah Muhammad, FBI file.

39 Gardell, *In the Name of Elijah Muhammad*, 72–73.

40 Clegg, *An Original Man*, 110, 114–15.

41 The *Los Angeles Herald-Dispatch,* February 13, 1960, quoted in C. Eric Lincoln, *The Black Muslims in America* (Grand Rapids: Eerdmans., 1994), 125–26.

42 Clegg, *An Original Man*, 131–32.

43 Cyril Glassé, *The Concise Encyclopedia of Islam* (New York: HarperCollins, 1989), 313.

44 DeCaro, *Malcolm and the Cross*, 56–57; Glassé, *The Concise Encyclopedia of Islam*, 313.

45 Rassoull, *The Theology of Time*, 78.

46 Clegg, *An Original Man*, 136–44.

47 Ibid., 141–42.

48 Louis E. Lomax, *When the Word Is Given* (1979; Westport, Conn.: Greenwood Press, 1963), 60.

49 Lincoln, *Black Muslims in America*, 223.

50 Ibid., 227.

51 Lincoln, *Black Muslims in America*, 227; DeCaro, *Malcolm and the Cross*, 56–57.

52 Clegg, *An Original Man*, 119.

53 Rassoull, *The Theology of Time*, 338.

54 Gardell, *In the Name of Elijah Muhammad*, 74. Gardell lists FBI file 105–24822–[?], 4/26/62 as the source.

55 FBI file on Elijah Muhammad, 8/17/64.

56 Gardell, *In the Name of Elijah Muhammad*, 76.

57 Bruce Perry, ed., *Malcolm X: The Last Speeches* (New York: Pathfinder Press, 1989), 121–22. For comment on this thesis, see Joe Wood, ed., *Malcolm X: In Our Own Image* (New York: St. Martin's Press, 1992), 77–78.

58 In the Old Testament it was an aspect of tribal society to have multiple wives. In part this gave women a place in the community. The same could be said of Islam. Elijah Muhammad's cultural situation was quite different from the situation in the Old Testament.

59 Malcolm X, with Alex Haley, *The Autobiography of Malcolm X* (1965; New York: Ballantine, 1973), 299. Quoted in Gardell, *In the Name of Elijah Muhammad*, 76.

60 FBI file 100–448006–[?]; Chicago FBI file 100–35635–Sub B, 4/22/68. Quoted in Gardell, *In the Name of Elijah Muhammad*, 76.

61 Clayborne Carson, *Malcolm X: The FBI File* (New York: Carroll & Graf, 1991), 425.

62 Wood, *Malcolm X*, 132.

63 Ibid.

64 File dated 8/17/64.

65 Clegg, *An Original Man*, 129–30.

66 Perry, *Malcolm X*, 122–23.

67 Ibid., 124.

68 Clegg, *An Original Man*, 154.

69 In 1959 the then Cassius Clay came into contact with the NOI and later attended NOI meetings. In 1964 he defeated Sonny Liston to win the heavyweight boxing championship. Days later Elijah Muhammad announced during a radio broadcast his hope that Clay would accept the name Muhammad Ali. Clay did. Ali, however, would later come to reject certain core teachings of the NOI after Elijah Muhammad's death in 1975, opting instead for the more orthodox Islamic teachings of Elijah's son Wallace. Ali is quoted as saying, "I don't believe in Mr. Yacub and the spaceship anymore. Hearts and souls have no color. I know that too" (see Thomas Hauser, *Muhammad Ali: His Life and Times* [New York: Simon & Schuster, 1991], 102, 294, 97).

70 Clegg, *An Original Man*, 270.

71 Ibid., 271.

72 Ibid., 272.

CHAPTER SIX: MALCOLM AND LOUIS: GROOMED FOR THE TASK

1 Michael Eric Dyson, *Making Malcolm: The Myth and Meaning of Malcolm X* (New York: Oxford University Press, 1995), 5.

2 Ibid., 4.

3 C. Eric Lincoln says that the Little household had eleven children. See C. Eric Lincoln, *The Black Muslims in America* (Grand Rapids: Eerdmans, 1994), 188.

Other researchers fix the number of children at seven. Lincoln counts the three children that Earl Little fathered before marrying Louise.

4 Dyson, *Making Malcolm*, 4. Lincoln says the house was burned down by the Klan (*Black Muslims in America*, 189). It is disputed whether or not the Klan drove the Little family out of Nebraska. Another account has Mrs. Little's sister-in-law, Rose, stating that Malcolm's father impersonated her husband and stole clothing from a department store, leaving her husband to deal with authorities and pay the bill (see Joe Wood, ed., *Malcolm X: In Our Own Image* [New York: St. Martin's Press, 1992], 127). Perhaps this was the reason the Littles moved to Michigan. Additionally, it is disputed whether or not the Little home was burned down by whites (see ibid., 129).

5 Wood, *Malcolm X*, 128.

6 Dyson, *Making Malcolm*, 5.

7 Clayborne Carson, *Malcolm X: The FBI File* (New York: Carroll & Graf, 1991), 58.

8 Dyson, *Making Malcolm*, 5.

9 Ibid., 6.

10 Lincoln, *Black Muslims in America*, 190.

11 Louis A. DeCaro Jr., *On the Side of My People: A Religious Life of Malcolm X* (New York: New York University Press, 1996), 75–76.

12 Ibid., 83.

13 Ibid., 84.

14 Ibid., 36.

15 Claude Andrew Clegg III, *An Original Man: The Life and Times of Elijah Muhammad* (New York: St. Martin's Press, 1997), 107.

16 Carson, *Malcolm X*, 60–61.

17 Ibid., 100–101.

18 DeCaro, *On the Side of My People*, 97–98.

19 Ibid., 108–9.

20 Clegg, *An Original Man*, 124.

21 Louis Farrakhan states this was the reason Malcolm did not go to Mecca at this time (see Steven Barboza, *American Jihad: Islam after Malcolm X* [New York: Doubleday, 1993], 149).

22 Clegg, *An Original Man*, 126.

23 Ibid., 190–91.

24 DeCaro, *On the Side of My People*, 159–60. DeCaro notes that Malcolm did invoke the authority of Elijah Muhammad on other occasions during the show (160). This does not change the fact, however, that Malcolm went beyond his leader's authority in this particular exchange.

25 Clegg, *An Original Man*, 192.

26 Bruce Perry, ed., *Malcolm X: The Last Speeches* (New York: Pathfinder Press, 1989), 121.

27 DeCaro, *On the Side of My People*, 186.

28 Quoted in Lincoln, *Black Muslims in America*, 191.

29 Carson, *Malcolm X*, 71.

30 Ibid., 72.

31 Ibid., 71.

32 Lincoln, *Black Muslims in America*, 191.

33 DeCaro, *On the Side of My People*, 197.

34 Carson, *Malcolm X*, 74.

35 See Cyril Glassé, *Concise Encyclopedia of Islam* (New York: HarperCollins, 1989), 313–16.

36 Perry, *Malcolm X*, 115–16.

37 Ibid., 134–35.

38 Ibid., 131.

39 Ibid., 136–37.

40 Ibid, 137.

41 Clegg, *An Original Man*, 229.

42 Talmadge Hayer admitted in 1977 that he was a member of the NOI when he murdered Malcolm X. Hayer, now Mujahid Halim, said that Thomas and Norman were innocent, but he named four members of Newark Mosque No. 25 as responsible for the murder. See Mattias Gardell, *In the Name of Elijah Muhammad: Louis Farrakhan and the Nation of Islam* (Durham, N.C.: Duke University Press, 1996), 81.

43 Clegg, *An Original Man*, 232.

44 Arthur J. Magida, *Prophet of Rage: A Life of Louis Farrakhan and His Nation* (New York: HarperCollins, 1996), 10.

45 Ibid., 9.

46 Barboza, *American Jihad*, 148–49; interview with Louis Farrakhan.

47 Magida, *Prophet of Rage*, 31. Magida lists Sterling X Hobbs, "Miracle Man of the Muslims," *Sepia* (May 1975): 28, as the source.

48 Magida, *Prophet of Rage*, 35.

49 Clegg, *An Original Man*, 249.

50 Magida, *Prophet of Rage*, 74–75.

51 Ibid., 76–77.

52 Ibid., 81–82.

53 Ibid., 83.

54 Ibid., 98.

55 Clegg, *An Original Man*, 279–80.

56 Abass Rassoull, *The Theology of Time: By the Honorable Elijah Muhammad, the Messenger of Allah* (Hampton, Va.: UBUS Communications Systems, 1992), xvi.

57 Ibid., xviii.

58 Gardell, *In the Name of Elijah Muhammad*, 123–24.

59 Magida, *Prophet of Rage*, 129–30.

60 Farrakhan often refers to Elijah Muhammad as his spiritual father.

61 Minister Louis Farrakhan, "The Coming of the Messiah," *The Final Call*, January 31, 1996, 21.

62 *The Final Call* often features pictures of Farrakhan meeting with foreign dignitaries. For example, *The Final Call* issues of March 20, 1996, and February 14,

1996, display photographs of Farrakhan talking with Gadhafi and meeting with Nelson Mandela. The March 6, 1996, issue has photographs of Farrakhan being honored in Nigeria and Gambia during his "World Friendship Tour of Africa and the Middle East." The March 20, 1996, issue claims that Farrakhan addressed more than five million people at the seventeenth anniversary of the revolution in Iran. The accompanying picture features Iranian President Rafsanjani seated behind Farrakhan as he speaks to the crowd. In the article (titled "Islamic Nations Welcome Muslims from the West"), author Askia Muhammad claims, "The myth of rejection of the followers of the Honorable Elijah Muhammad by the world's Islamic nations has been relegated to the trash-bin of history by the World Friendship Tour of Minister Louis Farrakhan."

63 I am indebted to Jerry Buckner for the following information and for pointing out the need to include the following brief section on some major splinter groups from the NOI.

64 Rassoull, *The Theology of Time*, lix.

CHAPTER SEVEN: THE BIBLE, QUR'AN, AND THE GOD(S) OF THE NATION OF ISLAM

1 Elijah Muhammad, *The Supreme Wisdom: Solution to the So-Called Negroes' Problem* (Chicago: University of Islam, 1957), 12, 13.

2 Ibid., 13.

3 Ibid. See also Elijah Muhammad, *Message to the Blackman in America* (Chicago: Muhammad's Temple No. 2, 1965), 95.

4 Muhammad, *The Supreme Wisdom*, 20.

5 Muhammad, *Message to the Blackman in America*, 87, 91.

6 Muhammad, *The Supreme Wisdom*, 15.

7 Muhammad, *Message to the Blackman in America*, 88.

8 Elijah Muhammad, *Our Saviour Has Arrived* (Chicago: Muhammad's Temple of Islam No. 2, 1974), 50–51, 176.

9 Ibid., 16.

10 Ibid., 39, 40, 41.

11 Abass Rassoull, *The Theology of Time: By the Honorable Elijah Muhammad, the Messenger of Allah* (Hampton, Va.: UBUS Communications Systems, 1992), 95.

12 Muhammad, *Our Saviour Has Arrived*, 66.

13 Ibid., 63.

14 Ibid., 115; see also 96.

15 Rassoull, *The Theology of Time*, 94.

16 Muhammad, *Our Saviour Has Arrived*, 61.

17 Muhammad, *Message to the Blackman in America*, 9.

18 Muhammad, *Our Saviour Has Arrived*, 67.

19 Ibid.

20 Ibid., 96.

21 Muhammad, *Message to the Blackman in America,* 9.

22 The Ministry Class of Muhammad's Temple No. 7, *Seven Speeches by Minister Louis Farrakhan* (Chicago: WKU and the Final Call, Inc., 1992), 141.

23 Muhammad, *Our Savior Has Arrived,* 119.

24 Muhammad, *Message to the Blackman in America,* 31, and *Our Saviour Has Arrived,* 98.

25 Quoted in C. Eric Lincoln, *The Black Muslims in America* (Grand Rapids: Eerdmans, 1994), 69.

26 Muhammad, *Our Saviour Has Arrived,* 35.

27 Malcolm X may have been alluding to this teaching when he publicly took Elijah Muhammad to task for ordering the bombing of his home where his babies were asleep. Malcolm retaliated with the words, "When you attack sleeping babies, why, you are lower than a god."

28 The Honorable Louis Farrakhan, *How to Give Birth to a God,* four-part videotape series (Chicago: Final Call, Inc.), part 1. Delivered on July 26, 1987, at the Final Call Building in Chicago.

29 Muhammad, *The Supreme Wisdom,* 38.

30 See the next chapter for more details.

31 This is not so for the white race. As we shall see in chapter 9, the white race is a hybrid of the original race. The white race was "grafted" from the originals' lower nature.

32 See Muhammad, *Our Saviour Has Arrived,* 98. On the other hand, Muhammad makes reference to "our God, Who is the Originator of the universe" (ibid., 13). Again, this is confusing, for according to Muhammad's scheme the first god who created himself out of darkness more than seventy-six trillion years ago cannot be Fard.

33 Muhammad, *Our Saviour Has Arrived,* 12, 98.

34 Muhammad, *Message to the Blackman in America,* 242.

35 Muhammad, *Our Saviour Has Arrived,* 125.

36 Minister Louis Farrakhan, "After the Million Man March, Now What? Guidance and Instruction to the Year 2000," *The Final Call,* March 20, 1996, 20.

37 Clifton E. Marsh, *From Black Muslims to Muslims: The Resurrection, Transformation, and Change of the Lost-Found Nation of Islam in America, 1930–1995,* 2d ed. (Lanham, Md.: Scarecrow Press, 1996), 195; from an interview with Abdul Alim Muhammad, national spokesperson for Louis Farrakhan.

38 Muhammad, *Message to the Blackman,* 68.

39 Farrakhan, "After the Million Man March, Now What?" 20.

40 Muhammad, *Our Saviour Has Arrived,* 50.

41 Muhammad, *Message to the Blackman in America,* 10, 20.

42 Ibid., 24–25.

43 Muhammad, *The Supreme Wisdom,* 43.

44 The Ministry Class of Muhammad's Temple No. 7, *Seven Speeches by Minister Louis Farrakhan,* 149–50.

45 Elijah Muhammad, "I Want to Teach You," *The Final Call,* June 20, 2000, 19; reprinted from Muhammad, *Our Savior Has Arrived.*

CHAPTER EIGHT: YAKUB AND THE WHITE RACE

1　Elijah Muhammad, *Message to the Blackman in America* (Chicago: Muhammad's Temple No. 2, 1965), 31.

2　Muhammad elsewhere states that there are twenty-five scientists, the twenty-fifth being a judge of the history writings of the other twenty-four (see Elijah Muhammad, *Our Saviour Has Arrived* [Chicago: Muhammad's Temple of Islam No. 2, 1974], 12).

3　See chapter 7 under the subtitle "Allah in the Beginning."

4　Muhammad, *Message to the Blackman in America,* 110–11.

5　Ibid., 111.

6　Ibid., 111–12.

7　Ibid., 112.

8　Ibid., 113–14.

9　According to the NOI, anyone who is nonwhite is considered black Asiatic. Thus the red, yellow, and brown peoples are blacks.

10　Muhammad, *Message to the Blackman in America,* 114–16.

11　Ibid., 118.

12　The Jehovah's Witnesses influenced W. D. Fard. Fard used to encourage his students to listen to the radio speeches of Judge Joseph Rutherford, at that time the president of the Jehovah's Witnesses. The Witnesses said that 1914 signaled the time of the end of all earthly governments.

13　Muhammad, *Message to the Blackman in America,* 116–17.

14　Ibid., 267.

15　Ibid., 133.

16　Ibid., 119.

17　Ibid., 120–21.

18　Muhammad, *Our Saviour Has Arrived,* 267.

19　Abass Rassoull, *The Theology of Time: By the Honorable Elijah Muhammad, the Messenger of Allah* (Hampton, Va.: UBUS Communications Systems, 1992), 193.

20　Muhammad, *Message to the Blackman in America,* 126.

21　There seems to be a contradiction here in Muhammad's theology. If the devil is the white race and Adam and Eve are the first parents of the devil race, then who is the devil that deceived *them?* The obvious answer would be Yakub, but how can this be if Yakub was an original? Even Muhammad admits this and refrains from calling Yakub a devil (see *Message to the Blackman in America,* 118, 133).

22　Muhammad, *Message to the Blackman in America,* 124. Muhammad at times erroneously refers to it as "Revelations."

23　Ibid., 125–26.

24　Thomas Halpern and David Rosenberg, *The Other Face of Farrakhan: A Hate-Filled Prelude to the Million Man March* (New York: Anti-Defamation League, 1995), 1.

25　Ibid. Farrakhan has also levied some harsh words to Jews in America, calling them "wicked deceivers," "not real Jews," and part of the assembly of "the synagogue of Satan" (Minister Louis Farrakhan, "After the Million Man March,

Now What? Guidance and Instruction to the Year 2000," *The Final Call*, March 20, 1996, 31).

26 Jabril Muhammad, "Judge Not That You Be Not Judged," *The Final Call*, March 6, 1996, 29.

27 The Ministry Class of Muhammad's Temple No. 7, *Seven Speeches by Minister Louis Farrakhan* (Chicago: WKU and the Final Call, Inc., 1992), 70.

28 Ibid., 73.

29 Muhammad, *Message to the Blackman in America*, 69.

30 Muhammad, *Our Saviour Has Arrived*, 50.

31 Ibid., 49–50.

32 Elijah Muhammad, *The Supreme Wisdom: Solution to the So-Called Negroes' Problem* (Chicago: University of Islam, 1957), 13–14.

33 Ibid., 14.

34 Muhammad, *Message to the Blackman in America*, 54, 22. Members also have X after their first names. This signifies that they no longer identify with names given to them by slave masters.

35 Muhammad, *Our Saviour Has Arrived*, 126.

36 Muhammad, *Message to the Blackman in America*, 55.

CHAPTER NINE: ARMAGEDDON: WHO WILL SURVIVE?

1 Elijah Muhammad, *The Supreme Wisdom: Solution to the So-Called Negroes' Problem* (Chicago: University of Islam, 1957), 6, 7, 8.

2 See Louis Farrakhan, "Allah (God) Hates Divorce," *The Final Call*, June 21, 1995, 20–21.

3 Here I must disagree with C. Eric Lincoln (*The Black Muslims in America* [Grand Rapids: Eerdmans, 1994], 76), who says there is no connection with NOI morality to any doctrine of salvation. Lincoln says on the same page that NOI members do not look forward to an afterlife. As we shall see, they do. Here, though, Lincoln is probably referring to the NOI's rejection of what it perceives to be the Christian understanding of the afterlife, complete with resurrection and a changed earth.

4 Elijah Muhammad, *Our Saviour Has Arrived* (Chicago: Muhammad's Temple of Islam No. 2, 1974), 116–17.

5 The Ministry Class of Muhammad's Temple No. 7, *Seven Speeches by Minister Louis Farrakhan* (Chicago: WKU and the Final Call, Inc., 1992), 145.

6 Elijah Muhammad, *Message to the Blackman in America* (Chicago: Muhammad's Temple No. 2, 1965), 60.

7 In order to avoid stumbling blocks in NOI members' walk with Allah, males and females sit in separate sections during meetings.

8 Lincoln, *Black Muslims in America*, 202.

9 The Fruit of Islam serves two basic purposes. It guards NOI officials from the physical attacks of unbelievers and takes part in the discipline process of

strayed members. It is composed of the physically and mentally finest young men in the movement. Captains are appointed to lead sections, which in turn are broken down into squads commanded by lieutenants. The captains report directly to the top. See Lincoln, *Black Muslims in America*, 201–4, for more information.

10 Ibid., 202–3.

11 James Baldwin, quoted from *The Fire Next Door;* back cover of Muhammad's *Message to the Blackman in America.*

12 Back cover of Muhammad's *Message to the Blackman in America.*

13 Sociologically and psychologically this may be looked upon as a reaction to the genealogies of blacks in this country. As noted in chapter 4, Elijah Muhammad's physical ancestry is part white, and his "slave name" comes from the white slave owner Middleton Pool.

14 See chapter 7 under the subtitle "God Is Born Incognito."

15 Muhammad, *Message to the Blackman in America*, 237.

16 Elijah Muhammad, "Days of Allah," *The Final Call*, January 31, 1996, 18; reprinted from Muhammad, *Message to the Blackman in America.*

17 Muhammad, *Message to the Blackman in America*, 290–91, 294.

18 Ibid., 290–91.

19 Ibid., 291. See also Abass Rassoull, *The Theology of Time: By the Honorable Elijah Muhammad, the Messenger of Allah* (Hampton, Va.: UBUS Communications Systems, 1992), 511.

20 See chapter 5 under the subtitle "Elijah Jailed."

21 Muhammad, *Message to the Blackman in America*, 291.

22 Rassoull, *The Theology of Time*, 510–11.

23 Ibid., 511–12.

24 Ibid., 512–13.

25 Ibid., 516–17.

26 Some people have noted the trend in the NOI to enter into the mainstream. For example, *The Final Call* of April 3, 1996, contains an article by Ja A. Jahannes, pastor of Abyssinia Baptist Church of Savannah, Georgia. The church welcomed NOI Minister Prince X Truell to deliver a speech. Truell later said to Jahannes, "I feel at home in your house." Jahannes responded, "You should, it's your house too." Indicative of this trend is the title of the article, "The Need for Muslim-Christian Unity."

27 Sura 2:217 in the Qur'an states, "And if any of you turn back from their faith and die in unbelief, their works will bear no fruit in this life and in the hereafter; they will be companions of the fire and will abide therein."

28 According to NOI author Tynnetta Muhammad, the Shriners, men who have reached the upper levels of Freemasonry, are sworn by oath to assist NOI believers in their cause of liberation "at the very tail end of the Judgment." (Those familiar with the Shriners know that the order is Islamic in nature.) Further, the Shriners know who NOI people are, but NOI people do not know who they are. Elijah Muhammad taught, "we will get acquainted with them at

a particular time." See Tynnetta Muhammad, "Freemasons and the Wisdom of the Nation of Islam," *The Final Call*, August 30, 1995, 27.

29 Muhammad, *Message to the Blackman in America*, 304.

30 Jabril Muhammad, "Judge Not That You Be Not Judged," *The Final Call*, March 6, 1996, 29. Abass Rassoull also claims to have seen Elijah Muhammad on a few occasions after his death. See *Theology of Time*, xvi, xxi.

31 See "Where Is the Honorable Elijah Muhammad?" review of *The Final Call*, June 7, 1995, 36.

32 Clifton E. Marsh, *From Black Muslims to Muslims: The Resurrection, Transformation, and Change of the Lost-Found Nation of Islam in America, 1930–1995*, 2d ed. (Lanham, Md.: Scarecrow Press, 1996), 182; interview with Abdul Alim Muhammad, national spokesperson for Louis Farrakhan.

33 Muhammad, *The Supreme Wisdom*, 26.

34 Muhammad, *Our Saviour Has Arrived*, 118.

35 Muhammad, *Message to the Blackman in America*, 303.

36 Rassoull, *The Theology of Time*, 519. See also Elijah Muhammad, *Message to the Blackman in America*, 304.

37 Muhammad, *Message to the Blackman in America*, 304.

38 Muhammad, *Our Saviour Has Arrived*, 114.

39 Ibid., 2, 117.

40 What does Muhammad say about whites who embrace Islam? They will escape destruction during Armageddon but will not enjoy the "new birth" (a term used to teach that the Asiatic race will continue forever). Even in the hereafter these white Muslims will die off without the blessing of reproduction. Though they are Muslims, they are Muslims by faith and not by nature (their nature, being white, remains evil).

In answering this question, Muhammad is yet again confusing. Chapter 17 of *Our Saviour Has Arrived* is titled "A Few White People Are Muslims by Faith." He then talks of the Islam of the prophet Muhammad of fourteen hundred years ago. He goes on to say that there are white people in Europe who are Muslims. He is right. But are they Fardian Muslims? Perhaps he is here assuming that his Islam is the same as traditional Islam. But in light of other statements Muhammad has made to the effect that one must believe Fard is Allah, it is difficult to imagine how he could state that white Muslims in Europe would survive Armageddon. Further, Muhammad could not be talking of whites who belong to the NOI, for they are nonexistent. Whites are not allowed to attend NOI meetings and are not evangelized.

CHAPTER TEN: A CHRISTIAN ANSWER TO THE NATION OF ISLAM

1 Elijah Muhammad, *Message to the Blackman in America* (Chicago: Muhammad's Temple No. 2, 1965), 94.

2 Ibid., 90.

3 Ibid., 87.

4 See the textual apparatus of the Nestle-Aland *Novum Testamentum Graece,* 26th ed. (Stuttgart: Deutsche Bibelgesellschaft, 1979), 278, 317.

5 This is not to say that God has not directly revealed himself to me. He has, and that was needed in order for me to be saved by him. What I am arguing is this: I have examined the reliability, historicity, and authority of the Bible and have found it to be true. To be sure, this came after my conversion experience (enabling me to see things from God's perspective) but the evidence has shown the initial experience to be true. My argument with Muhammad, however, does not take place solely on this ground, as is evidenced above.

6 Muhammad, *Our Saviour Has Arrived* (Chicago: Muhammad's Temple of Islam No. 2, 1974), 50.

7 Ibid.

8 Ibid., 176.

9 See the following for evidence: F. F. Bruce, *The New Testament Documents: Are They Reliable?* (reprint ed.; Grand Rapids: Eerdmans, 1984); F. F. Bruce, *History of the Bible in English* (New York: Oxford University Press, 1978); Josh McDowell, *Evidence That Demands a Verdict* (San Bernardino, Calif.: Here's Life Publishers, 1979); Norman L. Geisler and William E. Nix, *A General Introduction to the Bible* (Chicago: Moody Press, 1986); Benjamin B. Warfield, *The Inspiration and Authority of the Bible* (Phillipsburg, N.J.: Presbyterian and Reformed Publishing Co., 1948).

10 The Greek imperfect tense, third person for the verb "to be" is translated "[he] was." This signals continuous action in the past, thus the eternal existence of "the Word" (preincarnate Jesus).

11 For the created order, John does not use the verb "to be." Rather, he uses "to become" or "to come into being."

12 See Raymond E. Brown, *The Gospel According to John,* 2 vols. (New York: Doubleday, 1966), 1:360.

13 See C. F. Keil and F. Delitzsch, *Commentary on the Old Testament,* 10 vols. (reprint ed.; Grand Rapids: Eerdmans, 1983), 7:234–37.

14 Oftentimes God is a synonym for the Father. Not always, though, for Jesus is called God (John 20:28), and the Holy Spirit is equated with God (Acts 5:3–4). For further information, see Steven Tsoukalas, *Knowing Christ in the Challenge of Heresy: A Christology of the Cults, a Christology of the Bible* (Lanham, Md.: University Press of America, 1999).

15 Muhammad, *Message to the Blackman in America,* 27.

16 Muhammad, *Our Saviour Has Arrived,* 67.

17 Philip Schaff, ed., *The Creeds of Christendom,* 3 vols. (reprint ed.; Grand Rapids: Baker, 1985), 3:677.

18 See Tsoukalas, *Knowing Christ in the Challenge of Heresy,* 221–24, for a concise exposition of the doctrine of the Trinity.

19 See the Nestle-Aland *Novum Testamentum Graece,* 275.

20 The Septuagint is the Greek translation of the Hebrew Old Testament. It was translated around 250 to 150 B.C. The Septuagint of these two passages has the same phrase as John 8:24 ("that I am").

21 Elijah Muhammad, *The Supreme Wisdom: Solution to the So-Called Negroes' Problem* (Chicago: University of Islam, 1957), 43.

22 Here the NOI aligns with orthodox Islam. Islam also denies that Jesus is the Son of God (see Surah 4:171).

23 Muhammad, *The Supreme Wisdom*, 16.

24 See chapter 3 under the subtitle "The Shaping of a Theology."

25 The Ministry Class of Muhammad's Temple No. 7, *Seven Speeches by Minister Louis Farrakhan* (Chicago: WKU and the Final Call, Inc., 1992), 142.

26 Muhammad, *Message to the Blackman in America*, 27.

27 The phrase "the Word was God" should be taken to mean that the Word (preincarnate Jesus) was eternally God in his essential being. This is the thrust of the qualitative anarthrous predicate "God." In the Greek it appears before the verb (was), thus making it qualitative (speaking to the *nature* of the Word).

28 The Greek *ison* means "to claim for one's self the nature, rank, authority, which belong to God, Jn. V.18." See Joseph Henry Thayer, *A Greek-English Lexicon of the New Testament* (reprint ed.; Grand Rapids: Zondervan, n.d.), 307. See also W. Bauer, W. F. Arndt, and F. W. Gingrich, *A Greek-English Lexicon of the New Testament and Other Early Christian Literature* (Chicago: University of Chicago Press, 1979), 381.

29 Cf. Ps. 34:23 in the Septuagint. Here the psalmist, in reference to Yahweh, uses the same Greek phrase, though the order is reversed (Thomas: "My Lord and my God," and the psalmist: "My God and my Lord"). Leon Morris calls attention to the parallel. See *The Gospel According to John* (Grand Rapids: Eerdmans, 1971), 853 n. 76. Brown does as well (*The Gospel According to John*, 2:1047).

30 Morris also states that "the reference . . . is not to Christ's essential being" (*The Gospel According to John*, 658). See also Brown, *The Gospel According to John*, 2:632, 654–55. Brown links 14:28 to 16:13 ("No messenger is more important than the one who sent him") and connects it to the Jewish concept of "agent/sender." Brown cites P. Borgen, who, though shying away from philosophical speculations, nonetheless says that the sender and the agent share a "likeness of nature" (632).

31 See note 28.

32 See Robert L. Reymond, *Jesus, Divine Messiah: The New Testament Witness* (Phillipsburg, N.J.: Presbyterian and Reformed Publishing Co., 1990), 251–66, especially his exegetically based paraphrase on 264.

33 Muhammad, *Our Savior Has Arrived*, 50.

34 Bauer, Arndt, and Gingrich, *A Greek-English Lexicon of the New Testament and Other Early Christian Literature*, 886–87.

35 For much of the following I thank James Montgomery Boice, in *The Expositor's Bible Commentary*, ed. Frank E. Gaebelein, 12 vols. (Grand Rapids: Zondervan, 1976), 10:468–69.

36 Compare the Genesis account of the description of the garden of Eden and the curses contained therein (Gen. 2 and 3) with Revelation's account of the description of the new Eden and the reversal of the curses (Rev. 21 and 22).

37 See Jerry Buckner, "Witnessing to the Nation of Islam," *Christian Research Journal* (January-March 1998): 42.

38 Be ready for your NOI contact to attack the trustworthiness of the Bible at this point. Refer to the information already provided in this chapter for refutation.

APPENDIX: IS LOUIS FARRAKHAN CHANGING?

1 *Muslim Journal* 25.19 (February 18, 2000): 1.

2 Ibid., 14.

3 Ibid.

4 Ibid.

5 Jabril Muhammad, "The Good and Bad Roots of Critics and Questions," *The Final Call*, February 1, 2000, 26. Here Jabril Muhammad quotes from an interview in *The Atlanta Journal Constitution*, November 10, 1999.

6 Richard Muhammad, "Farrakhan Stresses Prayer, Family as Foundations of the New Country," *The Final Call*, January 4, 2000, 3.

7 Message delivered by Louis Farrakhan as an opening statement for a press conference on December 22, 1999, reproduced in *The Final Call*, January 4, 2000, 21. This perhaps is the press conference to which *Muslim Journal* was referring.

8 Page 20.

9 "Farrakhan Meets the Press." Cited February 24, 2001. Online: http://www.finalcall.com/national/mlf-mtp5-13-97.html.

10 Elijah Muhammad, "Four Great Judgements of America," *The Final Call*, January 9, 2001, 19; reprinted from Muhammad, *The Fall of America*.

11 Elijah Muhammad, "Time," *The Final Call*, January 2, 2001, 19.

12 Elijah Muhammad, "America Hastens Her Own Doom," *The Final Call*, December 12, 2000, 19; reprinted from Muhammad, *The Fall of America*.

13 Muhammad, "Four Great Judgements of America," 19.

14 Elijah Muhammad, "The Food and Its Eater," *The Final Call*, January 9, 2001, 28.

15 Louis Farrakhan, "The Black Man Must Turn Inward," *The Final Call*, February 1, 2000, 21.

Bibliography

Ali, A. Yusuf. *The Holy Quran: Text, Translation and Commentary.* 2 vols. New York: Hafner Publishing Co., 1934.

Ali, Noble Drew. *The Holy Koran of the Moorish Science Temple of America.* 1929.

Alexander, E. Curtis. *Elijah Muhammad on African-American Education.* New York: ECA Associates, 1989.

Anderson, Benedict. *Imagined Communities: Reflections on the Origin and Spread of Nationalism.* New York: Verso, 1990.

Ansari, Zafar I. "Aspects of Black Muslim Theology." *Studia Islamica* 53 (1981): 137–76.

———. "W. D. Muhammad: The Making of a 'Black Muslim' Leader (1933–1961)." *American Journal of Islamic Social Sciences* 2.2 (December 1985): 245–62.

Atyeo, Don, and Felix Dennis. *The Holy Warrior: Muhammad Ali.* New York: Simon and Schuster, 1975.

Austin, Allan D. *African Muslims in Antebellum America.* New York and London: Garland, 1984.

Baigent, Michael, and Richard Leigh. *The Temple and the Lodge.* New York: Arcade Publishing, 1989.

Baldwin, James. *The Fire Next Time.* New York: Dell, 1962.

Barboza, Steven. *American Jihad: Islam after Malcolm X.* New York: Doubleday, 1993.

Barnette, Aubrey. "The Black Muslims Are a Fraud." *Saturday Evening Post,* February 27, 1965, 23–29.

Beynon, Erdmann Doane. "The Voodoo Cult among Negro Migrants in Detroit." *American Journal of Sociology* 43 (May 1938): 894–907.

Bishop, Jim. *The Days of Martin Luther King Jr.: A Biography.* New York: Barnes & Noble, 1994 [1971].

" 'Black Supremacy' Cult in U.S.—How Much of a Threat?" *U.S. News & World Report,* November 9, 1959, 112.

Breitman, George. *The Last Year of Malcolm X: The Evolution of a Revolutionary.* New York: Pathfinder Press, 1984.

Brotz, Howard. *The Black Jews of Harlem.* London: Macmillan, 1964.

Burkett, Randall K. *Garveyism as a Religious Movement: The Institutionalization of a Black Civil Religion.* Metuchen, N.J.: Scarecrow Press, 1978.

———. "Religious Ethos of the UNIA." In *African American Religious Studies,* edited by G. S. Wilmore. Durham, N.C.: Duke University Press, 1989.

Carson, Clayborne. *Malcolm X: The FBI File.* New York: Carroll & Graf, 1991.

Cazembe, Lasana D. "Racist Views Travel through the 'Stargate.' " *The Final Call,* January 11, 1995, 29.

Chalmers, David M. *Hooded Americanism: The History of the Ku Klux Klan.* Durham, N.C.: Duke University Press, 1981.

Chism, Tina X. "Tuskegee Archives Document Over 5,000 Hangings." *The Final Call,* February 8, 1995, 10.

Clarke, John Henrik, ed. *Marcus Garvey and the Vision of Africa.* New York: Vintage, 1974.

Cleage, Albert B., Jr. *The Black Messiah.* Kansas City, Kans.: Sheed & Ward, 1968.

Clegg, Claude Andrew, III. *An Original Man: The Life and Times of Elijah Muhammad.* New York: St. Martin's Press, 1997.

Coil, Henry Wilson. *Coil's Masonic Encyclopedia.* New York: Macoy Publishing and Masonic Supply Co., 1961.

Cowans, Russell J. "Death List Found in Voodoo Cult." *Chicago Defender,* December 3, 1932.

Cronon, E. David. *Black Moses: The Story of Marcus Garvey.* Madison: University of Wisconsin Press, 1969.

Curry, Lamont X. "Native Americans Reveal Islamic Roots." *The Final Call,* November 16, 1994, 6.

Cushmeer, Bernard. *This Is the One: Messenger Elijah Muhammad; We Need Not Look for Another.* Phoenix: Truth Publications, 1971.

DeCaro, Louis A., Jr. *Malcolm and the Cross: The Nation of Islam, Malcolm X, and Christianity.* New York: New York University Press, 1998.

————. *On the Side of My People: A Religious Life of Malcolm X*. New York: New York University Press, 1996.

Dowling, Levi H. *The Aquarian Gospel of Jesus the Christ*. Marina del Rey, Calif.: Devorss, 1987 [1907].

Draper, Theodore. *The Rediscovery of Black Nationalism*. New York: Viking, 1969.

D'Souza, Dinesh. *The End of Racism: Principles for a Multiracial Society*. New York: The Free Press, 1995.

Dumenil, Lynn. *Freemasonry and American Culture, 1880–1930*. Princeton, N.J.: Princeton University Press, 1984.

Du Bois, W. E. B. *Writings*. New York: The Library of America, 1996.

Dyson, Michael Eric. *Making Malcolm: The Myth and Meaning of Malcolm X*. New York: Oxford University Press, 1995.

El-Amin, Mustafa. *The Religion of Islam and the Nation of Islam: What Is the Difference?* Newark, N.J.: El-Amin Productions, 1991.

Essien-Udom, E. U. *Black Nationalism: The Search for an Identity in America*. Chicago: University of Chicago Press, 1963.

Evanzz, Karl. *The Judas Factor: The Plot to Kill Malcolm X*. New York: Thunder's Mouth Press, 1992.

Farrakhan, Louis. "After the Million Man March, Now What? Guidance and Instruction to the Year 2000." *The Final Call*, March 20, 1996, 20–21, 30–31.

————. "All Opposition to Truth (Islam) Will Be Destroyed." *The Final Call*, October 19, 1994, 20–21, 30.

————. "Allah (God) Hates Divorce." *The Final Call*, June 21, 1995, 20–21.

————. "Allah (God) Hates Divorce: Part Two." *The Final Call*, July 5, 1995, 20–21.

————. "The Coming of the Messiah." *The Final Call*, January 31, 1996, 20–21.

————. *How to Give Birth to a God*. Four-part videotape series. Chicago: Final Call, Inc., part 1, July 26, 1987.

————. "Jesus Saves." *The Final Call*, March 15, 1995, 20–21.

————. "Jesus Saves: Part Two." *The Final Call*, April 12, 1995, 20–21.

————. "Principles of Religion." *The Final Call*, November 16, 1994, 20–21.

————. "The Sacredness of the Female." *The Final Call*, July 19, 1995, 20–21.

————. *A Torchlight for America.* Chicago: FCN Publishing Co., 1993.

"Farrakhan's Secret." *New York,* November 6, 1995, 24–25.

Fauset, Arthur Huff. *Black Gods of the Metropolis: Negro Religious Cults in the Urban North.* Philadelphia: University of Pennsylvania Press, 1971 [1944].

Friedly, Michael. *Malcolm X: The Assassination.* New York: Carroll & Graf, 1992.

Gardell, Mattias. *In the Name of Elijah Muhammad: Louis Farrakhan and the Nation of Islam.* Durham, N.C.: Duke University Press, 1996.

Garnett, Bernard E. *Invaders from the Black Nation: The "Black Muslims" in 1970.* Nashville: Race Relations Information Center, 1970.

Garvey, Marcus. *Marcus Garvey: Life and Lessons.* Edited by Robert A. Hill and Barbara Bair. Berkeley: University of California Press, 1987.

————. *More Philosophy and Opinions of Marcus Garvey.* Edited by E. U. Essien-Udom and Amy Jacques-Garvey. Totowa, N.J.: Frank Cass, 1977.

————. *Philosophy and Opinions of Marcus Garvey.* Edited by Amy Jacques Garvey. New York: Atheneum, 1986 [1923].

Gellner, Ernest. *Nations and Nationalism.* Oxford: Blackwell, 1983.

Glassé, Cyril. *The Concise Encyclopedia of Islam.* New York: Harper-Collins, 1989.

Goldman, Peter. *The Death and Life of Malcolm X.* Chicago: University of Illinois Press, 1979.

Gould, Robert F. *The History of Freemasonry.* 4 vols. New York: John C. Yorston & Co., n.d.

Haddad, Yvonne Y., ed. *The Muslims of America.* New York: Oxford University Press, 1991.

Halasa, Malu. *Elijah Muhammad.* New York and Philadelphia: Chelsea House Publishers, 1990.

Halpern, Thomas, and David Rosenberg. *The Other Face of Farrakhan: A Hate-Filled Prelude to the Million Man March.* New York: Anti-Defamation League, 1995.

Hardy, Michael, and William Pleasant. *The Honorable Louis Farrakhan: A Minister for Progress.* New York: New Alliance Publications, 1987.

Harrison, Barbara G. *Visions of Glory: A History and a Memory of Jehovah's Witnesses.* New York: Simon & Schuster, 1978.

Hauser, Thomas. *Muhammad Ali: His Life and Times.* New York: Simon & Schuster, 1991.

Hill, Robert A., ed. *The Marcus Garvey and Universal Negro Improvement Association Papers.* Berkeley: University of California Press, 1983.

Hobbs, Sterling X. "Miracle Man of the Muslims." *Sepia,* May 1975, 24–30.

Jahannes, Ja A. "The Need for Muslim-Christian Unity." *The Final Call,* April 3, 1996, 25.

Karenga, Maulana. *Introduction to Black Studies.* Los Angeles: Kawaida Publications, 1987.

Karim, Benjamin. *Remembering Malcolm.* New York: Carroll & Graf, 1992.

Kearney, Reginald. "Japan: Ally in the Struggle Against Racism, 1919–1927." *Contributions in Black Studies* 12 (1994): 117–28.

Khalifah, H. Khalif. *The Legacy of the Honorable Elijah Muhammad.* Newport News, Va.: UBUS Communications Systems, 1998.

Kly, Y. N. *The Black Book: The True Political Philosophy of Malcolm X (El Hajj Malik El Shabazz).* Atlanta: Clarity Press, 1986.

Knight, Fahim A. *In Defense of the Defender: The Most Honorable Elijah Muhammad.* Durham, N.C.: Fahim and Associates, 1994.

Lanternari, Vittorio. *The Religions of the Oppressed.* Chicago: Mentor, 1965.

Lee, Martha F. *The Nation of Islam, An American Millenarian Movement.* Lewiston, N.Y.: Edwin Mellen Press, 1988.

Lefkowitz, Mary. *Not Out of Africa: How Afrocentrism Became an Excuse to Teach Myth as History.* New York: Basic Books, 1997.

Lemann, Nicholas. *The Promised Land: The Great Black Migration and How It Changed America.* London: Papermac, 1992.

Lewis, Bernard. *Race and Slavery in the Middle East.* New York: Oxford University Press, 1990.

Lightfoot, Claude. "Negro Nationalism and the Black Muslims." *Political Affairs* 41.7 (July 1962): 3–20.

Lincoln, C. Eric. *The Black Muslims in America.* Grand Rapids: Eerdmans, 1994.

Litwack, Leon, and August Meier, eds. *Black Leaders of the Nineteenth Century.* Urbana: University of Illinois Press, 1988.

Lomax, Louis E. *When the Word Is Given.* Westport, Conn.: Greenwood Press, 1963.

Long, David E. *The Hajj: A Survey of the Contemporary Makkah Pilgrimage.* Albany: State University of New York Press, 1979.

Lynch, Hollis. *Edward Wilmot Blyden: Pan-Negro Patriot.* London: Oxford University Press, 1967.

Mackey, Albert G. *The History of Freemasonry.* 7 vols. New York: The Masonic History Co., 1906.

McCartney, John T. *Black Power Ideologies.* Philadelphia: Temple University Press, 1992.

Magida, Arthur J. *Prophet of Rage: A Life of Louis Farrakhan and His Nation.* New York: HarperCollins, 1996.

Malcolm X, with Alex Haley. *The Autobiography of Malcolm X.* New York: Grove, 1965.

—————. *The End of White World Supremacy: Four Speeches by Malcolm X.* Edited by Benjamin Goodman. New York: Merlin House, 1971.

Marsh, Clifton E. *From Black Muslims to Muslims: The Resurrection, Transformation, and Change of the Lost-Found Nation of Islam in America, 1930–1995.* 2d ed. Lanham, Md.: Scarecrow Press, 1996.

Melton, J. Gordon, ed. *The Encyclopedia of American Religions.* Detroit: Gale Research, 1989.

—————. *Encyclopedic Handbook of Cults in America.* New York: Garland, 1986.

Ministry Class of Muhammad's Temple No. 7. *Seven Speeches by Minister Louis Farrakhan.* Chicago: WKU and the Final Call, Inc., 1992.

Mitchell, Sara. *Shepherd of Black Sheep: A Commentary on the Life of Malcolm X with an On-the-Scene Account of His Assassination.* Macon, Ga.: Sara Mitchell, 1981.

Morris, Brian. *Anthropological Studies of Religion.* Cambridge: Cambridge University Press, 1987.

Moses, Wilson Jeremiah. *Black Messiahs and Uncle Toms: Social and Literary Manipulations of a Religious Myth.* Rev. ed. University Park: Pennsylvania State University Press, 1982.

—————. *The Golden Age of Black Nationalism, 1850–1925.* New York: Oxford University Press, 1978.

Muhammad, Abdul Akbar. "An Open Letter to the Third Popular Arab & Islamic Conference." *The Final Call,* April 26, 1995, 20–21.

Muhammad, Amin. "The Science of Self." *The Final Call,* January 31, 1996, 37.

Muhammad, Askia. "Islamic Nations Welcome Muslims from the West." *The Final Call,* March 20, 1996, 2, 18, 22.

Muhammad, Donald. "Christian Evangelists Hold All-Male Meeting in D.C." *The Final Call,* June 21, 1995, 36.

Muhammad, Elijah. "America Hastens Her Own Doom." *The Final Call,* February 14, 1996, 18 (reprinted from *The Fall of America*).

———. "Days of Allah." *The Final Call,* January 31, 1996, 18 (reprinted from *Message to the Blackman in America*).

———. *The Fall of America.* Newport News, Va.: National Newport News and Commentator, n.d. [1973].

———. *History of the Nation of Islam.* Cleveland: Secretarius Publications, 1994.

———. *How to Eat to Live.* 2 vols. Vol. 1. Newport News, Va.: National Newport News and Commentator, n.d. [1967].

———. *How to Eat to Live.* 2 vols. Vol. 2. Newport News, Va.: National Newport News and Commentator, n.d. [1972].

———. "Mary, Joseph, and Jesus." *The Final Call,* December 28, 1994, 19.

———. *Message to the Blackman in America.* Chicago: Muhammad's Temple No. 2, 1965.

———. "Old Wicked Going Out . . . New World Coming In." *The Final Call,* August 31, 1994, 19 (reprinted from *Our Saviour Has Arrived*).

———. *Our Saviour Has Arrived.* Chicago: Muhammad's Temple of Islam No. 2, 1974.

———. "Separation Is the Answer." *The Final Call,* November 16, 1994, 19 (reprinted from *The Fall of America*).

———. *The Supreme Wisdom: Solution to the So-Called Negroes' Problem.* Chicago: University of Islam, 1957.

———. *The True History of Jesus as Taught by the Honorable Elijah Muhammad.* Compiled by CROE. Chicago: Coalition for the Remembrance of Elijah, 1992.

———. "We Must First Be Brothers." *The Final Call,* September 28, 1994, 19 (reprinted from *Muhammad Speaks,* January 22, 1971).

Muhammad, Jabril. "Developing the Nature of God within Ourselves." *The Final Call,* August 16, 1995, 26–27.

————. "Farrakhan's Sermon on the Mount." *The Final Call,* June 21, 1995, 26.

————. "Judge Not That You Be Not Judged." *The Final Call,* March 6, 1996, 29–30.

————. "Paul and Aaron: Biblical Signs of Minister Louis Farrakhan." *The Final Call,* October 19, 1994, 26–27.

————. "Realizing the Divinity of Minister Farrakhan's Mission." *The Final Call,* December 28, 1994, 26.

————. "The Relevance of Theology in Today's World." *The Final Call,* July 19, 1995, 26.

————. "Theology: Whose Study of God?" *The Final Call,* July 5, 1995, 26.

————. "A Time of Divine Intervention and Universal Change." *The Final Call,* August 31, 1994, 26–27.

————. "Understanding Min. Farrakhan, His Mission and His Opponents." *The Final Call,* January 31, 1996, 26.

Muhammad, Tynnetta. "America's Moslem Sons, Prophecy and the Nation of Islam." *The Final Call,* August 16, 1995, 31.

————. "Freemasons and the Wisdom of the Nation of Islam." *The Final Call,* August 30, 1995, 27, 37.

————. "A Warning to Religious Communities." *The Final Call,* July 19, 1995, 29.

Muhammad, Wallace D. *As the Light Shineth from the East.* Chicago: WDM Publishing Co., 1980.

————. *Religion on the Line.* Chicago: WDM Publishing Co., 1983.

Muraskin, William Alan. *Middle-Class Blacks in a White Society: Prince Hall Freemasonry in America.* Berkeley: University of California Press, 1975.

"The Muslim Message: All White Men Devils, All Negroes Divine." *Newsweek,* August 27, 1962, 26–27, 30.

Nichols, Traci X. "The Power of Master Fard Muhammad: The Story of Bilal Muhammad." *The Final Call,* March 29, 1995, 29, 37.

Perry, Bruce, ed. *Malcolm X: The Last Speeches.* New York: Pathfinder Press, 1989.

Perry, Teresa, ed. *Teaching Malcolm X.* New York: Routledge, 1996.

Pinkney, Alphonso. *Red, Black, and Green: Black Nationalism in the United States.* New York: Cambridge University Press, 1976.

Porter, Frances E. *The Hajj: The Muslim Pilgrimage to Mecca and the Holy Places.* Princeton, N.J.: Princeton University Press, 1994.

Randles, Jenny, and Peter Warrington. *Science and the UFOs.* New York: Basil Blackwell, 1985.

Rashad, Adib. *Elijah Muhammad: The Ideological Foundation of the Nation of Islam.* Newport News, Va.: UBUS Communications Systems, 1994.

Rassoull, Abass. *The Theology of Time: By the Honorable Elijah Muhammad, the Messenger of Allah.* Hampton, Va.: UBUS Communications Systems, 1992.

Redkey, Edwin. *Black Exodus, Black Nationalist, and Back-to-Africa Movements.* New Haven: Yale University Press, 1969.

Reed, Adolph L. *W. E. B. Du Bois and American Political Thought.* New York: Oxford University Press, 1997.

"Return to the Motherland." *The Final Call,* October 19, 1994, 16.

Roberts, Allen E. *The Craft and Its Symbols: Opening the Door to Masonic Symbolism.* Richmond: Macoy Publishing and Masonic Supply Co., 1974.

Sahib, Hatim. "The Nation of Islam." Master's thesis. University of Chicago, 1951.

Thomas, Richard W. *Life for Us Is What We Make It: Building Black Community in Detroit, 1915–1945.* Bloomington: Indiana University Press, 1992.

Tsoukalas, Steven. *Knowing Christ in the Challenge of Heresy: A Christology of the Cults, a Christology of the Bible.* Lanham, Md.: University Press of America, 1999.

———. *Masonic Rites and Wrongs: An Examination of Freemasonry.* Phillipsburg, N.J.: Presbyterian and Reformed Publishing, 1995.

Turner, Henry McNeal. *Respect Black: The Writings and Speeches of Henry McNeal Turner.* Edited by Edwin S. Redkey. New York: Arno Press, 1971.

Washington, Booker T. *Up from Slavery.* New York: Bantam, 1956 [1900].

Washington, Joseph R., Jr. *Black Sects and Cults.* Garden City, N.Y.: Doubleday, 1972.

Watts, Jill. *God, Harlem U.S.A.: The Father Divine Story.* Berkeley: University of California Press, 1992.

"Where Is the Honorable Elijah Muhammad?" *The Final Call,* June 7, 1995, 36.

Whitehurst, James E. "The Mainstreaming of the Black Muslims: Healing the Hate." *The Christian Century,* February 1980.

Wilmore, Gayraud S. *Black Religion and Black Radicalism: An Interpretation of the Religious History of Afro-American People.* Maryknoll, N.Y.: Orbis, 1986.

Wood, Joe, ed. *Malcolm X: In Our Own Image.* New York: St. Martin's Press, 1992.

Index